COUNSELING SINGLE PARENTS

by

JOAN D. ATWOOD, PhD, CSW
Hofstra University

FRANK GENOVESE, PhD
Hofstra University

ACA

AMERICAN
COUNSELING
ASSOCIATION

American Counseling Association
5999 Stevenson Avenue
Alexandria, VA 22304

Cover Design by Sarah Jane Valdez

Library of Congress Cataloging-in-Publication Data

Atwood, Joan D.
   Counseling single parents / by Joan D. Atwood, Frank Genovese.
   p.   cm.
   Includes bibliographical references (p.   ) and index.
   ISBN 1-55620-125-7
   1. Single parents—Counseling of. 2. Single-parent family.
I. Genovese, Frank, II. Title.
HQ759.915.A86   1993
306.85'6—dc20

                                                            93-21659
                                                            CIP

Printed in the United States of America

ACKNOWLEDGMENTS

We would like to thank the following people for their help, support, and assistance:

- Daniel Araoz for his insightful and thoughtful comments on the sexuality chapters
- Andrew Schepard and Steve Schlissel for their dedication to furthering the best interests of children of divorce
- Nancy Cohan for her assistance with information for the social service system chapter
- Michelle Dunning for her assistance with the bibliographic materials
- Our families for their love, encouragement, and support.

DEDICATION

To all the single parents who over the years have shared their experiences, both joyful and painful: This book is a tribute to your strength and courage—J.D.A.

To the memory of George Krupp, mentor, colleague, and friend—F.G.

TABLE OF CONTENTS

ABOUT THE AUTHORS

Joan D. Atwood, PhD, is the coordinator of the graduate programs in marriage and family counseling and the director of the Marital and Family Clinic at Hofstra University, New York. She is an approved supervisor and the president elect of the Association for Marriage and Family Therapists. She is a clinical supervisor and diplomate of the American Board of Sexology. Dr. Atwood has published over 50 journal articles and six books in the field of marriage and family therapy. She is in private practice in Rockville Centre, New York.

Frank Genovese, PhD, is school psychologist at Xaverian High School and adjunct assistant professor of marriage and family counseling at Hofstra University. He has taught school psychology at St. John's University and has served as the clinical director of the Marriage and Family Therapy Clinic at Hofstra. Dr. Genovese holds certification in school psychology in New York and New Hampshire. He is a clinical member of the American Association of Marriage and Family Therapy and serves on the executive board of the Long Island chapter. He has published several articles and book chapters dealing with bereavment processes and with adolescence. Dr. Genovese is in the private practice in Rockville Centre, New York.

INTRODUCTION

For years professionals and the public have been warned by the "experts" about the pathological effects of disrupted bonds of attachment. Our theories and research served to validate the view that divorcing individuals have failed and that they and their children suffer psychologically from this trauma. In so doing, counselors everywhere focused their therapy sessions around the "emptying out" of feelings of anger, pain, sadness, and guilt. Today the term *divorce* still has connotations of failure and shame for many Americans. Emery, Hetherington, and DiLalla (1984) have stressed that it is crucial to keep in mind that social and political views affect both lay and professional opinion regarding the effects of divorce on adults and children.

The socially constructed definitions about divorce and the ensuing psychological reactions in terms of its negative connotations can be traced to an era in the United States before the Industrial Revolution when the two-parent family system was the norm. Evidence that these social definitions are changing is accumulating slowly. In the last decade there has been a gradual shift from the use of the term *broken home* to the more neutral term *single-parent family*. This term still does not depict the family situation accurately because in cases of divorce, for the most part, there are two parents present. They simply live in two different locations. This shift in language reflects the public's recognition and acceptance of the dramatic rise in the divorce rate that has cut across all socioeconomic classes. In many schools today at least half of the students come from homes headed by one parent, and the consensus is that most youth will spend some time prior to age 18 in a single-parent household (Demo & Acock, 1988). An analysis by Norton and Glick (1986) has projected that 60% of American children will live in a single-parent family before reaching age 18.

A changing view of marriage also has contributed to the decline of the judgmental attitude toward divorce (Morawetz & Walker, 1984, pp. 5-6). Although expectations around marriage are changing slowly, at the turn of the century the average age of death was approximately 45 years old. This meant that individuals were married for about 20 to 25 years. Today, with the average life span over age 80 for women and close to 80 for men, it is possible that couples will be married for 60 years, or even longer. Expecting couples to remain married for such a long period of time may not be reasonable. Being married to one person during the child-rearing years and another for the post-child-rearing years might be a more viable option. It appears that this is beginning to happen as evidenced by the serial monogamy picture of marriage that has recently emerged in American society. Another factor clearly affecting the changing values around marriage is the fact that more and more women are entering the labor force because of economic need. The result is that wives are no longer as financially dependent on their husbands as they once were.

The media also plays an important role in this change of attitudes. Early images of the family looked like "Little House on the Prairie." In the 1950s and 1960s, we all wished for homes like those in "Ozzie and Harriet" or "Father Knows Best." Few bothered to question why our mothers did not wear aprons while standing over the stove like June Cleaver in "Leave It to Beaver" or why the men on these shows never ventured into the kitchen except to offer some worldly bit of advice.

In the 1970s values and attitudes with regard to family structures shifted to a reality that had not been there before. "One Day at a Time" depicted a single mother raising two children. Although she may have suffered some setbacks, it was a lifestyle she chose. In fact, early in the show's run, she voluntarily rejected a marriage proposal because she wanted to remain a single parent.

In the 1980s this shift in family structures continued. Families became more open, actualized and experienced at expressing their feelings. "Kate and Allie" depicted two single mothers pooling resources to raise three children in New York City. "Who's the Boss" portrayed a male housekeeper, his daughter, a female corporate executive, and her mother and son all living together in a family. "Different Strokes" showed a single white man living with his two young black adopted children.

The 1990s went beyond these alternatives to the more traditional marriage or the results of the death of a spouse or divorce and brought us "Murphy Brown." Even when she had the opportunity to marry the father of the child, she made a conscious choice to be a single parent.

This book provides an in-depth exploration of the single parent family system. The book also explores—and explodes— the four societal assumptions underlying the "intact family myth." These assumptions are:

1. Staying together no matter what in long-term relationships is good; short-term relationships are bad. In other words, marriage should be forever.
2. A society in which people live to age 80 can operate with the same relationship commitments as a society in which people live to age 45.

3. The traditional family—mother, father, sister, brother—is the basic social unit and should be strengthened.

4. Only dysfunctional adults divorce, and divorce results in dysfunctional children.

The reality is that single parents are found in every age group and represent hundreds of thousands of individuals in American society. Among these single parents are those who have never married, those who have been divorced, and, most common past middle age, those whose spouses are dead. Those in the never-married category include *single parent by choice* and *single parent not by choice*. Those who are single parents by choice—the Murphy Browns—are generally older women who have not married for many reasons but around age 35 decide to have a child. These women tend to be financially secure and involved in their careers. Although they face many of the same problems that other single parents face, they generally do not experience the feelings of failure that divorced women experience or the feelings of loss that widowed women experience. They also do not experience the psychologically uncomfortable identity transition that divorced and widowed women face in moving from the married world to the world of singles. This is not to say that these single parents by choice have an easy time of it. Even though many have thought through the decision to have a child, and for some the transition to parenthood is smooth, for others the enormous responsibility of caring for a child is overwhelming.

For those who become single parents not by choice, usually in their teenage years, the picture is not as rosy. The United States has the highest teenage pregnancy rate (Jones & Placek, 1985) in the developed world, reporting 96 pregnancies per 1,000 (or 1 in 6) young women between the ages of 15 and 19, with the highest rates among low-income black adolescents (Franklin, 1988). This represents approximately 1 million young women in this country (nearly 11% of this age group) who become pregnant every year (Hayes, 1987). Of these premarital pregnancies, 39% end in abortion, 12% end in miscarriage, and just under 50% result in live births. Approximately 184,000 of these births are legitimized by marriage and roughly 261,000 end in out-of-wedlock births (Hayes, 1987).

The consequences of teenage pregnancy are often disastrous. It increases health risks to both mother and child. Adolescent mothers have a death rate 60% higher than the rate among older women (Thorburg, 1979). They are also liable to have numerous health problems and are at high risk for abuse and neglect of their children (Alan Guttmacher Institute, 1976). Single adolescent mothers have less chance than their peers of getting married and a much greater chance of divorce if they do. Among girls who keep their babies (90%), only 2 out of 10 marry the father (Furstenberg, Brooks-Gunn, & Morgan, 1987; Glick & Norton, 1979; Hayes,

1987). The teenage fathers often prematurely leave school to work in order to care for their families.

The baby also faces increased risks. Babies born to adolescent mothers are more likely than babies born to older mothers to have low birth weights, neurological defects, and childhood illnesses, all of which are major causes of infant mortality (Bolton, 1980). The social and economic consequences can be enormous. Adolescent mothers are twice as likely to drop out of school, less likely to be employed, and more likely to be dependent on welfare. Fully half of all payments made under the Aid to Families With Dependent Children (AFDC) go to women who bore children during their adolescent years (Gilchrist & Schinke, 1983).

This book, however, does not focus on never-married single parents— by choice or not by choice. Although single parents of all types share similar experiences, and some sections of this book are relevant to never-married single parents, (for example, chapter 10's discussion of the feminization of poverty), other sources do better justice to their situation (Atwood, 1992; Atwood & Donnelly, 1992; Atwood & Kassindorf, 1992).

This book also does not include differentiation among cultural groups. Culture is indeed a critical counseling consideration but economic status seems to us to be more relevant. Nor is this book about men. Although some chapters certainly apply to the single-parent father, over 90% of single parents in this country are women, and it is to them that we direct the majority of our comments.

This book is instead directed toward helping those counselors who work with middle-class divorced and widowed clients—that is, those individuals most likely to seek the services of mental health counselors in private practice. Rather than providing a superficial overview of all groups fitting into the single-parent categories, and in order to provide an in-depth analysis of the single-parent situation, we have decided to focus on the particular segments of the single-parent population—the divorced and widowed—where our expertise lies and where we feel we can make the most appropriate contribution. In no way do we mean to minimize the importance of other segments.

The uniqueness of this book is that it is the first on counseling single parents that includes a focus on the strengths of the single-parent family rather than the more typical focus on the deficits. We do not ignore the psychological problems often experienced by the members in such families; but rather, we present a more balanced picture in light of more recent, methodologically sound research findings. Our view is that the single-parent family is a viable, healthy family form. Our assumption is that ideas we hold about what it means to be a member of such a family system are socially constructed. We believe that one nurturing and loving parent can produce healthy productive individuals if society's prejudices do not interfere. As competent professionals we need to examine society's assumptions (and our own) in order to provide these families with counseling that empowers them. This book assists counselors in the examination process and is thus a book for counselors on both personal and professional levels.

People who have gone through a divorce or who have experienced the death of a spouse must confront life in a completely new role that creates special problems as well as presents new challenges for growth. Single parents (as well as many nonsingle parents) have three major concerns: loneliness, children, and money. The problems and pressures around these issues generally evolve and build over time. The difficulties of providing for their own and their children's physical, psychological, and social needs may result in task overload and exhaustion. In addition, the single parent's relational-sexual part of life is affected. When, where, and with whom can they have intimacy and sex? Many single parents are reluctant to have their dates meet with their children or have a difficult time finding baby-sitters. Clients who are involved in these readjustments encounter important social and psychological issues as they try to find a new place for themselves as social and sexual beings. As for the children, many of them grow up "faster" than their peers in two-parent family situations. These children have many competencies and resources, and tend to be quite resilient, but in some cases, they experience responsibilities beyond their capabilities.

One focus of this book is thus to explore both parent and child experiences by describing the most commonly reported experiences reported by single parents and examining these from the single parent's perspective as well as the child's perspective. In this way, the professional counselor can understand the many, often overwhelming problems faced by their clients. Discussion is primarily from a social psychological point of view because a major task of the single parent is to redefine social roles. These social redefinitions have psychological consequences, which are also described and discussed in detail.

Another focus of this book is on interventive strategies that are relevant to treating specific single-parent family issues, that take into account current research findings, and that provide a deeper understanding of the single-parent family system. Specific counseling strategies are proposed throughout to assist counselors in therapeutic direction. The theoretical orientation of the book is primarily systemic and looks at persons in context, whether that context be intimate relationships, the family as a system, or larger outside systems such as schools, workplaces, or social services.

For the most part, the book uses nontechnical language. All case material is real but disguised, and originates from the authors' clinical practices and many years of experience. Throughout our goal is a progressive deepening of the counselor's knowledge and awareness of the special issues faced by divorced and widowed single-parents. The implications for reflective psychological therapy during the process of intimacy dissolution are explored and the psychological stages of the separation and remergence process presented. Suggestions for facilitating growth at each of these stages are given so that this life-cycle transition can eventuate in a time of freedom, challenge, exploration, and growth.

Yet another focus is on deepening the counselor's understanding of the therapeutic process, on challenging the counselor's assumptions around the counseling process and what it means to work with this type of family. For example, counseling strategies are initially presented from a more traditional family therapy model utilizing structural family therapy assessment and techniques. Next, the internal dynamics of individuals in this type of family, including attachment bond dissolution and the ensuing feelings of loss, are described. Social constructionist assumptions are made throughout, and a new six-point social constructionist therapy model for working with this type of family is presented in chapter 11.

There are four broad areas of concern in this book. The first is the social and psychological experiences of those who are single again. Chapter 1 primarily explores single parents who are separated or divorced, focusing on the typical psychological and social issues faced by this growing population. The objective here is to assist the counselor in understanding the experiences of these individuals. Chapter 2 explores the psychological and social issues of single parents whose spouses have died. Differences between psychological responses to divorce and widowhood are examined, with an emphasis on presenting problems and emotional responses, and therapeutic considerations for empowering these clients are discussed.

Chapter 3 includes case histories that illustrate many of the special concerns of divorced and widowed single parents and demonstrates by example specific counseling techniques. Structural family therapy assessment and techniques are the basis for counseling.

Chapter 4 looks at children of divorce and their resiliency and competence. The factors that are predictive of the good divorce and that provide for positive outcomes in children and their parents are discussed.

Chapter 5 considers redefining relationships, a major component of the readjustment process after divorce or widowhood. Establishing new relationships with ex-spouses, in-laws, extended family, and single and coupled friends, and dealing with ghosts are discussed. The typical problems presented by clients around these issues and the potential for growth are described, and therapeutic assessments and counseling interventions are presented from a more psychodynamic theoretical base.

The next broad area of concern is around dating and sexuality. Chapters 6 and 7 present the relational and sexual issues of the divorced and widowed single parent in more detail, illustrating the complexity of these family systems in more depth. The chapters also present information to facilitate the counseling process in assisting clients with values clarification. Chapter 8 educates professional counselors about the AIDS virus, examining the impact of AIDS on sexual behavior in the 1990s, discussing the special worries and concerns of divorced and widowed persons who are sexually active, and describing how counselors can best educate their clients on how to protect themselves. High-risk behaviors and psychosocial concerns are discussed and counseling strategies investigated.

The third broad area concerns dealing with the larger systems. Chapter 9 explores how the professional counselor can assist the single parent in dealing with school personnel. Educators who are insensitive to the single parent's plight may further add to the emotional devastation. Research on children of divorce indicates that some children experience academic problems when there is a disruption in the family system. Others do not. The many ways that counselors can educate parents about school personnel issues, and how counselors can best mobilize the competencies and strengths of parents and their children with regard to these issues, are described.

Chapter 10 examines single parent work and welfare issues. Most single parents experience serious financial decreases. The problems that arise from these decreased finances are explored as are the problems that can arise when a newly single person decides to return to work. The counselor's role in providing psycho education and in uncovering strengths is discussed. The changes in life style after divorce or widowhood often necessitate the single parent's dependence on the social welfare agencies. Ways in which professional counselors can facilitate through education the process of securing social services for their clients are described.

A final broad area is social constructionist therapy for single-parent families. Concepts from social construction theory have recently entered the field of marriage and family therapy. Social constructionists believe that how we know what we know is not through an exact pictorial duplication of the world: "The map is not the territory." Rather, reality is seen experientially in terms of how we subjectively interpret the constructions. In this sense, we are responsible for what we believe, feel, and see. Chapter 11 explores how these notions can be applied to counseling the single-parent family and presents a model of therapy that creates an environment for change. Chapter 12 summarizes some of the points made throughout the book and gives additional suggestions for counselors.

PART I

SOCIAL AND PSYCHOLOGICAL EXPERIENCES OF THOSE WHO ARE SINGLE AGAIN

Chapter 1
SINGLE AGAIN
THROUGH DIVORCE

The offices of professional counselors are filled with persons who are either thinking about divorce, are divorcing, or are postdivorce. The high rate of divorce and the complexity of the emotional reactions to divorce lead many to seek professional help. In order to understand the complexity of the single-parent family system, it is first useful to examine the divorce rates and propose certain hypotheses about the composition of this group. This chapter examines incidences of divorce in the United States and explores the divorcing process from social and psychological frames of reference, describing how the social definitions of divorce influence psychological reactions.

Divorce Rates

The divorce rate (number of divorces per 1,000 marriages) began to increase in the United States early in this century. It seemed to peak after World War II and then to drop back a bit. But it has been rising again in recent years (Ditzion, 1978) with an increase of 34% in the 1960s and about 80% during the 1970s ("Commerce Department Survey," 1978). Most of this increase in divorce during the 1970s was among younger couples. In 1975 there were 460 divorces per 1,000 marriages. Since then this rate has been rising, and current estimates indicate that there are approximately 500 divorces per 1,000 marriages, or approximately one divorce for every two marriages. Each year, there are approximately 2.2 million marriages and 1.1 million divorces in the United States. As a result, more than 1 million persons yearly return to single status. The divorce rate is higher for non-whites than whites and generally higher among lower class whites than middle and upper class whites (Glick, 1988). The average age at divorce from first marriage in the United States today is 27 for females and 29 for males. Divorce appears to have become so common that 60% of Americans who get married today report that they do not expect the marriage to last the rest of their lives (Yankelovich, 1981).

In addition to the already divorced, a sizable number of people are in between marriage and divorce. At any given time, individuals who are separated from their spouses constitute a very large population. In March 1984, the census reported 1.5 million men and 2.4 million women who were separated (Norton & Glick, 1986). According to Hanson and Sporkowski (1986), the U.S. Bureau of the Census in 1985 indicated that 25.7% of all family groups were headed by one parent in 1984.

> . . . based on current trends, Sandra Hofferth of the Center for Population Research at the National Institute of Child Health and Human Development recently made the startling projection that 70% of white children and more than 90% of black children born in 1980 will spend sometime living in a single-parent home before their 18th birthday. (Clapp, 1992)

These figures probably represent underestimates inasmuch as an unknown number of persons report that an absent spouse is "visiting relatives." It is impossible, then, to measure separation, either through agreement to separate or desertion, because there are no formal reporting techniques except for the few couples who go through the formalities of legal separation.

Current figures (Arditti, 1992) indicate that over 11 million people in the United States are divorced, and more than 2 million join the ranks each year. Divorced people represent over 40% of the population. One quarter of all children growing up today will have more than two sets of parents by age 18. Further, 80% of divorced people remarry, 60% have more children, and 40% of second marriages end in divorce in the first 4 years.

These statistics mean that American society has the highest divorce and/or separation rate of all industrial countries and that most of this population involves children. Thus from both the available divorce statistics and the estimates of separations, it is clear that a large segment of the population is confronted with the task of readjusting to postmarital life.

Interpreting Divorce Rates

It is obvious that more marriages are ending in divorce. What is less obvious is what this means. Rising divorce rates are a common topic in the popular media, and they often are interpreted as a sign of societal rejection of the institution of marriage. This explanation, however, is questionable. One reason is that available divorce statistics are not necessarily an entirely reliable indicator of the current state of marriage. It may be true that fewer people value the commitment of marriage, but it is also possible that expectations of marriage are higher than they were historically and that people are more easily disappointed. In the days of arranged marriages, many people tolerated unhappy or unsatisfying situations and adjusted to them. Today fewer people are kept from divorce by religious prohibitions, legal barriers, and social disapproval and sanctions. Therefore couples who are dissatisfied with their marriage are more likely to terminate the union. Another reason that divorce is more common today may be because women have more opportunities economically, and emotionally, to support themselves and their children and to receive financial aid from government agencies. (About one family in seven now has a woman as the head of the household.) Yet another reason is that changes in gender roles and gender role expectations may have led to increased dissatisfaction with the institution of marriage in general. However, it is important to keep in mind that the number of divorces may reflect dissatisfaction more with a particular marriage and a specific relationship than with the institution of marriage itself. The great majority of people who divorce—five out of every six divorced males and three out of four divorced females—eventually do remarry. There is no simple summation of the positive and negative features of divorced life as compared with married life.

Several other factors may bear on the way divorce statistics are interpreted. As mentioned earlier, only half of the states in this country have developed uniform standards for divorce record-keeping (Glick & Norton, 1971). What this probably means is that the records may reflect variable data collection procedures. In addition, there have been many legal changes regarding divorce. Thus the recent rise in divorce rates may result from the increased ease with which divorces are obtained rather than from an increased dissatisfaction with marriage itself. In recent years, obtaining a legal divorce has become a relatively simple, less expensive legal process. Added to this is the fact that a significant percentage of the divorce rate is composed of individuals who have had more than one marriage and divorce. This means that a higher percentage of first marriages than is obvious at first glance remains intact. Using most measures, though, the research does appear to indicate that the proportion of marriages ending in divorce has almost doubled since the 1950s, lending credence to the fact that a large and still-growing divorced population is confronted with the emotional task of adjusting to a new social, psychological, and sexual role.

Social Definitions and Reactions to Divorce

There are many social stereotypes of the divorced or separated person. The divorced male or female has traditionally been seen as a social loser, sitting alone in his or her apartment with four or five cats and newspapers piled to the ceiling. This stereotype invokes an image of a sad, depressed, psychologically devastated victim of divorce, struggling over the trauma of this life change and experiencing devastating problems in his or her interpersonal and sexual relationships. Today, this image has changed. The divorced single is now typically viewed as a young, swinging, upwardly mobile career person without a worry in the world, living out the sexual fantasies of which others only dream. This is the image of a gay divorcee, of a person who feels released from the bonds and burdens of marriage and supposedly lives amidst constant parties and entertainment, plentiful sex (hopefully safe), and general abandonment in sexual and other areas of life. Of course, neither the social loser or gay divorcee stereotype is accurate, but both probably contain elements of truth applicable to many people's adjustment to divorce or separation. Becoming single again for most people falls somewhere between these extremes.

> *Lois, a 39-year-old social worker, was married for 15 years. She separated from her husband when she learned that he was involved in a long-term extramarital relationship. Now, 5 years later, she lives with her 11-year-old son in a condominium on the beach, realizing her long-time dream. For the most part, she is happy with her life. She is currently dating someone she likes but reports that there are many times when she feels lonely and misses the sharing and intimacy of married life.*

As with almost everything else, individuals report both desirable and undesirable aspects of singlehood. On one hand, it offers the independence that some feel is rarely obtained in marital relationships. Singlehood also offers time alone, giving persons the opportunity to examine individual needs and desires (a concern of many young people today). Thus for those who value privacy and time alone, singlehood is defined as a very positive life style. They can come to know what kind of person they are in the absence of the day-to-day living with partners who may be the primary focus of their self-definition. Singlehood also offers variety in terms of both interpersonal and sexual relationships. Some people believe that only singles can truly experience the human diversity in interpersonal sexual relationships, an opportunity that many people find rewarding in terms of the uniqueness of each person and each relationship.

On the other hand, many people report disadvantages to being single. Some people define singlehood as being lonely rather than as being alone. Perhaps more important for the average single person are the many times when the price paid for independence and time spent alone is the absence of intimacy and not having anyone with whom to share day-to-day living. Little necessary life events may become problematic, for example, errands during the day, doing laundry, and washing the car, because they must be accomplished alone.

Changing status from being married to being single again may involve varied social adjustments. Many individuals have established friendships and social relationships as couples rather than as individuals, and the divorcing individual may feel awkward being with others who are in couples. At the same time, other couples may not be comfortable including single persons in their activities. The divorcing individual may also feel uncomfortable being alone as the sense of security or belonging that accompanies being part of a couple is replaced with sudden autonomy.

Mel, a 54-year-old business executive, divorced Ellen, his wife of 25 years, because he wanted to experience other women. Initially feeling secure with the support network of friends they both had known for many years, he did not feel lonely. Over time, however, his friends tended to side with Ellen. Mel became increasingly uncomfortable in their presence, so he stopped seeing them. Eventually he began to experience depression—feeling alone and abandoned by his friends. After 2 years of therapy, Mel began to establish a support network of his own that consisted mainly of persons who were single again like himself.

Males and females experience the divorcing process differently. Initially, men report that they feel relieved—of obligations and responsibilities. Many experience a sense of euphoria. They have more time alone, enabling them to watch television leisurely or stay late at work. They are free from the obligation of having to come home on time for dinner or having to help Johnny with his home work. Many women, who more typically define themselves in terms of relationships, experience loss—of a husband, of the married status, of the relationship. They take on many of the financial, parental, and familial responsibilities their husbands gave up. Initially, many women report that they feel overwhelmed, fear for their financial and emotional security, and worry about their future.

Over time, the picture appears to change. Men report that they begin to miss the structure that marriage afforded them. The highest rate of suicide is among divorced men, and men seem to have more difficulty establishing social support networks and creating a day-to-day living structure for themselves. Women, however, generally have no place to go but up emotionally. They typically have to find employment outside the home, which tends to enhance their feelings of self-esteem and competency. Settling in with the children tends to become systematized, and over time their lives, although changed, remain much as they were before the divorce. Durkheim (1951) was one of the first to believe that marriage gave men the benefits of structure but placed women in "chains." Divorce, Durkheim believed, represented freedom from those chains for the woman but threw the man into a state of anomie, that is, into feelings of helplessness and despair, which he saw as accounting for the high suicide rate among divorced men. Epstein's (1974) work on divorce found that women, although initially depressed after divorce, reported high rates of happiness 1 year later. Men, however, reported high levels of happiness immediately after divorce, but those levels plummeted 1 year later.

Divorcing individuals often need to establish new social contacts, which include new groups of single people. Many cities have organizations where single people can meet and form new friendships. However, for many individuals giving up old relationships and seeking out new friendships can be a frightening experience.

Divorced men and women undergo a radical change in social role—from wife or husband (and thus part of a couple) to an unattached person for whom society has established no definite role or expectations. For this reason, recently divorced people often feel anxious and rootless. They may watch helplessly as the friends who saw them as half of a couple drift away. These social definitions, expectations, and assumptions about marriage and divorce that delineate the appropriate contexts for sociosexual behavior create the setting within which individuals experience the psychological reaction to the divorcing process.

Psychological Reactions to Divorce

Although the chain of events leading to marriage is varied, most people marry with the hope and expectation that the marriage will last. Divorce often represents loss of this hope as well as loss of one's spouse, sometimes of one's children, possibly of a life style, often of the security of familiarity, and, perhaps most importantly, of part of one's identity. Even though in many cases a choice is involved and single parents see this choice as making their lives and the lives of their children more positive, often the single-parent family system is born of loss, either through death or divorce. Although most families successfully negotiate the developmental tasks involved in the dissolution of intimacy bonds, some do not. In these cases, there appears to be a persistence of the marital bond, regardless of the quality of the marriage. These people may feel anxious, fearful, or terrified when contemplating their separated or divorced situation, and they often feel trapped in time, unable to grow.

The disturbances that most clients feel at this time are almost always associated with the disruption of the attachment bond. Marital dissolution is an extremely disruptive event, not only ending the accessibility to the spouse but also changing the client's social role and his or her relationships with children, relatives, and friends. Psychological reactions to the dissolution of the marriage may become intertwined with reactions to many other disruptions. Although these reactions are experienced by many, they are not experienced by all, and it is wise for counselors to keep in mind the varied reactions of individuals entering this process. The emotional descriptions provided in this chapter are best used as guides for those counselors who work with these types of families.

The loss of attachment may, however, be seen as the primary cause of the distress that persons experience in single-parent situations. This distress includes the need to reorganize attention around the image of the lost spouse and the working through of the urge to contact the lost spouse as well as anger or guilt toward the lost spouse and hypervigilance around issues involving the lost spouse. The distress is indicated by feelings of fear or panic at the thought of contact with the spouse. It can also manifest in sleeplessness or loss of appetite.

Children from single-parent homes may also exhibit these symptoms. In the school situation, for example, distress presents as failure to concentrate, drifting off into fantasy, academic decline, withdrawal from social relationships, and/or acting out with peers. Thus the manifestations of the core problem of loss of attachment can be numerous and subtle. Counselors and families may fail cognitively to connect presenting problems with mourning issues.

For those who are single due to widowhood the presenting issues are similar. Persons experience numbness and disbelief accompanied by feelings of denial, a nonacceptance of the fact that the person is really dead. This is often followed by emotional reactions such as crying, psychosomatic symptoms, insomnia, and feelings of guilt ("If I had . . . maybe he wouldn't have died"). Some clients become immersed in anger ("Why me! Why did this happen to me!" or "The doctors killed him"). Next come the feelings of sadness, loneliness, and often incapacitating depression because of the loss of habit patterns, such as not being able to have coffee together in the morning. A variety of persistent grief reactions (for example, reconstructing idealized versions of the lost spouse) may be experienced if the person does not express emotion or refuses to deal with the loss. In addition to the psychological issues are such concrete factors influencing the plight of the widowed single parent as financial problems, finding new roles, and the disruption of family relationships.

Whether caused by death or divorce, changing status from being married to being single inevitably presents varied difficulties in emotional adjustments (as well as in the social adjustments already noted). It usually takes 2 to 3 years to form a strong attachment to a partner, and if separation occurs after this time, it usually involves separation shock for the individual. It is a myth for people to assume that couples who are married 30 years suffer more than couples who are married for 7 years.

Divorcing Process Stages

Individuals going through the divorcing process typically pass through a series of psychological stages. We want to emphasize that not all clients go through these stages, and not all clients go through them in order. However, because many individuals do report experiencing these emotions, counselors need to be aware of these stages in order to help clients in this social-psychological process. The four stages are labeled *denial, conflict, ambivalence,* and *acceptance.*

Denial. Stage I of the emotional divorcing process—denial—is mainly manifested by separation shock. If the individual is experiencing separation shock, he or she experiences relief, numbness, or panic. Relief is often felt when the divorce has been a drawn-out process. The most typical reaction to separation is fear of abandonment, and the emotional response to this fear is often apprehensiveness and anxiety.

> *Linda, a 32-year-old housewife, separated from her husband of 8 years because of constant arguing. For the most part she was comfortable with her decision; however, she said that she felt shaky, not on solid ground, about once a week. During these times, she doubted her decision to divorce, feeling that she had made a mistake. Often she went to bed, feeling anxious and upset, and stayed there for days, leaving the care of her children to her mother. Eventually, she felt a little better and got up and functioned as usual. She was fine for awhile, but after a few weeks, the pattern repeated.*

These anxious feelings may be accompanied by disturbances of sleep or appetite patterns. Increases in food intake and decreases in number of hours spent sleeping usually mean the person is experiencing anxiety. Decreases in food intake and increases in time spent sleeping are probably related to depression. In any case, the symptoms are indications of separation shock. During this stage, individuals often report that they are unable to concentrate on work activity or carry on conversations with people. They think about other things while people are talking to them, often about conversations or activities with their former partners. Each memory brings a different experience that may result in sudden outbursts of tears or anger. They seem unable to "get outside of themselves."

> *Linda reported that once she had to leave the supermarket because she started to cry "for no reason." This added to her "shakiness" because she felt that she couldn't control or predict her emotions.*

Other people report that they often lose control of their anger and, for what later seems to them to be an insignificant reason, explode into sudden flashes of rage.

> *Jim, a 49-year-old advertising manager, said that he snapped at a waitress in a rage because she forgot to bring him milk for his coffee. The*

strength of his anger frightened him and precipitated his coming to therapy. He said he felt as if he wanted to kill her.

Many individuals, however, experience numbness or the absence of feelings. Numbness is a way of muting or denying feelings that if experienced would be too overwhelming for the individual to handle.

When Linda felt shaky and went to bed, if anyone asked how she felt, she replied, "I feel nothing. The world feels numb. I don't love anyone or hate anyone. I just don't feel anything."

In this case, Linda is overwhelmed by the reality of the situation and responds with denial, temporarily turning off her psychological system. During this stage, the person may vacillate among emotions—feeling anxious, then angry, then numb. These emotions are often combined with and compounded by feelings of optimism about the new life. This stage of separation shock can last anywhere from a few days to several months.

Often one partner desires the divorce more so than the other. Reactions to the impending divorce depend upon whether or not one initiates the divorce, and it is important to be aware of the specific emotional reactions to each situation. For example, the person who leaves is often burdened with enormous amounts of guilt and self-blame, whereas the remaining person may feel more anger, hurt, self-pity, and condemnation of the other. The person who requests the divorce may fear being labeled a deserter, whereas the person who is left may feel embarrassment and fear being labeled a loser. Both individuals suffer.

Linda requested the divorce. The arguing in the marriage had nearly escalated to physical violence. Steve, her husband, often came home at 2 or 3 a.m. This enraged Linda. On these nights, she waited up for him and questioned him extensively as to his whereabouts because she was convinced (rightly so) that he was having an affair. Then she felt guilty about arguing and accusing him. During and after the divorce she also felt tremendous guilt over depriving him of his family and hurting him.

The process of divorce can have effects far greater than simply the dissolution of an unworkable marriage. Even when the marriage ends because one of the partners has fallen in love with someone else, there can be profound pain in the partner who asks for the divorce. In sum, Stage I emotionality involves coming to grips with the fact that the marriage is ending. The emotional task of the person at this stage of the divorcing process is to accept the reality of the separation. Once this occurs, the divorcing person enters the next stage.

Conflict.   The only thing predictable in Stage II is the unpredictability of feelings. The individual may begin to experience a multitude of conflicting emotions, one occurring right after the other. One minute, one day, people may feel perfectly comfortable with their new-found freedom and their new lifestyles; a minute or a day later they may find themselves in tears, reminiscing about their former spouse; and shortly thereafter, they may remember a negative event or an argument and feel enraged.

> *After being in therapy for about 6 months, Linda started to feel good about herself. She had taken up racket ball, lost 10 pounds, and started a part-time job. She reported to the therapist that for the first time since she was married, she was focusing on herself—her own needs, her own wants and desires. She was learning who she was as a person. Before she always focused on Steven's needs, trying to anticipate them to avoid conflict. These feelings of well-being lasted about 2 weeks. Then Linda came to therapy reporting that "she didn't know what she was doing; she had made a mistake; being married and miserable was better than not being married at all." Her feelings had "fooled" her again. Just when she thought she was doing better, she came crashing down.*

Individuals in this stage typically feel as if they may fall apart at any time. Volatile, explosive emotions may unexpectedly surface. Feelings of guilt and anger become strong. Persons may feel angry at their spouse and then, a few hours later, feel ashamed and guilty about their angry feelings. They may experience periods of anger at themselves and their spouses for failing their marriage, or at being left alone. They may wonder if they made a mistake; they may feel regret. Such feelings usually come in waves, and they may catch the person off guard. Because this stage is typified by conflicting emotions, the individual cannot predict which feeling he or she will be experiencing at any given time.

During this second stage of the divorcing period, individuals may also do what is called *scanning* (Krantzler, 1975). In this process, they reminisce about what went wrong with their marriage, wonder who was to blame, and consider what their own role was in the failure. It means that they are reliving the best times in the marriage and mourning the loss of its more intimate aspects. Scanning, in many ways, may be a way of preserving the attachment bonds; it may also provide important insight to individuals about their own constructive and destructive patterns in relationships. This may be a valuable learning experience. This review process may go on for months and contribute to the mood swings the divorcing person experiences. Each memory and each new awareness causes the person to feel different emotions. This process, although emotionally uncomfortable, enables individuals to release the pent-up feelings that might otherwise cause them much distress at later points in their lives.

During the emotional upheaval of this stage, a sense of loss and loneliness may develop. Loneliness manifests itself in many ways: Some individuals may sit in front of the television set for hours. Others may gradually withdraw from social contacts. Still others may experience a more active type of loneliness, and instead of sitting at home, they frequent old restaurants, pass by their spouses' homes or go from one singles' bar to another, desperately looking for solace for their loneliness. In addition, negative feelings and emotions experienced as a child, such as separation anxiety, low self-esteem, or feelings of worthlessness, may resurface, causing the individual much distress.

Although individuals at this point typically experience strong emotional swings, they may also at times experience periods of euphoria. Hunt and Hunt (1977) found that after separation a small percentage of individuals in their sample felt a sense of relief, increased personal freedom, gained competence, and were able to reinvest emotional energy in themselves, energy that was previously directed toward the marriage. These euphoric feelings tend to appear suddenly and for no apparent reason, causing the person to feel "on top of the world." These happy feelings may last for days or weeks. The danger during this phase is that the person may think that the worst is over, only to suddenly plunge into the depths of depression. Unfortunately, it is during this time when emotions are changing so rapidly that the person is usually required to deal with lawyers and make major decisions. For most people, Stage II represents an emotional see-saw, usually characterized by psychological conflict. The emotional task of individuals at this stage is to achieve a realistic definition of what their marriage represented, what their role was in its maintenance, what their responsibility was for its failure, and where they were "stuck" psychologically.

Ambivalence. Stage III is characterized by ambivalence and involves changes in the person's identity. In many ways, this is the most psychologically stressful aspect of the divorcing process. Being married is a primary source of self-identity. The two individuals involved co-develop identities about who they are as a couple and where and how they fit into the world. They co-create social definitions that are consonant with the social definition of marriage. When their relationship ends, they may feel confused and fearful, as though they no longer have a script telling them how to behave. Often during this time period, they may try on different identities, attempting to find one that is comfortable for them. At this time, the divorcing person faces a major change in self-perception. Instead of being a husband and father, a man may find himself living in a small apartment only seeing his children every other weekend. Instead of being a wife and homemaker, a woman may find herself labeled as a *divorcee*, a term that sometimes means promiscuous and loose to the uninformed person.

Linda typifies feelings experienced while going through these emotional stages. As stated earlier, originally she wanted the divorce. She was tired of fighting and felt that she wanted to find a loving relationship. Most days she felt this way. Occasionally, however, she remembered the good times, a party they went to together, a funny episode that occurred with one of the children. Sometimes when her husband came to pick up the children, she felt a resurgence of tenderness. A moment later she experienced the rage she felt when he stayed late at work after promising to be home early. Then she felt certain of her decision once again. But the emotions she experienced during those few seconds were extreme. When she felt tenderness toward him, she also felt guilty about having deserted him; then remembering all the hatred and arguing, she felt rage at his behavior. These emotional swings left her exhausted. So she spent the next few days in bed.

Sometimes, during this period, people go through a second adolescence. They may become very concerned about how they look, how they sound. They may buy new clothes or a new car. Many of the struggles that they experienced as a teenager may reappear, and persons may find themselves trying to decide how to handle sexual advances or when to kiss a date good night. Sexual experimentation may occur as individuals attempt to explore their new sexuality outside of the marital situation. The emotional task for the person at this stage involves making the psychological transition from being married to being single again. This identity transformation for many is psychologically the most difficult and stressful undertaking of the divorcing process.

Acceptance.   Finally (usually not until after several months or a year), the person may enter Stage IV, in which individuals typically feel a sense of relief and acceptance about their situation (Krantzler, 1975). After a while individuals start to experience a new sense of strength and accomplishment. For the most part, in this stage, they feel quite content with their life style and no longer dwell on the past. They now have a new sense of awareness and knowledge of their own needs. If after months of separation, a sense of acceptance of the past is not developing, the person may seek professional help. According to Hunt and Hunt (1977) and Weiss (1975), the most painful aspects of divorce peak within the first several months of a divorce and then tend to level off by the end of the first year. The complete emotional resolution of a divorce occurs when the spouses are no longer significantly influenced by the previously described reactions. This usually takes between 2 and 4 years. Although many of the feelings triggered by divorce are painful and uncomfortable, they ultimately lead toward resolving the loss so that, if the individual desires, he or she will be emotionally able to reestablish an intimate relationship.

In therapy, Linda's feelings eventually began to stabilize. Her feelings of well-being began to take precedence over her feelings of anxiety and anger. She was able to pursue her own interests and put her ex-spouse and ex-marriage in a perspective that she was comfortable with. She had started to date someone that she liked, and although she felt he was not the "right" one, she was content in her situation.

Unfortunately, not all people reach Stage IV and achieve acceptance. Some individuals get "stuck." Although most people benefit from therapy while going through the divorcing process, it is those who get stuck who will find therapy most useful.

Terry, an attractive 57-year-old bookkeeper, couldn't accept the idea that her husband had left her to move in with his young, pretty secretary. After her husband moved out, Terry withdrew from all her friends, and eventually they stopped calling her. She spent all her evenings at home alone preoccupied with thoughts of her ex-husband and his girl friend. All she could think about was the two of them together. Becoming obsessed with these thoughts, she was determined to discover what they were doing in their daily lives. She decided to set her alarm clock for 2 a.m., at which time she awakened, dressed, and drove to their home. She snuck out of her car, stole their garbage, took the garbage home, and examined it on her kitchen table. In therapy, she exclaimed to her therapist, "You'd be surprised how much you can learn from people's garbage. I know when they're sick, what they eat for dinner, when she has her period!"

After 2 years of therapy, Terry was able to develop her own support structure, become involved in meaningful activities, and begin dating. Eventually, she gave up the possibility of a reunion with her ex-husband.

Stress

Under the best of circumstances, separation and divorce represent a major life-cycle transition. Even in mutually agreed-upon, friendly terminations of a marital situation, many significant life-style changes occur. The newly single person often faces adjustments in social, psychological, and sexual relationships as well as in financial arrangements, living arrangements, and, in most cases, parenting roles. Most divorces, however, do not occur under the best of circumstances. Divorces are typically not logical or rational agreements. Rather they are emotional, irrational conflicts full of bitter contention. During this time, individuals' self-confidence may be shattered because they believe they have failed at the marriage. In a society where the "family value" is the outmoded and unrealistic two-parent norm, persons opting for divorce often define their situation as deviant. The psychological consequences based on this social definition then ensue. Extensive changes such as these, even if accomplished by the relief of ending an undesirable situation, typically cause stress. Holmes and Rahe (1967) found that divorce and marital separation rank second and third behind death of a spouse as events that produce the highest degrees of stress in individuals' lives.

The stress of divorce shows in many ways. Compared with married (or remarried) people, divorced men and women drink more often, smoke more marijuana, are lonelier and more despondent, and are more likely to feel anxious or guilty (Cargan & Melko, 1982). It is likely that this is why Mohammed said, ". . . divorce is the most detestable of all permitted things" (quoted in Epstein, 1974, p. 19)."

Interview and clinical data indicate that most divorced individuals go through a period of social and psychological readjustment as they redefine themselves as single again. For many, this is difficult, and for a few, it is traumatic. After this period, however, the person's life settles down into its own pattern.

Counseling Strategies

Chapter 1 has looked at parents who are single again through divorcing, examining social definitions and reactions to divorce as well as psychological reactions to divorce. In discussing these reactions, as well as in describing the four stages of the divorcing process (denial, conflict, ambivalence, and acceptance), basic issues, structures, and counseling strategies are presented. The next chapter, which looks at parents who are single again through widowhood, amplifies many of these strategies.

Chapter 2
SINGLE AGAIN THROUGH WIDOWHOOD

Psychological Differences Between Divorce and Widowhood

Divorce represents a unique kind of a loss—called a relationship loss—for many people. The reaction to loss is the mourning process. The road back to emotional stability is the healing process. The loss a person feels in divorce is comparable to the loss an individual experiences when a significant other dies. In both cases, a grieving process occurs, but there are important differences. In divorce, even though there is the loss of a person, the focus is primarily on the loss of a relationship. In death the focus is on the loss of a person. In divorce, the lost spouse continues to exist, and in many cases, continues to interact with the spouse around legal, financial, and parenting matters. In death, there is no interaction. When the grief is caused by a death, there are social rituals and supports available that may aid the remaining spouse in his or her emotional adjustment in the mourning process. Unfortunately, there are no recognized grief rituals to help the divorced person.

The postmarital adjustment of widowhood is also different from the situation commonly found in divorce. Widowed individuals typically do not have the sense of having failed at a marriage. In addition, the anger and resentment that often help to facilitate the emotional separation after a divorce is frequently lacking when a partner dies. The grief may be more intense, and the emotional attachment to the deceased mate may be quite high. For some people, this emotional tie remains so strong that other potential relationships appear dim by comparison.

Rathus and Nevid (1992) indicated that divorce may require a more difficult adjustment than the death of a spouse. They stated that when a spouse dies, legalities in most cases are less drawn out, and there are often clear-cut dictates in a will or insurance document that specify the wishes of the deceased. In divorce, persons generally experience financial decreases because two households need to be supported. Generally, when a partner dies, insurance monies are available, and in some cases, the mortgage on the house is paid off. Divorce often seems to require reams of legal documents and endless waiting periods. When someone dies, the family remains intact. In divorce, children and others may choose sides and assign blame. For the parent who does not have custody of the children, divorce signals changes in the parental as well as the marital role. After a death, people receive compassionate leave from work and are expected to be less productive for a while. After divorce, people are often criticized. Death is final, but divorce may nourish "what if's?" and vacillating emotions for many years. It is important for the counselor to keep in mind that personal reactions to both these processes vary and that few typologies or general statements can be made with regard to the trauma suffered in each.

U.S. Widowhood Rates

Of the more than 22 million people in the United States who are 65 years and older, almost one half of the women and one fifth of the men have lost their marital partners (Leslie & Leslie, 1977). Because of the differential longevity of men and women, an increasing preponderance of widows in the aged population can be expected over the years to come.

One out of every 12 women in the United States over the age of 14 is a widow. There are over 11.5 million widows and widowers in the United States. The overwhelming majority (by ratio of 5:1) are women. By contrast, there are only 6 million divorced persons, of whom five sixths are men and three fourths are women. Widowed men and women tend to be much older than divorced people. More than 43% of the women between 65 and 74 are widows (Strong & Reynolds, 1979).

Only 12% of the 11 million single people over the age of 65 are never married; 3% are separated, 77% are widowed, and 7% are divorced. Thus it appears that widowhood is shared by a large number of women. In the United States well over 10 million, or about 13% of all women over the age of 18, are widows (Bureau of the Census, 1989). Growth in the number and proportion of women who are widows is likely to continue for the rest of this century because census projections indicate an increase of 43% in the size of the total population over 65 by the year 2000.

By far the majority of marriages end with one partner's death. Although a spouse can die during early or middle adult years, widowhood usually occurs later in life. Thus widows and widowers are likely to be older than divorced persons. In most cases, it is the man who dies first, a tendency that has become more pronounced in this century. The ratio of widows to widowers has increased from less than 2:1 in the early 1900s to 5:1 in the 1970s (Hoult, Henz, & Hudson, 1978), which means the pool of available men is small relative to the number of women looking for partners. The larger percentage of widows compared to widowers can be attributed to the fact that women live longer than men and tend to marry men who are older than themselves. Widows, particularly if they are older, tend to be less active sexually than widowers. Older widows are often reluctant to begin new relationships and may be influenced by loyalty to the departed husband and by negative family pressure. It is also easier for widowers to remarry, and they tend to marry younger women. This reinforces the cultural stereotypes, shared by elderly women themselves, that physical attractiveness is more important in women than men and that aging women are less attractive than aging men.

Currently American women have a life expectancy of 79, about 7 years longer than American men. If demographic patterns were used to suggest marital arrangements, it would make sense for older women to marry younger men. However, our cultural norms, socially constructed definitions around mate selection, and opportunities are such that the initial mortality differences are compounded by the tendency for women to marry older men. Because only about 5% of previous cohorts of American women never married at all, the inevitable result is that ever larger proportions become widows and remain so for an increasing number of years.

Though the average age for widowhood is over 50, a recent detailed study by the Bureau of the Census (1989) showed that the majority of women whose first husbands die are widowed before age 50. The younger the age at widowhood, the more likely a woman is to marry, but overall, fewer than one third of these widows ever remarry.

Social Aspects of Widowhood

Most preindustrial societies have clear roles for widows. For example, in traditional Indian society, a Brahmin widow was supposed to commit suttee by throwing herself on her husband's funeral pyre. If she did not do this, she was condemned to live out her life with shaven head, dressing in a coarse garment, eating only one meal a day, and being shunned by others as unlucky. Another solution, practiced by many African societies, was an immediate remarriage to a younger brother of the deceased or to some other heir, so that the widow and her children became part of a polygamous family.

Widowhood can thus be defined more by the collapse of old roles and structural supports than by norms and institutions that specify or provide new role relationships and behavior patterns. Lopata (1975) concluded from her data that American society has been phasing out the traditional status role of widow as an all-pervasive lifelong identity: "Usually, widowhood is a temporary stage of identity reconstruction, and this is a major problem. The direction of movement out of it is not clearly defined" (p. 47).

The widow in American society and other Western industrialized societies has lost not only a husband, but in many cases, if she is not working, her own main functions, reason for being, and self-identity. In spite of "women's liberation," most women who become widows today have defined themselves primarily as wives and mothers.

Remarriage is not a likely solution. There are fewer than 2 million widowers in the United States, one for every five widows, and they are likely to marry younger women. Thus fewer than 5% of women widowed after age 55 ever remarry (Cleveland & Gianturco, 1976). However, even though a woman is likely to spend as much time as a widow as she does raising children, the subject is taboo, and few women prepare ahead of time for widowhood.

A younger widow is apt to be lonelier than an older widow, who is more likely to have many more friends in the same position. Furthermore, older people may be better prepared psychologically for widowhood because they have experienced the death of friends and relatives and "rehearsed" for the deaths of spouses.

"Anticipatory socialization" had not occurred for the 40 Kansas widows studied by Gibb (1979), however. Even though all were over 50 years of age, they were little prepared for widowhood. Intensive interviews with widows in three age groups (30 to 40, 41 to 59, and 60 and older) revealed both common problems and problems that differed by age (Wyly & Hulicka, 1975). All complained of loneliness and of difficulties in maintaining homes and cars. The two younger age groups also mentioned problems with decision making, child rearing, sex, and money. The oldest widows had trouble learning how to manage money and find transportation, and they feared crime. Although some younger widows acknowledged that they felt more independent and free than while they were married, the oldest widows saw no advantages to their condition. To some extent, cohort differences were more important than age differences. For example, younger women were more likely to have participated in money management and to have driven cars.

Other investigators have found that although younger widows have lower levels of well-being, they are more likely to remarry (Cleveland & Gianturco, 1976). Further, Wyly and Hulicka's older subjects reported nothing good about their state (1975)—but a Los Angeles study (Morgan, 1976) found that older widows had higher morale than did older married women.

Psychological Aspects of Widowhood

The death of a spouse is one of the most serious life crises a person faces. The immediate emotional crisis of bereavement, if not fully worked through, may result in psychological symptoms. During the first few days of bereavement, sacred and secular guidelines define the proper mourning role for the widow. However, over the longer term the widow's life generally needs to be restructured as she finds herself much poorer, socially isolated, and without a meaningful life style.

In traditional situations, perhaps because of their greater dependence on the deceased, the stress of bereavement tends to be greater for women than for men. Men also seem to accept death more readily than women and find it harder to express grief (Glick, Weiss, & Parkes, 1974). However, whether the survivor is a man or a woman, the death of a loved one deprives the survivor of various kinds of satisfaction both physical and emotional. Over the years the bereaved's sense of identity and the meaning of his or her life may have become intertwined with the personality of the deceased. Somehow he or she must now learn to cope with the loss and the resulting stress.

The period of greatest stress for the bereaved is usually immediately after the death of the deceased when the reactions of the bereaved are most intense. Among the behavioral reactions observed during the first month of mourning are periodic crying, difficulty sleeping, loss of appetite, and problems in concentrating or remembering. A study of 109 widowed persons found that the emotional disturbances and insomnia associated with bereavement can also lead to dependence on tranquilizers, sleeping pills, and or alcohol (Clayton, Halikes, & Maurice, 1971).

The emotional reactions of a surviving spouse, who in 75% of the cases is the wife, may be so intense that severe physical illness, a serious accident, or even death—occasionally from suicide—occurs. A study of 4,500 British widowers aged 55 and over found, for example, that 213 died during the first 6 months of their bereavement (Parkes, Benjamin & Fitzgerald, 1969). The rate of death, most instances of which apparently resulted from heart problems, was 40% higher than expected in this age group. Concluding from a series of related investigations that grief and consequent feelings of helplessness make people more vulnerable to pathogens, Seligman (1973) suggested that individuals who have recently lost a spouse should be very careful about their health. He recommended monthly medical checkups during the first year after the loss.

Although anxiety and depression are the most common reactions to bereavement, anger, guilt, and even psychotic symptoms have been observed. Depression is a normal response to any severe loss, but it is augmented by feelings of guilt in cases where interpersonal hostilities and conflicts with the deceased have not been resolved. Anger may be expressed—toward nurses, physicians, friends, and family members whom the bereaved believes to have been negligent in their treatment of the deceased. For various reasons, survivors may also experience anger toward the deceased or relief at his or her death—both of which can lead to feelings of guilt.

The emotional and psychological traumas of grief and mourning involve letting go of the emotional ties and roles centered on the spouse. If this working through of grief is successfully accomplished, the widow can face a second set of problems having to do with building a new life, a new set of role relationships, and constructing a new identity.

Maggie, at 46, had been married for 21 years. She and her husband Michael had three children. The two older boys were away in college, and the youngest, age 17, was still at home, finishing high school. Maggie and Michael enjoyed their life together. For a while she had worked in his family business, an interstate trucking company that was doing very well financially. But after 2 years in the firm, she yearned for the painting and sculpting that were her true vocational interests and pursued them with great dedication and with Michael's complete support. Her artistic work was exhibited in a few well-known galleries in So-Ho. Their life was happy, worry free, and cheerful. Both were in excellent physical health and went regularly for medical checkups. Michael had seen the doctor just the week before, and nothing amiss was found with his health. However, that night he felt what he thought was indigestion and slight nausea. He went to bed in this condition and died in his sleep of a massive heart attack. He was 47 years old.

Maggie was in a state of shock, unable to function or think clearly. The boys and her older brother, whose family was very close to theirs, took care of all the arrangements for Michael's funeral and burial. Maggie could not stop crying; her speech was incoherent, and she looked 20 years older than her chronological age. Even 2 weeks after Michael's death, she needed someone— usually her daughter, Chrissie—to watch over her. Otherwise, Maggie forgot to eat, take a shower, get out of bed. After a month of this, her brother told the children that he thought Maggie should be seen by a doctor for her depression. She was under psychiatric care for 5 months.

When we talked to Maggie, about a year after Michael's death, she explained that she still missed Michael very much but that she knew she had to focus on the future, not on the past. She thought that their happiness together had made them such a close couple that his death made her feel lost, panicked, and helpless. She realized now that she had not achieved the balance between closeness and separation that she thought she had between her husband and herself. Her whole life had not made her ready for being without her husband even though, because of her artistic career, she looked as if she was "independent." She was now organizing a self-help group, not for widows but for married women. She wanted to prepare women for the possibility of having to cope with the type of circumstances she had gone through.

Bowlby (1969) found evidence for five stages in mourning: (1) concentration on the deceased, (2) anger toward the deceased or others, (3) appeals to others for help, (4) despair, withdrawal, and disorganization, and

(5) reorganization and direction of love toward a new object. There has been relatively little research on Bowlby's stages, but it is recognized that not all mourners go through them in the order listed.

Kavanaugh (1974) also described stages in the process of grieving or mourning for a loved one: shock, disorganization, volatile emotions, guilt, loss and loneliness, relief, and reestablishment. Kavanaugh also recognized that a particular mourner may not go through all these stages or in the order listed.

Gorer (1967) presented a four-stage conception of mourning:

1. Initial shock is the first stage that lasts only a few days and is characterized by loss of self control, reduced energy, and lack of motivation. The mourner is bewildered, disoriented, and loses perspective. The person cannot accept the fact that "he is really dead, gone forever." This numbness often extends for several weeks beyond the funeral.

2. Intense grief is the second stage. It is characterized by emotional reactions such as crying, a confused inability to comprehend what has actually happened (often accompanied by such psychosomatic symptoms as headache and insomnia), feelings of guilt ("If I had done so and so, maybe he wouldn't have died"), expressions of anger, ("Why me! It was so unfair!"), hostility or blame ("The doctors killed him"), and often preoccupation with memories of the deceased and an idealization of him. The second stage can last for several months, but it gradually gives way for the next stage.

3. Feelings of sadness and loneliness are the third stage. These feelings, which are often incapacitating, include depression and loss of customary patterns of behavior and of motivation to try to go on living.

4. A recovery phase is the fourth and final stage. Here there is a general recovery of interest. The mourner accepts the reality of the loved one's death and all that it means. As Glick et al. (1974) have concluded from their extensive studies on bereavement, "the death of a spouse typically gives rise to a reaction whose duration must be measured in years rather than in weeks" (p.10).

A variety of grief reactions may occur when the mourner does not express emotions or refuses to deal with the loss. These include delay of the grief reactions for months or even years, overactivity without a sense of loss, indefinite irritability and hostility toward others, sense of the presence of the deceased, acquisition of the physical symptoms of the deceased's last illness, insomnia, apathy, psychosomatically based illnesses such as ulcerative colitis, and such intense depression and feelings of worthlessness that suicide is attempted (Parkes, 1972, p. 211; Van Coevering, 1974, p. 6).

One tendency is for the bereaved to reconstruct an idealized version of the deceased husband and of the relationship with him before the death. Lopata (1972) referred to this as "husband sanctification" and reported that three quarters of the Chicago area's current and former beneficiaries of Social Security defined their late husband as having been "extremely good, honest, kind, friendly, and warm." Sanctification is especially likely among women who rank the role of wife above all others. It is an attempt to continue defining oneself primarily in terms of the now-ended role relationship. Lopata viewed this as an effort to "remove the late husband into another worldly position as an understanding but purified and distant observer" (p. 30), so that the widow is able to go about reconstructing old role relationships and forming new ones.

Several factors are related to severe or prolonged grief. When 68 widows and widowers under the age of 45 were interviewed shortly after the spouse died and again a year later, the researchers found three classes of strongly correlated variables predict continued severe bereavement reactions 13 months after the death (Parkes, 1975, pp. 308-309):

1.   Low socioeconomic status, that is, low weekly income of the husband
2.   Lack of preparation for the loss due to noncancer deaths, short terminal illness, accident or heart attack, or failure to talk to the spouse about the coming death
3.   Other life crises preceding spouse's death, such as infidelity and job loss.

It is interesting that a poor income is likely if the marriage relationship was troubled before the death; folk wisdom has it that the widow should "be glad to be rid of him." However, psychologically debilitating guilt over having wished the death of the husband could be very strong in such cases. Another problem is the amount of unfinished business (Blauner, 1968) left by the removal of the husband through death. Parkes (1975) concluded that for his young respondents, including widowers as well as widows, "When advance warning was short and death was sudden, it seemed to have a much greater impact and to lead to greater and more lasting disorganization" (p. 313).

Given the severe and persistent emotional, psychological, and psychosomatic aspects of even normal grief, it becomes impossible for a widow to carry out her usual role relationships and to cope with the problems of change in financial and social status that are thrust upon her.

The Widow

Ruth and Ralph had been married for 38 years. Their three "girls" and two "boys" were all married and had given them nine grandchildren. Only the oldest son, 37, had stayed nearby. The others were living as far away as California, South Carolina, and Illinois. Ruth's marriage was of the traditional type in the most negative sense: Ralph was a psychologically abusive husband who disregarded her rights and feelings, engaged in many extramarital affairs for the duration of the marriage, and had little to do with the children's upbringing other than providing them with a negative role model. During the 2 years of Ralph's illness (cancer of the bladder), Ruth was a model of devotion to her husband, disregarding her own feelings and remaining at the beck and call of a very unreasonable and demanding "husband/master."

When he finally died, she was the dutiful mourning spouse; however, immediately after the funeral she felt a raw and powerful hatred and rage that she tried to repress because these feelings were so new and so much against her value system. Her unconscious repression turned into conscious suppression that took the form of alcoholism. Her children reacted with great righteousness to their mother's "misconduct" and became punitive and disrespectful. This only gave her more reasons to increase her drinking. The situation became so bad, causing social embarrassment to the family, that she was hospitalized for detoxification after she was arrested for urinating in a children's playground while inebriated. In her first few days at the hospital Ruth fought every inch of the way, refusing even to answer questions or eat. She was given a series of electroshock treatments, after which she cooperated with the hospital routine and therapy.

At the age of 63, as she told us, she finally realized the marital abuse she had been exposed to during almost four decades of her life. Her therapy had allowed her to accept as valid the fury that she had so well repressed during her marriage and that came up after her husband's death. It had also helped her to change her values and to become a "new woman," as she proudly called herself. She had to travel a long and painful road to arrive at the point where she was now, 5 years after Ralph's death. His death had caused turmoil in her life and in the lives of her children, but Ruth now realized that was the high price she had to pay to become the new woman she was now.

One of the accomplishments she was very pleased with was that she had cultivated new relationships with her daughters. She had visited each of them and prepared for her visit by telling them that she wanted to have plenty of time to talk privately. The three visits were successful, and a new, mature, adult relationship was started with each one of her daughters. The two sons offered a great amount of resistance to her new image, and Ruth resigned herself to less intimate relationships with them, as compared to the new interactions with her daughters.

Ruth told us that she still had feelings of love for her former husband, that she had been able to forgive him "because he didn't know better," and that she didn't know any better in terms of not accepting his sexist treatment of her. She said that she attained a state of inner peace by selectively remembering good and pleasant events of those 38 years. Ruth sounded a very wise, calm, and happy person, indeed.

The subsequent life changes and problems faced by the widow indicate that widowhood is a role for which there is no comparable role among males. Glick et al. (1974) summarized the difference between their samples of widows and widowers:" Insofar as the men reacted simply to the loss of a loved other, their responses were similar to those of widows; but insofar as men reacted to the traumatic disruption of their lives, their responses were different" (p. 262). This differential impact is found in the financial impact after death. For the widow it almost always means the loss of the main source of financial support for the family and a consequent lowering of the standard of living. The incomes of the widows' families were down an average of 44% from previous levels 2 to 3 years after the onset of widowhood, and 58% had incomes that fell below the amount necessary to maintain their family's former standard of living.

In addition to financially devastating final expenses that wipe out savings, widows are entitled to no Social Security benefits at all unless they have dependents or are over 60. After 60 years of age, they are entitled to only a portion of what would have been their husband's benefits. The final explanation for the high probability of poverty among widows is that because of age, general low level of skill and education, and lack of experience, they are often unable to obtain employment. In other words, neither the private economy nor the public welfare system is currently structured to provide economic support in late middle age.

Before widowhood, a traditionally married woman defines herself and relates to others mainly in terms of her status as somebody's wife. At widowhood, most of her role relationships have to adjust and some terminate. She has to establish new role relationships if her life is to be a satisfying one. For example, she is unlikely to maintain close ties with friends and relatives who belonged to social circles maintained with her husband. Changes in finances can require changes in other spheres of life, such as movement into the work force. A change in residence may result in loss of contact with neighbors. Often, in settling her husband's estate, she has to deal with lawyers and insurance agents and has to take on the role of business woman (Lopata, 1975, p. 48).

The difficulties an older woman in our society is likely to encounter in establishing such a new set of role relationships are affirmed by Lopata's research. She found that half of the widows in her sample considered loneliness their greatest problem, and another third listed it as second. Social isolation was listed by 58%, who agreed that "One problem of being a widow is feeling like a 'fifth wheel'" (Lopata, 1972, p. 346).

Lopata's work focused on the widow's role relationships in regard to motherhood, kin relationships, friendship, and community involvement, including employment. Among her findings were that "women who develop satisfactory friendships, who weather the transition period and solve its problems creatively, tend to have a higher education, a considerable income, and the physical and psychic energy needed to initiate change" (1972, p. 216). These women are not the average widows, who are likely to have a high school education or less, low income, depleted physical energy due to advancing age, and depleted psychic energy due to the trauma of bereavement and its associated problems. Thus, Lopata (1973) found that while the death of the husband created greater personal disruption in the lives of her more educated respondents than was the case for less-educated women, and also greater dislocation of the friendship network because it had been based on couple companionship, the better educated women had greater emotional and financial resources. They were able to move about and meet others whom they could choose as friends, and they also had less stressful relationships with their children than did the less-educated women. The same advantages may characterize reintegration in friendship networks after separation and divorce.

The importance of maintaining or establishing supportive role relationships with an understanding "other" such as an old friend, neighbor, or supportive professional or paraprofessional has been emphasized in many studies. For example, Maddison and Raphael (1975) emphasized their "conviction that the widow's perception of her social network is an extremely important determinant of the outcome of her bereavement crisis" (1975, p. 29). "Bad outcome" women had no one to whom they could freely express their grief and anger.

The Widower

The impact of widowhood on men has received little systematic attention, and the role of widower is probably even vaguer than that of the widow. Because widowers who have not remarried are not very common in the community until after about age 75, they are not as likely to join each other in groups. Like widows, they are expected to preserve the memories of their wives and are expected not to show interest in other women. Indications are that many widowers adhere to the former but ignore the latter, as can be inferred from the remarriage rates cited earlier.

Clearly something other than simple numbers is operating with respect to sex differences in coping with widowhood. Men who have led their entire lives playing instrumental, at the expense of expressive, marital roles are poorly prepared for widowhood. Most men who had traditional marriages have been so dependent upon their wives for the performance of the most basic maintenance tasks, such as preparing a meal or running a washing machine, that they often feel totally helpless in tending to daily necessities. There is also a general unwillingness among some of these men to perform "women's work" if there is any way they can avoid it (Rainwater, 1965). They have difficulty breaking lifelong attitudes toward sex-role behaviors.

In addition, those men who have taken most seriously the traditional cultural position regarding emotion or sensitivity among males have often not developed genuinely close friendships. One reason is that they may have been preoccupied with their image of what it is to be a man at the expense of true same-sex intimacy. Another reason may be that they have been socialized in such a way that they feel uncomfortable risking their feelings or expressing fears and concerns among peers, whereas within a traditional/subordinate type marriage, a wife can be used as confidante without the husband fearing a loss of face (Balsweick & Peek, 1971). For whatever reasons, studies have indicated that among middle and lower socioeconomic groups, male friendships resemble play or meet work-oriented goals rather than genuine interpersonal needs. However, there is evidence that men, especially in late middle age, experience awareness of the superficiality of their friendships and express regret (Lowenthal & Robinson, 1976).

Perhaps because women have been permitted, indeed have been culturally coerced, to play expressive roles within families and have been socialized to display such attributes as emotionality and sensitivity to others, they show more flexibility in the object of their close relationships. Women often have intimate same-sex friendships at various life stages. Thus the prevalence of friendships among older widows not only reflects the dearth of available widowers at that age but also their prior experiences and comfortability within such relationships. Both in terms of same-sex friendships and in ability to run a household on a day-to-day level, widowed women tend to be better prepared for living alone than their male counterparts.

Further, women who are widowed do not seem to experience that life event in the same way that men do. In a study of 403 community residents aged 62 and over (Barrett, 1978), six major areas of life functioning were assessed: psychosocial needs, household roles, nutrition, health care, transportation, and education. Widowers were found to experience lower morale, feel lonelier and more dissatisfied with life, consider community services more inadequate, need more help with household chores, have greater difficulty getting medical appointments, eat more poorly, and possess stronger negative attitudes about continued learning than widows. Moreover, widowers were more reluctant to talk about widowhood or death than widows were, and stated that they did not want a confidante.

Although the problems of adjusting to the loss of a spouse are often worse for a woman than for a man, an elderly widow usually has more friends available to her than an elderly widower, who may discover that he was more dependent on his wife for physical and emotional support than he realized when she was living. Because men are usually not as close to other people as women, widowers are apparently more lonely and consequently need marriage more than widows do. This is one reason why the great majority of widowers remarry within a year or so after their wife's death.

Because men traditionally acquire their identities only partly from being husbands, widowers are probably not as apt as widows to face acute identity crises when they lose their wives. Yet because they are likely to have seen their wives as important parts of themselves (Glick et al., 1974), they, too, can feel lost. Their wives were probably their main confidantes and their links to family and friends. There is little evidence that widowhood is any less devastating for men than for women.

Glick et al. (1974) reported that widowers have more difficulty on the job than do widows during the mourning period. Because jobs are primary in men's lives, widowers may be more sensitive to job disruption than are widows.

Widowers do not differ from widows in feeling isolated from kin or friends. Nor are widowed men and women, on the whole, more isolated than are their married peers. In fact, after being widowed those who have friends tend to see them more often (Petrowsky, 1976). When Atchley (1975) controlled for social class, he found that widowhood tends to increase contacts with friends among middle-class widowers and to decrease them among lower class widowers. It could be that the large surplus of women in senior centers and similar social groups for older people—generally used more by working-class people than by middle-class people—may inhibit working-class widowers from developing new kinds of community activities. Widowers tend to be embarrassed and even to feel harassed by the competition among widows for their attentions. Moreover, they are unaccustomed to participating in such preponderantly female gatherings, where women dominate discussions and other activities. Petrowsky (1976) found that widowers were less involved in religious activities than were widows, an effect that is probably due to a continuation of religious participation sex differences established earlier in life.

Between the ages of 65 and 74, widowers in general tend slightly more than widows to live in group quarters, such as hotels or rooming houses, rather than in independent households. After age 75, there is little sex difference in type of residence. Widowers who live in their own homes are only slightly more likely to live alone than are widows and are only slightly less likely to be living with their children. When they live in multiperson households, however, widowers are much more likely to be considered heads of such households.

Harry and Odile had been married for 42 years. Odile died of intestinal complications after several operations that unfortunately made her more and more disabled. Harry, in spite of his 76 years, was a consultant to several big industries and kept giving seminars, traveling, and maintaining a busy schedule. His health was strong, and his hobbies were many, including boating, car racing, tennis, and acting in a local theater company. After about 6 months of mourning, during which he hardly saw any friends and did not socialize at all, though he kept himself professionally occupied, he started to accept invitations from friends to parties and get-togethers. He kept many souvenirs of Odile in the house, such as pictures, objects, and books. His house was near the ocean, and he started inviting people over to keep him company. He told many stories of the many wonderful years he and Odile had traveled all over the world, attended important congresses, and lived in many different parts of the country. They never had children, and he had little contact with relatives. But he formed a large circle of friends around him. Through his friends, he met several available widows or divorced women and soon he started dating. About 2 years after Odile's death, he was dating Connie exclusively.

When we interviewed Harry, he explained that he felt "too old to marry Connie," but that they were practically sharing their lives as if they were married. Although Connie kept her own house, she spent much of her time at Harry's. However, she ran her own business and did not want to depend on Harry. He explained that widowhood had been a very painful shock to him: "I had never really thought of death before." But he made an effort to go on with his life and work, grateful for the great life he and Odile had together, rather than allowing her death to depress him or slow him down. Connie knew how important his wife had been and accepted the fact that Harry kept so many fond memories and told so many stories of his wife. He mentioned several of his friends whom he described as "losers" because they kept on living in the past. "I remember Odile with fondness and gratitude, but I realize she is now a memory. The person is gone, and now I have the great fortune of sharing my life with another wonderful person. I love Connie, I'm fond of her, we enjoy each other's company, and I even suspect that when I am 80 years young, I'll decide to get married. I am too old now, but by 80, I've heard, one enters his second youth."

Harry had refused to feel helpless. He thought that joining clubs and groups of old people was a sign of helplessness and had decided to form his own network of friends from among the many people he had met in his long career as a business consultant. He had persevered and the result was his new love and his continued professional involvement and activity. He told us that he had several models for this stage of his life, including Casals, Picasso, Irving Berlin, George Burns, and Bob Hope. He considered them his teachers: "They live or lived fantastic in their senior years. They are my teachers. I try to live exactly the way they do or did."

Widowhood and Children

Jim was 77 years old when his wife Sylvia died. It happened suddenly. One day she was fine and the next she was in the hospital attached to tubes. As he stood watching her breathe, he remembered that she had been complaining of a pain in her back for the past week, but neither of them thought it was anything serious. He talked about this in counseling for the next 2 years, feeling guilty, feeling that he could have possibly saved her life if he had acted sooner. But they both thought she had pulled a muscle playing golf. She died 2 days later, a consequence of the damage done from a massive heart attack. Everyone was shocked when she died because she was such a vivacious woman. On some level Jim and their children thought she would live forever. She rarely was ill, and she remained active after she retired from her job as an office manager. In fact, she had continued to help out at the office up until a few weeks ago.

After the funeral, Jim emptied the house of all her personal belongings. This was so painful for him. As he went through her personal belongings, he remembered when she had worn a particular dress last or when they had bought a certain piece of jewelry. He kept feeling that at any moment she would walk into the room and ask him what he wanted for dinner. He missed her.

They had many friends, so he was kept occupied by people who lived in the retirement community stopping over to make sure he was all right. Many women in the community brought over food and baked goods, trying to help him as much as possible.

In a few months, his friends began to introduce him to other "ladies." At first he felt very guilty and ashamed, but soon he welcomed the company. It helped him not to think about Sylvia. His children were appalled that he was dating other women. They thought he was having a nervous breakdown. One of his daughters even tried to talk to him about safer sex practices. He was very embarrassed.

Then he met Ester. Ester was a good woman, kind and sensitive. Her own husband had died a year earlier. He liked Ester right away. She had a quiet way about her, helping him to feel calm and content. When he was with her, he didn't feel the incredible loneliness and sadness he had been feeling since Sylvia died. Their relationship escalated quickly, and they began spending more and more time together.

When Jim told his children that he was seriously dating Ester, they were outraged. "How could you do this to Mommy?" his oldest daughter screeched. His middle daughter said she could go along with anything he wanted, but Jim knew she was deeply depressed about the situation. They felt he was not being loyal their mother. Jim felt that he didn't know how much time he had left to live so he didn't want to waste time.

Six months after Sylvia died, Jim and Ester married. They had a small wedding, and only the immediate family attended. Her children were delighted at the marriage and treated him very kindly. Although his children were very polite to Ester, he knew they were extremely upset. His oldest daughter, who generally verbalized everything that was on her mind, told him she understood why he wanted to marry Ester, but she was having a hard time handling it. She still felt he was being disloyal to their mother. She said their mother wasn't even dead a year.

A few months later, when Jim and Ester were traveling, they stayed for a few nights at this daughter's home. One evening, when Jim and his daughter were alone, his daughter told him that it was making her sick that he was traveling all over the world with Ester when that was what their mother had wanted to do. It also made her sick that they were sleeping in the same bed together. She couldn't believe that he had just "thrown Mommy away." She was so upset. Still grieving for her lost mother, she couldn't understand why he wasn't feeling the same sadness. She didn't understand that his sadness was different from hers and that the fact that he had such a good, rewarding marriage to her mother helped him to seek out another marital partner.

As is illustrated in this case history, there are also problems when the widowed individual has adult children living in the area. The death of a husband tends to cause strain in relationships with children, in-laws, and even one's own siblings and other relatives. Thirty-nine percent of the clients of the Widows Consultation Center reported that relationships with family members were a problem at the time they came to the center (Hiltz, 1975). Problems with children were reported by more clients (31%), compared to in-laws (8%) and siblings (6%).

The problems with children were twofold: a perceived coldness or neglect to give the widow as much "love" and support and time as she thought she was entitled to (17%), and what the widow considered serious behavioral problems with the children, such as taking drugs or withdrawing from employment and from communication with the mother (15%) (Hiltz, 1975, pp. 65-65).

The neglect or coldness the widow sees may be viewed as an unfair and unpleasant burden by a child, especially sons. For example, Adams (1968) found that grown middle-class sons perceived their obligations to their mother as a "one-way" or unreciprocated pattern of aid and support giving.

This typically results in the son's loss of affection for the mother and his resentment of her dependence on him.

For younger widows with dependent children, there are difficulties in maintaining the maternal role of effectively responding to the child's needs. Silverman and Englander (1975) found that most parents and children avoided talking about the death to one another. Common reactions for the children were fear that they could lose the surviving parent too; the assumption by the children of new family responsibilities; and poor school work related to rebellion and social withdrawal (Silverman & Englander, 1975, p. 11).

Role relationships to in-laws may be cut off entirely if the widow does not find them pleasant and supportive. As Lopata (1973) pointed out, this is a unique kind of institutional arrangement because the patriarchal family traditionally had vested rights over the wife and the offspring of a marriage. However, "American widows are free to move away from their in-laws, if they were living nearby, and even to lose all contact with them. They are free to cut the ties between their children and that side of the family and even to remarry and change the name of the unit" (p. 3). However, none of the studies seem to include the impact of such decisions on the role relationship between paternal grandparents and grandchildren, and on the emotional pain that may be caused if the relationship is severed.

In these cases, there also may be divided loyalties between the dead parent and the new person the remaining parent is dating, possibly creating hostility toward the new partner. Sometimes adult children feel they must protect themselves from the new relationship. In these cases they tend to deny the existence of the relationship and in very patronizing ways laugh at their parents "childish" behavior. Many adult children also have difficulty in viewing their widowed parents as sexual persons.

Counseling Strategies

Lopata (1973) has concluded that the greatest short-range needs of widows are:

1. Expressing emotions and coming to terms with widowhood through "grief work" with the help of family, friends, and counselors.
2. Finding companionship, especially if the widow is living alone for the first time in her life.
3. Being protected from the hordes of people who want to give her advice. "Every one around her is full of advice, and the bits she receives are often contradictory and irrelevant or unbeneficial from her point of view (p. 273).

4. Getting assistance in building self-confidence and competencies, assis-
    tance that can consist of not giving too much advice and avoiding
    actions that might encourage dependency.
5. Receiving help in reengaging, that is, in becoming involved in social
    activities that will be stimulating and meaningful.

Group counseling is an effective method for dealing with these issues.
In looking for ways in which groups can be used to facilitate the grief
process, Barrett (1977) organized three different kinds of groups of widows.
Half of her sample said they had never thought about the death of their
husband before it occurred, and two thirds had never considered what it
might be like to be a widow. Their average income, even though half of
them worked, was about one half of what it had been at the time of their
husband's death.

The first group was called a *self-help group* because the leader was a
facilitator, not a teacher, and helped members of the group help each
other. This type is generally referred to as a widow-to-widow group in
England and in some cities in this country.

In this intervention approach, experienced widows (and widowers) are
matched for certain characteristics (age, education, economic status) and
then serve as helpers with new or newly bereaved group members, assisting
in the transition period and in acquiring the new role. This approach
appears to be generally successful (Silverman & Cooperband, 1975).

The second group was called the *confidante group*. The leader used
intimate techniques and group activities where individuals were paired and
participated as couples. In this group the leader tried to facilitate a "helping
relationship" for each pair.

The third group was labeled a *woman's consciousness-raising group*. In
discussions, the focus was on ways in which sex roles were viewed by widows
in the group. Such topics as "Sexuality among widows: Are you still a wife?"
characterized the interaction. Each of the groups gathered for 2 hours a
week for some 8 weeks.

Barrett (1978) assessed three different therapeutic group interventions
dealing with consciousness raising for 70 urban widowed women. The
effects of the intervention were evaluated, and the women were compared
to a waiting-list control group. Treatments were designed to meet the needs
of widows of all ages because research suggests that stresses may be greater
for younger widows (Kraus & Lilienfeld, 1959), even though the frequency
of widowhood is higher among older women. Eighteen personality, attitude, and behavioral measures were obtained by written report on three
occasions: pretest, posttest, and follow-up 14 weeks later. At posttest and
follow-up, higher self-esteem, increased intensity of grief feelings, and increased negative attitudes toward remarriage were reported by all groups.
Intervention groups showed improvements in their ratings of their future

health, and they became less other oriented in their attitudes toward women relative to the controls.

Chapter 3
SINGLE PARENT FAMILY ISSUES

Since 1970 the number of single-parent households has doubled. Of these households, 70% are the result of divorce, 14% are the result of death of a parent, 6% are temporary because one parent is away, and 10% have not been involved in a marriage (Weiss, 1979). Because of the problems inherent in this type of family system, the single-parent family frequently comes for counseling. This chapter describes systemic and behavioral theory relevant to single-parent family counseling and discusses a single-parent case history illustrating behavioral and systemic counseling strategies.

Most parents, whether they be in a two-parent or a single-parent family situation, are not aware of the functions of a family. According to Parsons and Bales (1955), the functions of the family are to socialize the children, provide models for relationships with others, establish cultural norms, provide religious and ethical values and emotional support, politically indoctrinate the children, provide financial care, give guidance, and educate the young. When these tasks are accomplished, a functional family provides the children with a healthy sense of self (Walsh, 1982). It teaches them how to relate to other people by providing them with the nurturing, support, and security necessary for each member of the family to develop to his or her fullest potential. The single-parent family with a problem is generally not carrying out these tasks satisfactorily and so is assumed stuck in its definition of the situation (Walsh, 1982).

These are not easy tasks even with the traditional two adults in the parenting role. The situation becomes yet more difficult in a single-parent family household, with only one person responsible for providing the young with an adequate foundation for psychological development. In addition, there are many variations among single-parent families, particularly with respect to their access to economic and social resources. As mentioned in chapter 2, widows tend to have higher incomes and experience less social disapproval than do other groups, whereas never-married mothers (mainly adolescent women) have the fewest resources and are most likely to become dependent on government welfare assistance (Kohen, 1981). In 1983, one of two children in female-headed households was poor. (See the discussion of the feminization of poverty in chapter 10.)

General Concerns Among Single-Parent Families

Although there is no one type of single-parent family system (Mendes, 1979), certain generalities about the problems inherent in this system can be made. For example, Weiss (1979) has identified three levels of possible overload for the single parent. First is *responsibility overload*. The single parent has to make all decisions regarding family life and the children's behavior. From financial details to daily domestic duties, there is no one else to turn to for direction. The parent can feel overwhelmed by these demands. Children often begin to take on some of the responsibilities, but they are unable to make some of the bigger decisions regarding their lives, which are left up to the lone parent. It is in this area of increased responsibility that the single parent may feel the greatest effects of having lost a system of interaction in which many decisions are shared. Although some single parents feel freer in making decisions without interference, others may feel tension, pressure, and confusion (Ahrons & Rodgers, 1987).

The second level is *task overload*, or, simply, too much to do. The parent has to earn money, make meals, clean the house, discipline the children, make doctor and dental appointments, make rental, insurance, care, and other payments—all alone. Most single parents have little time for friends or a social life, which often leads to social isolation.

Weiss's (1979) third level is *emotional overload*. The single parent has to be available to his or her children emotionally, even when exhausted or drained of all available reserves. Some single parents do have family, friends, or an ex-spouse to consult with, but for many there is no one else to turn to for needed attention, no one with whom to discuss the children's growth and personality development. There also may be no other person to step in at times when the parent is feeling so stretched as to be irrational or thoughtless with regard to the children (Isaacs, Montalvo, & Adelsohn, 1986). In some cases, emotionally overburdened parents may lash out, physically as well as verbally, against a child, not because he or she has done anything wrong but simply because he or she is there (Isaacs, Montalvo, & Adelsohn, 1986).

The loss of the other parent is significant in other ways as well. The parent may no longer have an ally to help him or her in disciplinary efforts. The single parent, with new responsibilities, can suffer in ways that are passed on to the children and are detrimental to the functioning of the whole family. If the single parent is depressed, hostile, or aggressive, and if his or her children are acting out some of their own distress, the single parent may be unable to stop them because there is no other adult around to help. The major point is that the single parent is the focus, especially for younger children, around which all task performance occurs and through which all anxiety and stress must be processed (Beal, 1980).

Other pressures on the parent in the primary home include the conflicts between parents regarding child-rearing practices and how time and monies are spent on children. The absent parent may actively sabotage the other parent's efforts by trying to get the children aligned with him or her against the primary parent. In all situations the absent parent must be included in consideration of the system (Beal, 1980). Grandparents and other relatives may take sides with one of the parents, serving to confuse the children with divided loyalties. Or they may align with the children against the custodial parent, creating a cross-generational coalition that leaves the family system ripe for dysfunction. Whether brought about through necessity or choice, single-parent families share certain basic problems: how to cope single handedly with day-to-day decisions and with supervision and discipline of children, and how to compensate for the absence of the other parent.

Systemic family therapy applies general systems theory to family constellations. The systemic approach to family counseling looks at the symptoms or problems presented in a counseling situation in terms of the whole family. Systems theorists assume that behavior is a communication about relationships (Haley, 1977) and that behavior can only be understood within the context in which it occurs. Behavior is defined by (as well as defines) and influenced by (as well as influences) all other behavior in the context or system in which it occurs.

The basic assumption of the family systems counselor, then, is that all parts are interrelated. Change in any one part of the system can effect change in another part of the system. Each part of the system has a unique role or function, and these parts work together to achieve common family goals (Hoffman, 1981). Families also have boundaries that separate them from the environment. Each family's boundary is structured by the values, norms, and attitudes derived from the family's cultural heritage (Minuchin, 1974). Boundaries are the rules and regulations that govern interactions among family members and between the family and the surrounding society. These rules and regulations define how specific family functions get carried out (Minuchin & Fishman, 1981). For a detailed examination of general systems theory, see von Bertalanffy, 1968; and for a description of its application to family therapy, see Bateson, 1979; Bowen, 1978; Haley, 1973, 1977; Hoffman, 1981; Madanes, 1981; and Minuchin and Fishman, 1981.

Systems counselors believe that to counsel only the identified patient is missing the point. Persons exist in environments, and to look at the problem presented from an individual frame of reference is taking the person out of context, seeing the person as existing in a vacuum.

According to systems theory (von Bertalanffy, 1968), family systems have the property of self-regulation. Any input to the family (i.e., change on any one member) is acted upon and modified by the system itself through the mechanism of feedback. Family stability or equilibrium is generally maintained through negative feedback mechanisms, but change (learning, growth, or crisis) is maintained and increased through positive feedback (Walsh, 1982).

A typical traditional two-parent nuclear family system might look like the following: There is a mother and a father, representing an executive authority block from which all authority flows. The mother and father have a bond stronger than all other bonds. The bonds with the children are relatively weaker. Chronologically, the bond between the mother and the father, who generally have greater wisdom and judgment, comes first and endures longer (Nichols, 1984), thereby establishing the authority hierarchy. The natural division occurs always along generational lines. In any given family system, there are at least four subsystems: the children (the sibling subsystem); the husband-wife interactions (the marital subsystem); the parent-child interactions (the parental subsystem); and the nuclear family interactions with external systems and individuals (the extrafamilial subsystem). (See figure 1.)

Figure 1. Structural Diagram of the Two-Parent Family

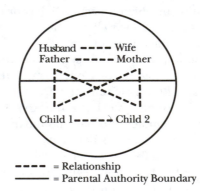

In a healthy, functioning system, the boundaries are clarified. There are relationships among the mother-father subsystem, the mother-children subsystem, and the father-children subsystem. In a single-parent family system, the husband-wife subsystem no longer exists; however, the mother-father subsystem does (Ahrons, 1980). In this single-parent family system, the father of the children is an important part of the children's lives, and he is available to the mother as a resource person in terms of caretaking and decision making concerning the children (Wallerstein & Kelly, 1980c). (See figure 2.) It is helpful to stress when working with single-parent families that the couple relationship may be dissolved, but the parental relationship will remain forever, and the two persons will become grandparents at exactly the same time. Stressing the parental relationship assists the parents in focusing on the best interests of the child and helps to defocus on the problems that they were experiencing in the marital relationship. Also important is the idea put forth by feminist family therapists that when there is a male in the family, as is generally the case in the two-parent family, the family is based on hierarchy; when there is a female running the family, the hierarchical structure generally gives way to a more collaborative structure, based on affection and emotional support.

Figure 2. Structural Diagram of the One-Parent Family

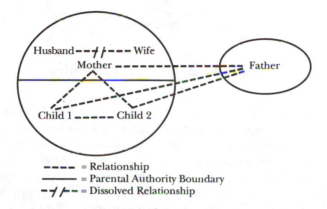

The single-parent family system has one parent absent from the household, or there is a single-parent ghost (i.e., the influence of a dead husband on a family that is kept alive by the wife) in the case of death or birth out of wedlock. A parent-ghost can also exist for either the children or the parent in a single-parent home when there is no contact with the absent parent. In any case, there is a gap that is present in this type of family system, and it typically becomes filled by one of the children. This child is called the *parental child.* Usually the parental child is the oldest child, but not always (Ahrons, 1980).

The presence of a parental child can lead to the cross-generational coalition; it almost always leads to the formation of a pseudoadult who can be overwhelmed and burdened by adult responsibilities (Weiss, 1979). As mental health professionals, it is important to recognize the presence of parental children and to encourage the return of the child to the sibling subsystem, reinforcing the sibling coalition. (See figure 3.)

Thus the systemic approach enables counselors to conceptualize how the family structure looks. In addition, counselors can assess the hierarchy within the system, examine the boundaries of the family members, explore the nature of the subsystems, and look for coalitions.

Figure 3. Structural Diagram of the One-Parent Family With a Parental Child

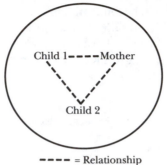

---- = Relationship

Cognitive-Behavioral Principles

Cognitive-behavioral psychological principles may be useful for the therapist not only because they provide information about the family system but also because they can help in utilizing behavioral therapeutic interventions in order to induce systemic change. Cognitive-behavioral approaches have been shown to be an effective strategy for treating marital distress (e.g., Jacobson & Margolin, 1979; Weiss, 1980). Until recently, little attention has been paid to the potential success of applying it to family therapy. The behavioral approach contributes the specific, step-by-step intervention strategies through which the underlying goals of the family are accomplished via the use of positive and negative reinforcers and punishers (Jacobson & Margolin, 1979). Because one of the basic assumptions of cognitive-behavioral therapy is that emotional disturbance is caused by the persistence of beliefs that are irrational or untrue, cognitive-behavioral interventions may be used to help produce perceptual shifts in thinking, feeling, or acting (Jacobson & Margolin, 1979). Thus the family is assessed at the systemic level, and the specific therapeutic interventions used are cognitive-behavioral. The level of analysis is systemic; the interventive strategies used to accomplish structural change are behavioral.

Single-Parent Family Case History

The case history that follows depicts a "typical" white, middle-class single-parent family system, provides a systemic analysis of the family structure, and describes the behavioral goals utilized to accomplish change in the structure.

Nancy M, a 39-year-old assistant banking manager, was referred for counseling by her family physician. She was divorced for about 3 years and was having a hard time coping with her two sons, Steven (age 8) and Craig (age 5). Prior to the present counseling, she was in group counseling for a drinking problem.

In the present counseling situation, although Nancy stated that her marriage was not good before the divorce, she often expressed both "negative and positive feelings in abrupt alternation" about Roger, her ex-husband. The main reason Nancy gave for her divorce was Roger's infidelity, his ongoing affair with his secretary. At the beginning of counseling, the relationship between Nancy and her former husband was antagonistic. They constantly argued about financial arrangements, visiting arrangements, or any other topic. Because of this, the two children began to suffer, each in his own way. Steven, for example, started to do poorly in school. He did not listen to his mother, frequently called her names, told her he hated her, and had frequent temper tantrums. Craig, the younger child, also had temper tantrums, after which he hid in his closet for many hours.

Most of the time, Nancy aligned herself with Craig. He was behaviorally a better child who achieved more in school and had more friends at home. Steven looked like his father. This carried over into Nancy's interactions with Steven and was the basis for a somewhat distant relationship between the two. Steven was a loner, and although there was no learning disability involved, schoolwork was difficult for him. Complicating the matter even further, Nancy and her ex-husband argued incessantly about whose fault Steven's low school grades were. Steven frequently heard these arguments.

Nancy was from an upper middle class family background, and all her needs were taken care of while growing up. At the time of the divorce, Nancy had not psychologically separated from her mother, who fostered attachment and dependency. She invited Nancy and the boys to live with her. She told Nancy that she would take care of her, something which at times was quite appealing to Nancy, even though their relationship was generally conflict ridden.

As Weiss (1975) has pointed out, "For the separated woman the parental invitation is not without attractions. Going back home can offer a brief moratorium from responsibility, a breathing space during which the woman can pull herself together without feeling guilty for neglecting her children. But . . . the cost would be reduced autonomy" (p. 141). For Nancy, this could be psychologically costly. In certain European cultures with an accepted extrafamilial subsystem, the psychological cost of moving back home might be much less. In this culture, the move might further widen the power gap between Nancy and her children.

Throughout her marriage, as well as while she was growing up, Nancy had few extrafamilial responsibilities. She had little job training and was quite unprepared psychologically and technically for the work force. However, upon her divorce, it became necessary for her to return to work to help support the children financially, and she began working at a low-paying clerical position. For Nancy, this was the first time in her life that she was totally responsible for her own needs and the needs of her children. She appeared fragile, overwhelmed by the slightest thing. She was unsure of her role, sometimes rationalizing that "it's okay not to cook dinner for the children because I'm exhausted. I've had a hard day and I need to relax. It won't kill them to eat bread and butter for one night." This happened on more than a few nights and was becoming problematic for the children.

The basic pattern of the family was chaotic. All fended for themselves. Things went along smoothly for a while, but then a crisis occurred, and problems arose. Nancy seemed to suffer from each and every one of the specific problems as presented by Bloom, White, and Asher (1979): ". . . difficulties with children, the need to work, sexual problems, problems with reestablishing social relationships, financial difficulties, and the feelings associated with failure and shame" (p. 193). The communication issues involved either Nancy pleading for the boys to behave or giving in to their whims so as to prevent them from annoying her. Nancy gave little positive reinforcement to the boys, with their positive behavior going generally unnoticed and their negative behavior punished, sometimes. Because most of the attention they received from Nancy was in a negative form, the boys' bad behavior increased, for it was the only time they received attention from their mother. Transactions occurred mainly surrounding functional issues, such as "Did you do your homework?" or "Put your toys away!"

There was, however, some consistency within the chaotic mass of family interactions. Although for the most part Nancy tolerated the children's misbehavior, becoming upset but disciplining them in an inconsistent fashion, when their behavior became excessively disruptive, she called Roger and argued with him about his lack of responsibility for the children.

Nancy's report of her seeming inability to consistently reward and punish the children thus seemed to be insuring Roger's participation in their lives. The children contributed their misbehavior to insure that Nancy became upset enough to call Roger. Roger then came to the rescue but only made slight attempts to resolve the problems with children, managing usually to blame Nancy. This insured that the children continued to misbehave, and thereby determined that Nancy called Roger again in the near future.

This is an example of how dynamics, as viewed from a behavioral approach, act to mold the family system in a way that is problematic for the members. This also illustrates the sequence of events that leads to family problems. It is called *tracking the symptom*. Once we understand the cycle of interaction, we can find alternate, healthier ways of being.

In a typical single-parent family with a problem, such as the one just described, the husband-wife bond is usually dissolved, but there is generally conflict and hostility between the two parents and the siblings. Sometimes, one of the children has entered the executive subsystem as the parental child, creating a cross-generational coalition, replacing the absent father and taking on adult responsibilities.

Counseling Strategies

As noted earlier, there are many types of single-parent households. The case history in the preceding section represents one type: a white middle-class single-parent family system with young children. It is not typical of other types of single-parent family systems, and therefore the principles stated here are not generalizable to other single-parent family systems. Even among middle-class single-parent family systems there are many variations (Mendes, 1979); but there are also similarities, and therefore certain principles can be used by mental health professionals to deal effectively with such family systems.

Cognitive-Behavioral Interventions

The focus in this type of counseling is always on the family. The goals are to change the structure of the family and the behavioral sequence that has led to the problems, and to teach more effective coping skills necessary to accomplish the functions of the family as listed earlier in this chapter (see Minuchin & Fishman, 1981). This goal is accomplished through the use of planned behavioral counseling techniques and based upon a systemic analysis of the family's hierarchy, boundaries, and subsystems. In Nancy's case, the goal was to find ways of addressing her dependency needs and lack of power that did not put her sons' development in jeopardy.

The specific cognitive-behavioral interventions that follow were used in this family in order to create systemic change. Because there are structural similarities among single-parent systems (Minuchin & Fishman, 1981), these counseling strategies are generalizable, even though these interventions are discussed in relation to the specific case history.

Reinforce the parental role. Because most parents are unaware of the functions of the family, it is most useful in a counseling situation for the mental health counselor to teach and educate. In single-parent families, a child may take on one of two roles in order to maintain the postdivorced family's equilibrium (Ahrons, 1980). That is, a child may become a parental child who relinquishes childhood play and takes over many adult responsibilities, or a child may take on a spousal role and become an emotional confidante to the single parent. Both of these situations indicate cross-generational problems in the custodial parent-child subsystem and are indications for counseling (Ahrons, 1980).

Another problem in the custodial-parent subsystem may occur if the parent does not have the coping skills necessary to care for the children. In the case description in the preceding section, it was important to reinforce the caretaking role (Berman & Turk, 1981). This became a long-term goal of the therapy. Nancy, initially, was still dependent on her own mother, and had not been dependent on her husband. She could not become independent without first learning basic caretaking skills. This was accomplished by using short-term behavioral goals (Jacobson & Margolin, 1981). For example, the therapist worked with her on setting up a schedule so that she could utilize her time more efficiently. This was reinforcing for her because she was able to spend more time with the children, which helped her to feel less guilty about what she called her "mothering" capabilities.

She was helped to set up a behavior modification chart with the boys. Topics on the chart included brushing teeth, making beds, putting toys away, clearing off the dinner table, doing homework, studying, and getting good grades. Each topic was fully explained to the boys. For example, after school from 3 to 4 p.m., the boys were to do their homework and study. If they accomplished this, they got a gold star for the day. For every six gold stars (they did not have to study on Sundays), they received a prize. The prizes were reasonable ones, such as a trip to Friendly's for ice cream.

The purpose of the chart was to create some structure, some order in the children's lives; and the chart not only accomplished this but also taught the boys to be independent and take care of some of their own needs, something that Nancy originally was not modeling for them. This freed up some of Nancy's time. No longer was it necessary for her to yell at the boys to do their homework when she came home from work. Her interactions with them started to become more positive, and she began to enjoy spending more time with them.

Help the parent become nurturing and supportive. The divorce crisis creates systemic disequilibrium. Although this is often a period of increased strain on the family members, it can also be a time of growth and development (Beal, 1980; Isaacs, Montalvo, & Adelsohn, 1986). When a system is in flux, it is most conducive to change. Much can be accomplished during this crisis time when roles are ambiguous, when boundaries are permeable, and when rules are temporarily suspended (McPhee, 1984).

Nancy needed to establish a nurturing, supportive relationship with the boys. Once again short-term behavioral goals were utilized to accomplish this. Nancy needed to maximize the time she spent with the boys so that it was beneficial to all and did not turn into an argument. The counselor suggested that Nancy make a list of places that she was interested in visiting. Then the counselor suggested that Nancy plan weekly day trips to these places. In this manner, she did not feel resentful about "not having any time to do the things I want to do," and the boys also had the chance to spend enjoyable times with their mother.

In counseling Nancy learned how little things could make small amounts of time valuable for both mother and children. For example, although Nancy had to drive the children to their various afterschool activities, it could be a fun time for all. She learned to create quality moments for the children in the car. It was a time when they had her attention. She realized that she did not need to spend large blocks of time with the boys in order to have a meaningful time with them. This also helped to alleviate some of the guilt she was feeling about her mothering abilities.

Another behavioral goal was to help her to cook efficiently for the boys. Interestingly enough, Nancy loved to cook but was feeling overwhelmed by it on the nights when she came home from work. She decided that it might be more enjoyable for her to cook the meals all at once. The counselor suggested that she do the cooking on Sunday mornings when the boys generally were with their father. In this way, she could focus completely on the cooking, which she loved, without interruptions from the boys.

Soon Nancy was cooking all the meals for the entire week at once, then packaging and freezing them. During the week, she took them out one at a time and used the microwave oven to heat them up. Because she was cooking decent meals for the children, all family members benefited. Nancy felt positive about her capabilities as a cook, and the boys were finally eating nutritious meals. Because Nancy did not have to shop and cook during the week, she also had more time for herself and boys.

Help the client with separation/individuation issues. The issue of separation/individuation from the family of origin can be an important one in therapy with single parents. It is therefore important that there are clear boundaries around the single-parent family system—that the single-parent family system is not confused with the extended family system (Isaacs, Montalvo, & Adelsohn, 1986). Nancy was responsible for many things, and the overwhelming feelings that she was experiencing were perfectly normal. In counseling, she realized that even though sometimes things seemed overwhelming, they could be broken down into small parts and accomplished easily. In so doing, she also learned that she did not have to depend on her mother for help with everyday activities and chores.

Nancy's mother represented a problem because she wanted Nancy to move back home. Nancy's father had died about 5 years before Nancy's divorce, and her mother was lonely. This is the typical trap into which single parents often fall. Single-parent families are often economically disadvantaged, so the single parent's family of origin, as in Nancy's case, may represent a rescue from financial ruin. If Nancy moved back to her family of origin, her mother could take care of food shopping, cleaning, chores, and baby-sitting. But the psychological price might be high. Nancy's mother was controlling, demanding to know Nancy's whereabouts at all times. There was only one right way to do things; no other way was acceptable. Nancy's mother was critical of her and wished to change her; if Nancy moved back, her mother was sure to set Nancy up for constant failure.

Another problem involved with moving back concerned authority. When Nancy's mother was visiting, she became the person in charge, and Nancy's authority with her children was often undermined. This created a triangle that produced conflicting feeling in the children, who got confused over whom they were supposed to obey because mother and daughter had different ways of doing things. All sorts of alliances might be created, with Nancy never being quite sure whether she was the child or the mother. This pattern might be a repeat of her relationship with her ex-husband. So even though the offer to move back in with her mother initially seemed quite appealing, upon closer investigation, it seemed sure to be a psychological disaster for Nancy. In future counseling sessions, Nancy learned to assert herself with her mother and to remain in the authority position when her mother came to visit. During one of the sessions, Nancy verbalized that she finally felt "grown up."

Thus in single-parent family systems, the power hierarchy may become blurred. It is important for mental health counselors to ask, "Where is the power base? Are the children mothering the mother? What is the role of the mother's mother, the mother's father, of other family members?"

Help dispel feelings of abandonment. Nancy's own feelings of abandonment were crucial and were discussed throughout the sessions. Weiss (1980) also discussed the problem: "The disruption of attachment is a major source of emotional disturbance following a separation" (p. 205). When Nancy felt overwhelmed or abandoned, she wrote her feelings in a journal that she then brought to the counseling session to discuss. The counselor then pointed out the connections between unrealistic expectations and unnecessary painful feelings.

Nancy's children were also experiencing fears, as exemplified by not wanting to stay with a sitter. Often they asked their mother, "Are you sure you're coming back? What time will you be home?" In counseling, Nancy learned to help her children get through these feelings. She reassured them of her love often. She also involved them in planning future activities in which they could all participate. In this way the children were able to project themselves into future situations, reassured that their mother would be there with them.

Help the mother involve the children in her goals. At the beginning of counseling, Nancy and her children were alienated from each other. They seemed to be simply living in the same residence, with very little positive communication and/or affection flowing among them. During the adjustment period after a separation or a divorce, this is often typical. One way to help increase the positive aspects of the parent-child relationship is to help the mother involve her children in her goals. Nancy accomplished this when the boys joined with her on every other Sunday and helped her prepare the meals for the week. They were given choices and encouraged to cooperate. Soon after this process began, preparing the meals became a fun-filled family activity. Through such behavioral activities, the roles of the family members became defined, the responsibilities of each member became known, and the family system began to function more effectively (Ahrons, 1980).

Help the mother develop outside support structures and social interests. It is important for mental health counselors to help the client make contact with and attach to another system. A single-parent system can be quite successful if there are other strong systems to which the client looks for support (Morawetz & Walker, 1984). These outside systems could be women or men friends, a group of single parents that meets on a regular basis, a sports activity, or even courses at a school. Such networks can provide resources in the form of people as well as material resources, helping the single parent to reach out and form new relationships with supportive people (Warren & Amara, 1985). Initially, Nancy was so overwhelmed that she had little time left for anything but basic survival. Her entire world consisted of working, cleaning, cooking, and shouting at the boys to behave. Her life was devoid of fun and relaxing activities. She felt she had little to look forward to and was in a state of depression. What she missed most was not having anyone with whom to discuss her day. Her life was filled with either professional conversations with people with whom she worked or conversations with her children about things that were important to them. There was no one in her life with whom she could have an adult conversation, no one with whom she could share an intimate relationship. In short, there were no reinforcers in her life; and according to cognitive behavioral psychology (Beck, 1970), depression is defined as a lack of reinforcers in an individual's environment.

During counseling, Nancy was encouraged to seek out other single parents in her neighborhood so that she could begin to develop friends. In this way she was able to share her career dreams, her life's trials and tribulations, and the fun moments that also began to occur more frequently. She was beginning to develop a support structure of women, that is, a network of comrades who helped make her life more pleasant. Her children were now free to play with their friends and engage in the extracurricular activities that young boys enjoy. The sibling subsystem was reinforced, and the boys no longer had to feel guilty about leaving a sad and depressed mother.

Help the client work out a reasonable relationship with the ex-partner. Wallerstein and Kelly (1980c) found that a supportive and cooperative divorced coparenting relationship is an essential ingredient for continued growth and development of the children involved in single-parent homes. Many problems arise, however, in the coparental subsystem. Some of these are concerned with raising children, one of the parents using the child as a go-between, competition with the other parent, the other parent spoiling the children, and lack of support and caring by the other parent (Morawetz & Walker, 1984). There may also be unresolved anger and hostility between the two parents, and too often the children become involved in this anger and hostility (Isaacs, Montalvo, & Adelsohn, 1986). Typically the child feels that he or she cannot express anger to the noncustodial parent out of fear of losing that parent forever. Thus the child expresses anger and complains to the parent with whom he or she is living, which in turn can cause resentment toward the child on the part of the parent (Wallerstein, 1984). In counseling sessions with single parents, it is important to discuss these issues in order to help the client work through feelings of resentment and anger and further understand the necessity of not conveying that anger and resentment to or at the children (Jacobson, 1978).

In some cases, clients present a different reaction to the ex-spouse, denying the impact of their divorce and reporting no strong feelings associated with the loss of their marriage or partner—as if the marriage or the divorce never happened. This has been likened to Bowen's (1978) concept of emotional cutoff. Here the individual cuts off the ex-spouse either by physical distancing, keeping contacts with him or her brief and infrequent, or total withdrawal and avoidance. Bowen's solution to emotional cutoffs was to have the client recontact the family member involved. Sometimes divorced spouses may need to reestablish contact in order to truly divorce—which can be a complicated process.

Working through her relationship with her husband Roger was another goal in counseling with Nancy. After discussing this in a session, Nancy attempted to speak with her ex-husband about taking on some of the extra responsibility with the boys and the possibility of coming for some joint therapy sessions. Involving the absent parent and helping increase the involvement of the noncustodial parent are other goals of therapy when working with single-parent families. Seeing the primary parent alone, in this case, the mother, reinforces the erroneous notion that the problem is hers alone. Roger did seem to want to be involved with the boys, so the counselor suggested that one of the ways he could increase his involvement with them was to drive them to and watch them do their sport activities. Thus, Nancy could stay at her job at the bank, thereby alleviating some of her anxiety and pressure. At the same time, Roger could become more involved, something that ultimately means positive consequences for the whole family.

Help the client mourn. Counselors need to help their clients deal with issues of unresolved mourning. Often when depression is the presenting problem, issues of relationship loss underlie the sadness. Clients in these situations need to mourn the loss of relationship (Walsh, 1982). The process of mourning is discussed more fully in chapter 5. In the case of divorce, these losses are experienced by all members of the family system. Fulmer (1983) believed that the single-parent family is especially vulnerable to problems resulting from unresolved loss. Hoffman (1981) described children's misbehavior as being "collusive mischief" to offset the mother's depression. Seeing her depression, they become anxious, begin to misbehave, and, therefore, "impel (her) to take an active position" (p. 84) by their disobedience. This was typified in Nancy's family. Whenever Steven sensed his mother's depression, he acted out by not doing his homework or by fighting with his brother. This behavior functioned to mobilize Nancy, taking the focus away from her depressed state.

In counseling, Nancy expressed her sadness around the loss of the relationship, the loss of her dreams and expectations around her marriage, and the loss of Roger. In family sessions the boys also expressed their sorrow of no longer having a traditional two-parent family and of not seeing their father as often as they used to before their parents separated.

Help the client recognize single-parent family system differences and strengths. As Mendes (1979) pointed out:

> One of the most important tasks for counseling with single-parent families, regardless of their life style, is to help liberate families that are tyrannized by the two-parent family model. They need to see that is impossible for one parent to be both father and mother (p. 195).

In this society, people are socialized to believe that the two-parent family is the norm. Although this is true in many cases, in just as many cases it is not. For example, between 1970 and 1978, there was a 46% increase in female-headed family systems. When the two-parent system is considered to be the ideal, the single-parent family system, which cannot fulfill this norm, is by definition considered a failure (Beal, 1980). Such social definitions of "failures" define the psychological condition of being in a "failed" situation. In the counseling situation, it is important to talk these issues through with clients and help them resolve some of their uncertainty, ambiguity, and loss of self-esteem. Each individual needs to evaluate his or her definitions of what a single-parent family system should be like—emotionally and realisti-cally—and to challenge unrealistic "shoulds." This is true for the counselor as well as for the client. The counselor can help the client evaluate the cost of doing everything and understand that by sharing family tasks the inevi-table anger felt by an overburdened parent can be reduced. For a considera-tion of other therapeutic issues with the single-parent family system, see Morawetz & Walker (1984).

Of course, some of the problems depicted in the case history would be alleviated if there were two people to share the responsibilities of the children, finances, and household chores. The interparental conflict would be much less. There also would be another person to share emotions with, for Nancy to talk with about the frustrations of her day. If this were a two-parent parent family, the focus of the therapy would be to help Nancy share her feelings of being overwhelmed with her husband and basically work out a task-sharing situation between the two adults. However, some of the same issues would still exist, for example, the lack of separation from the family of origin, the lack of coping skills on Nancy's part, and the detach-ment and aloofness on Roger's part.

Since the beginning of therapy, the structure of Nancy's single-parent family system has changed. The boundaries between the generations be-came are clearer. The father has become more involved, less alienated from the family situation. The children are in a more "normal" environment, with a strong sibling subsystem. There is more structure, more rules and regulations. The executive boundary is reinforced. Nancy is more nurturing and supportive to her children. She feels less overwhelmed. She has become more bonded to her children, which makes them feel more secure and helps her feel more fulfilled, more needed, less isolated and guilty. As a result, the children have fewer temper tantrums, and the anxiety level in the house has lessened somewhat. Nancy has even found time to go to an occasional movie with her friends.

Reissmann (1990), who interviewed many divorced persons in *Divorce Talk,* stated that "most of those interviewed had no difficulty identifying divorce's benefits, which they summarized as 'freedom' " (p. 163). "I feel like living again, I feel like I was dying a slow death in that relationship. There's a joy in my life . . . I feel a real emotional release" (p. 165). Reissman (1990) also stated that "as most women understand, divorce is not only a loss but a gain" (p. 161). She indicated that the positive change is in three general areas: competence in the management of daily life, changing meanings of social relationships, and a fuller sense of a whole identity.

Some of the long-range goals with Nancy are to help her continue to establish a support network, administer career-oriented tests and help her with career planning (something in which she was very interested), and help her reenter the dating situation (something that she also mentioned as desirable). Emotionally, Nancy still sometimes relies on alcohol to relax her, so more help is needed in this area. She also needs to continue to work through her anger at Roger for abandoning her. Much more work is still left to do with this single-parent family, but positive changes have started to occur.

A single-parent family is a difficult organization to run, but it can be done well even in the most difficult of cases. For example, it may be easier to make executive decisions when there is one executive. Cashion (1982) found that children from female-headed families are just as likely to have "good emotional adjustment . . . self-esteem . . . intellectual development ... and no higher rates of juvenile delinquency" as other children of comparable socioeconomic status.

Other Interventions

When working with a single parent family system, there are many areas to investigate. Assessing the family on a systemic level as well as using behavioral intervention strategies to realign boundaries and extinguish cross-generational coalitions are principal ways for counselors to work with these families. The emphasis on assessing the family as a whole is an obvious one. Also important is the role of the counselor as an educator who helps the family to restructure and clarify boundaries and roles. A useful model for intervention is facilitating "good enough" arrangements between divorced parents and their children (Isaacs, Montalvo, & Adelsohn, 1986). The basis of this approach is to include children's open access to the noncustodial parent and to assure that two parents are raising the children. Part of the family counselor's role is to teach the family good child-rearing practices and help them learn age-appropriate behaviors. The basic theme of single-parent family counseling is to stimulate psychological growth, always a developmental process, and to encourage the future psychological maturation of all family members.

Some single-parent women define divorce as an opportunity for reworking developmental tasks or unfinished business. They see it as a chance to achieve separation from historical parents or a spouse in the parental role and to develop new, more mature relationships. Counselors can assist in this process in the sense that part of the experience of the divorce process may be structured by the expectations of the professionals' single-parent encounters. Counselors' definitions of marital changes as disappointments balanced by new opportunities, as losses balanced by gains, can create comparable expectations in the minds of their clients.

It is here that counselors can change their lens in their approach to divorce and develop a new language, one in which the orientation of divorce as a disaster is augmented—or replaced—by that of divorce as a developer.

Chapter 4

RESILIENCY AND COMPETENCE IN THE CHILDREN OF DIVORCE

Hetherington (1989) reported that although there are losers in the process of divorce, survivors and winners also exist. In fact, if anxiety and stress are not continuous, most family members will recover in as little as 2 to 3 years. Wallerstein (1984) reported a series of negative outcomes in her 5-year longitudinal study of California children of divorce, but she also reported that about 34% of the children studied were happy and thriving. *Happy and thriving* are not the typical words that are associated with children of divorce, and these results warrant elaboration. What are the factors involved in good postdivorce adjustment? How can counselors assist the single-parent family in fostering these factors? How can counselors help their clients divorce in a competent manner—a manner that creates an environment facilitating growth and happiness? That is, how can counselors assist their clients in the competent divorce?

The Competent Divorce

Many variables influence the competent divorce. As noted throughout this book, social science literature discussing the single-parent family has traditionally focused on the deficits of such a family system. This is not the focus here; rather, we propose that counseling models that focus on deficits serve to reinforce the deficits. (For a comparison of these two approaches to counseling, see chapter 11.) Because of the tremendous social changes that have taken place in the family within the past hundred years, a competency-based model is more appropriate. In order for counselors to focus on the competencies of single-parent family systems, certain widely made assumptions must be challenged.

The purpose of this chapter, then, is to present recent, methodologically sound research that either found no significant differences between children from one- and two-parent households or research that pointed to the strengths of the one-parent family. In so doing, the factors that influence good adjustment processes in parents and children, or the competent divorce, are stressed. This side of the picture may be just as biased as the gloom-and-doom picture that is more typically presented; however, we believe that counselors are not typically familiar with the positive outcome research on children of divorce and that this presentation is crucial in order for them to assess their own biases.

Weiss (1979) studied the experience of growing up in a single-parent household and found that the absence of the traditional hierarchy that characterizes single-parent homes allows children a greater share in the responsibility for the household, thus allowing children to develop new responsibility, self-esteem, independence, and confidence. He noted that the parents as well as the children generally saw the changes produced in the children because of this change in traditional roles to be largely beneficial to the entire family. For many children, both younger and older, the new demands on them for autonomy and responsibility led to growth.

Weiss (1979) also reported that consequences for children in a one-parent household may foster an early maturity. One aspect of family life that reflects this maturity is the child's role in the decision-making process in a one-parent household. In a two-parent family, both parents typically share in the decision making, and children are supposed to abide by this decision. In the absence of a second parent, the single parent is likely to incorporate children into the decision-making process, if only because it is the most expedient way to manage a household (Weiss, 1979). These parent-child partnerships often lead to close ties in the enactment of reciprocal friend/confidant roles (Kurdek, 1981). In a one-parent family the parent does not need to check with a second adult before acceding to the children's wishes. No longer is there a structure in which the parent is unable to make common cause with the children for fear of betraying a prior understanding with the other parent. There is more acceptance of the additional responsibility when the child has a voice in the decision-making process. Children can be asked not only to perform additional chores but also to participate in deciding what is to be done. Children in single-parent households are often encouraged to develop a relationship with their custodial parent that is more like that of a peer and confidante, elevating the child to a coparent status (Kalter, Alpern, Spence, & Plunkett, 1984) or cooperative colleague (Ahrons, 1980). This means that the structure of this type of family is different from the two-parent variety in that there is a hierarchy with the single-parent mother in charge, but the rules, roles, and boundaries are more collaboratively based. Weiss (1979) concluded that the single-parent family, insofar as it requires children within it to behave responsibly, may in this respect be a better setting for growing up than the two-parent family. Hetherington (1989) agreed, adding that the nontraditional organization of the single-parent home can actually enhance responsibility, communication, and closeness between child and parent.

Hutchinson and Hirsch (in Everett, 1989) suggested that children of divorce tend to be good decision makers and are stronger and more mature as an outgrowth of divorce. Blades, Gosse, McKay, and Rogers (1984) concluded that children who are seen as partners in the single-parent household in which they are raised tend to be more capable and self-reliant. In times of crisis they rise to the occasion because they believe in their ability to handle things. Emery, Hetherington, & DiLalla (1984) noted that divorced families can tap into the experiences of the transitional situation and strengthen a child's ability to cope and be independent. They also believed that adolescents living in single-parent families are characterized by greater maturity, feelings of efficacy, and an internal locus of control (see also Guidubaldi & Perry, 1984; Kalter, Alpern, Spence, & Plunkett, 1984; Wallerstein & Kelly, 1974; Weiss, 1979).

Schwebel, Barocas, Reichmann, and Schwebel (1990) believed that parental divorce forces children to engage in personal adjustment. First, the person attempts to relate effectively to the environment in which he or she lives by developing skills, traits, and behaviors that will bring success, happiness, and other valued goals. Second, the person attempts to master the environment and modify it to his or her own advantage. This statement implies that children might develop strengths as a result of attempting to adjust to their parental divorce. They may develop skills or abilities to meet new challenges, and they may develop new self-cognitions as a result of these new challenges (Gately & Schwebel, 1991).

Cashion (1982), in a review of other studies, found that children in female-headed families are likely to have good emotional adjustment, good self-esteem (except when they are stigmatized), intellectual development comparable to others in the same socioeconomic status, and rates of juvenile delinquency comparable to others in the same socioeconomic status. Other research (in Everett, 1989; Hutchinson, Valutis, Brown, & White, 1989) examined depression, self-concepts, and ability to handle stress and found no statistical differences between children from one-parent and two-parent families. Warren, Illgen, Grew, Konac, and Amara (1982) also reached the same conclusions.

Research has indicated that children from single-parent homes are more creative than children from two-parent families. Albert (1971), Besdine (1968), and Roe (1953) studied the gifted and historically important people in history who had experienced loss and found that some of them were children of divorce. Preschoolers who live in single-parent families seem to be very imaginative, exhibiting divergent thinking and creative potential (see Cornelius & Yawkey, 1985). Wallerstein and Kelly (1980) explored the relationship between divorce and creativity potential and found that children of divorce exhibited flexibility, tolerance for change, a delay of gratification, and enhanced creative capacity. Guidubaldi, Cleminshaw, Perry, and McLoughlin (1983) concurred with the idea that originality is positively related to a positive postdivorce adjustment. Explanations for these findings vary: Jenkins (1988) seemed to question if intensification of feelings and emotions experienced in the divorce process may account for the heightened creative talent of children of divorce; Albert (1971) cited emotional distancing as causation for creativity; and Becker (1974) explained it as a result of the father's departure from the home.

With the changes in the family that come with divorce are changes in parental roles. Some of these changes can be related to changes in child discipline practices. On a more speculative level, parental roles may change as adults opt for more androgynous life styles (Kurdek, 1981). These changes may alter both the nature of the models to which the child is exposed and the types of child behavior that is regarded as desirable.

With divorce comes role allocation. Children are expected and required to take on new roles. Favorable outcomes occur if **children are assigned new roles appropriate to their abilities**. In so doing, they are more likely to experience success, increased competencies, and greater self-esteem (Gately & Schwebel, 1991). If children are assigned new roles based on their abilities rather than on traditional sex roles, it is more likely to foster androgynous sex-role orientations and increase behavioral flexibility.

MacKinnon, Stoneman, and Brody (1984) examined the impact of maternal employment and family form (married/working, divorced/working) on children's sex-role stereotypes and mothers' traditional attitudes. They found that the children from single-parent homes were less concerned about traditional sex-roles stereotypes. The shedding of restrictive sex-role orientation could be a positive growth factor, opening new doors for the newly single and their children.

According to a study by Kurdek and Siesky (1980), children of one-parent families were significantly more androgynous than children of two-parent families, who tend to be traditionally sex typed (Demo & Acock, 1988). The tendency of children in single-parent families to display more androgynous behavior may be interpreted as a beneficial effect. Children in female-headed families, because of father absence, are not as strongly pressured as children in two-parent families to conform to gender roles. These children frequently assume a variety of domestic responsibilities to compensate for the absent parent (Weiss, 1979). Because of this they broaden their competencies and skills as well as their definitions of gender-appropriate behavior (Demo & Acock, 1988).

This positive research promotes a "reframing approach" that focuses on seeing children of divorce as healthy and successful. It is significant that many mental health workers and educators hold the misleading assumption that children of divorce often display behavioral changes and perform lower academically (see chapter 9 for a review of children of divorce and the academic system). But whether or not children of divorce have personal or social problems depends on the resources and supports that the child receives. It is more helpful for counselors to view problems that result from divorce as a potentiality rather than an inevitability.

Factors Associated With the Competent Divorce

Examining factors influencing good postdivorce adjustment is as appropriate as focusing on the problems of children of divorce. Wallerstein (1984) noted that perhaps the most crucial factor influencing a good adjustment in children after divorce was **a stable, loving relationship with both parents, between whom friction had largely dissipated, and having regular, dependable visiting patterns**. She found that grandparents provided some support for both divorced mothers and their children. She also noted that a number of other factors seemed common to the children who dealt most resiliently with divorce. One was **a strong personality to start with**.

The microsystem represents interactive processes operative in the pre- and postdivorce family system and has been the focus of much research. For children, the threat of divorce lies in the disruption of the relationship with their parents. According to Wallerstein and Kelly (1980c) **positive continuity in relationships with both parents** is related to the psychological health of the child during the postdivorce years. Children of higher levels of interpersonal understanding and internal locus of control have also been shown to experience more positive postdivorce outcomes than do their peers.

One common theme that surfaced in situations in which children did meet with positive results relates to **how the parents approached divorce and how the children perceived the divorce**. Favorable outcomes are more likely in children **when people significant to them judge the single-parent home as a viable—rather than deviant—family form**. Feelings of well-being are a result in an atmosphere in which there is **nonstigmatization of the single-parent status and divorce** (Gately & Schwebel, 1991).

Kelly (1988) reviewed research on the impact of divorce on the adjustment of children and suggested that the conditions created by the divorce rather than the divorce itself determine the child's adjustment. This is supported by Stolberg and Garrison (1985) who found that more **effective parenting** was positively associated with better social skills, more involvement in prosocial activities, and less internalized problems in children.

Barry (1979) found that children's positive adjustment to divorce was related to four factors: (1) **parents having a good rapport with their children**, (2) **open communication within the family**, (3) **a sense of sharing and working together**, and (4) **the ability to accept and support one another in a loving manner**.

Portes, Haas, and Brown (1991) analyzed four general factors related to children's adjustment, including child coping skills, family functioning, stability, and family support systems. These factors have been studied by other researchers who noted that long-term effects of marital transitions are related more to new stresses encountered by the child, the individual attributes of the child, the qualities of the single-parent or stepfamily home environment, and the resources and support systems available to the child than to divorce or remarriage.

In 1980, Wallerstein and Kelly (1980c) identified variables that had a positive effect on the adjustment of children in a divorce situation and concluded that factors that appeared to influence good adjustment in children of divorce after 5 years were similar to those that make for good adjustment in a two-parent home. Guidubaldi (1983) noted seven similar variables. These combined variables had to do with the parental conditions and qualities as well as the qualities and needs of the children in general. But the most important variable of all may be the amount of marital conflict or discord and how the parents themselves handle it. Hetherington, Cox, and Cox (1985) concluded that in some cases divorce may reduce parental conflicts so that children are less distressed. It seems that with **reduced marital conflicts and warm parent-child relationships in which discipline is stressed**, children of divorce receive adequate support and are therefore well adjusted.

Brown, Eichenberger, Portes, and Christensen (1991) and Portes, Haas, and Brown (1991) conducted two separate studies to identify which of a number of interactive processes related to parental divorce are the best predictors of children's adjustment. The results of this study showed that roles, child reaction and insight into the divorce, and postdivorce adjustment (lack of conflict between parents) account for nearly half of the variance in the children's adjustment to the divorce. In the second study the authors hypothesized that family processes have a profound effect on the children's ability to adjust to divorce. They found that four factors were important: (1) **child coping skills**, (2) **family functioning and stability**, (3) **strong support systems**, and (4) **postdivorce conditions (tendency to agree and get along without turmoil and aggression)**. This study served to confirm the hypothesis that a child's susceptibility to socioemotional and behavioral problems can be due to faulty predivorce family functioning and that social support systems can help to ameliorate the effects of dysfunctional family functioning.

Tschann (1989) cited six predictors that may be most responsible for children's adaptive functioning during divorce: (1) family structure and other demographic variables such as child age, gender, number of siblings, socioeconomic status, and length of separation, (2) difficult baby temperament, (3) preseparation marital conflict, (4) postseparation parental conflict, (5) hours spent with the visiting parent, and (6) parent-child relationship. The conclusion of this study was that **parents who were warm and supportive** of their children helped their sons and daughters to become better adjusted. Tschann (1989) concurred with findings that girls demonstrated better postseparation emotional adjustment than boys but that there were no differences in behavior adjustments according to gender in either one-parent or two-parent family models.

Emery (1982), Everett (1989), and Magrab (1978) agreed with Tschann's viewpoint (1989) that parents who had less marital conflict had better relationships with their children after separation. This in turn was associated with more adaptive child functioning. Further, Tschann (1989) stated that children in high-conflict two-parent families show fewer favorable adaptations than do children of divorce in the social, emotional, and behavioral areas.

Another aspect of divorce that needs to be considered is the circumstances that led up to the divorce. It has become apparent that the consequences of a divorce are far less damaging to a child than living in a poor two-parent family system. Unhappy, conflicted families may have more negative effects for children than voluntarily divorced family units that successfully avoid further prolonged conflict (Kulka & Weingarten, 1979). Garber (1991) studied 324 college students from two-parent and one-parent homes in order to examine the long-term effects of family structure and conflict at home on the self-esteem of these students. The results indicated that interparental conflict may have long-term effects on general and social self-esteem of young adults but family structure does not.

One reason that these conflict-ridden two-parent families may be more harmful to children is that they are unable to resolve successfully the difficulties within them, whereas divorce may in fact do just that. Furthermore, it is reasonable to assume that children of divorce who come to consider their parents choice to separate as exemplifying successful problem solving will have fewer barriers to overcome if later confronted with irreconcilable conflicts of interest in their own significant relationships (Kulka & Weingarten, 1979). If divorce comes to be construed as a successful strategy rather than as a personal failure, a potential barrier to leaving a similar stressful situation in an individual's own adult life could thereby be removed and a more flexible set of coping mechanisms and appreciation for the complexity of relationships learned.

The support of others outside the family is another factor influencing positive postdivorce outcome that cannot be underestimated in fostering positive outcomes for single parents and their children. Brown, Eichenberger, Portes, and Christensen (1991) described this factor as *external support systems*. Portes, Haas, and Brown (1991) cited these external support systems as one of the four major factors contributing to children's positive adjustment to divorce. Kurdek (in Everett, 1989) believed that siblings may have an important consoling effect on children of divorce. Hetherington

(1989) stated that because children in the divorce arena are in a painful, unstable situation during which time trust in the adults may be shaky, they may rely on their siblings for support. They form an alliance, sometimes also in a friendship with another child outside the family unit. Grandparents, another extension of the unit, were not found as important in buffering roles unless they actually lived with the child. She also found that the age of the siblings had a great deal to do with adjustment. Older siblings fared better than younger ones, perhaps because their understanding of the divorce process was greater. In terms of gender, female siblings were able to understand conflict resolution better than their male counterparts, and so their reactions were more positive. In addition, parents rated their older children as less dependent on the adults than the younger siblings.

Studies have identified family functioning and stability as one of the most important factors in determining positive outcomes in children of divorce. One of these studies was by Thirot and Buckner (1991) of 204 single custodial parents. Another, conducted by Brown et al. (1991), also noted that the family's abilities to **maintain family rituals, provide a sense of security** to its members, **support each other emotionally**, and, overall, **maintain the organization of the family system** are critical. Thus providing resources, nurturance and support, life development skills, and system management and maintenance are essential, and healthy families are characterized by **adequate fulfillment of all family functions, appropriate allocation of responsibility**, and **clear accountability**. It appears that the maintaining of important family rituals helps to provide emotional support and can help stabilize the family following divorce. In coping with a family transition such as divorce, many of those involved are protected by factors such as positive personality dispositions, a supportive family milieu, and support from external sources.

Legal aspects of the divorcing process also have an effect on postdivorce outcomes. They affect children in terms of the extension or dissolution of conflict associated with the divorce process. Saayman and Saayman (in Everett, 1989) saw the court system as detrimental to the adjustment of children. They suggested **mediation** as a viable alternative. They additionally noted that in the cases they reviewed family functioning improved once the divorce process was expedited. Courts are expressed as adversarial and mediation as supportive. In relation to courts, custody issues (including who gets the child and when) and coparenting arrangements especially exert a positive influence in the child's life following divorce. Neugebauer (in Everett, 1989) found that children whose parents were able to arrange **successful coparenting** were unlikely to suffer distress. They did not experience the loss of either one of the parents and seemed to be well adjusted overall. They also found that **nonadversarial postdivorce parental relationships** are related to increased self-esteem and more positive adjustments.

Perhaps no other factor in the single-parent family's postdivorce adjustment is as important as the economic situation of the family. Chapter 10 discusses this phenomenon in more detail. Economic considerations are crucially important to the successful adjustment of children of divorce. A study by Guidubaldi (1983) noted that divorce often results in reduced economic status, especially for single-parent families with women as the head of household. If the parent's employment needs are met, often the adjustment of the parent is better, which in turn facilitates better adjustment in the children.

Consistent with research by Guidubaldi and Perry (1984), Tschann (1989) believed that lowered socioeconomic status can manifest in greater behavioral problems. This is further supported by Schnayer and Orr (in Everett, 1989) in their discussion of family structures and interactional patterns. These researchers believe that socioeconomic status may be a better predictor of children's behavior problems than the sex of the single parent.

When a single parent experiences economic hardships, all aspects of life are affected. As previously mentioned, in families that are financially comfortable, a moderate postdivorce financial decline may foster increased maturity in adolescents, characterized by reasonable adult-like attitudes toward financial matters and a greater appreciation for the value of goods (Wallerstein, 1984).

Thus a major impact of divorce involves economics, and the economic situation of a family has a tremendous bearing on the children's postdivorce adjustment. Specific measures designed to improve the economic condition of single-parent families should have a positive impact on many children's postdivorce adjustment and foster more favorable outcomes (Braver, Gonzalez, Walchik, & Sandler, 1989). For a summary of the factors influencing the competent divorce, see the list in this chapter's Counseling Strategies section.

In a recent review of the literature, Veevers (1990) identified 17 factors that may contribute to successful adjustment in the parent, and to growth, rather than trauma, as an outcome of divorce. Most importantly, she found that defining divorce as a normal event is essential. Given the current percentages of divorce in the United States today, the social stigma and psychological stain associated with divorce as a "deviant" activity no longer apply: She stated that "Antithetical to this (pathogenic) model is the contention that divorce per se need not always be a trauma, but may be **stren**, a strengthening experience" (p. 101). Further, "the extreme trauma felt by some divorcing persons does not belie the fact that for others the experience is merely a short-lived unpleasantness, and for some, it is actually defined in positive terms" (p. 125). Her review also showed that divorced persons may experience divorce on a continuum ranging from being relatively painful to causing relief.

The factors that appear to be associated with the psychological response to divorce more as a strengthening experience than as a trauma are perceiving divorce as normal; having such personality characteristics as self-assurance, ego strength, and dominance; being relatively younger; being female; perceiving that one is coming from an abusive rather than an ordinary marriage, being the initiator of the divorce; and being geographically mobile. Other strengths include having had a marriage of shorter duration, a relatively long period from decision to actual divorce, a low level of attachment to the ex-partner, a satisfactory relationship with the ex-mate, adequate income and material resources, higher levels of education (for females only), nontraditional ideas about gender and/or marital roles, access to supportive social networks, access to professionally organized support groups of peers, and a dating relationship and/or a love affair with a significant other.

Gately and Schwebel (1991) proposed a challenge model for the process of adjusting to divorce that fosters favorable outcomes in adults and children. They believed that the outcomes of parental divorce, whether favorable, neutral, or unfavorable, are shaped by the nature of the challenges that the children face, and by such moderating factors as the children's characteristics and the level of coping resources, including the social support available to them.

Certain types of parental behavior foster favorable outcomes in children following divorce. Kaslow and Hyatt (1981) stated that parents who cope well model for their children how to deal with strained interpersonal relationships and major life crises and provide vicarious experience that may increase children's feelings of self-efficacy. Santrock and Warchak (1979) found that an authoritative parenting style characterized by warmth, clearly specified rules, and extensive verbal give and take between parent and child is associated with social competence and maturity. A high level of parenting skills is also related to a higher level of social competence in children (Gately & Schwebel, 1991). Parenting styles, especially the authoritative approach, were associated with a higher level of social competence, lowered behavioral problems, and overall better adjustment. According to Hetherington (1989), a supportive, structured, predictable parent-child relationship plays a critical protective role.

Thirot and Buckner (1991) found that the **custodial parent's own subjective sense of well-being** was the strongest single predictor of divorce adjustment. These researchers pointed out that parents who feel good about themselves also feel good about their parenting skills as single parents.

From the studies just described and from other research presented in this book we can conclude that divorce per se does not have a negative effect on children and that there are factors that can influence a competent divorce. This idea is further supported by the empirical sociological studies of Ganong and Coleman (1984) who hypothesized that divorce is not confirmed as having an effect on emotional well-being. They found that there was a failure to confirm large negative effects on different family structures and that divorce does not necessarily result in the deterioration of children's well-being. These researchers raised the questions of whether, in light of the theoretical, clinical, and empirical studies conducted, we can really expect emotional maladaption in divorce, and also whether we can objectively measure for the analysis of nonfactual and dynamic variables like well-being.

Thus there is little evidence for the existence of any long-term effects of divorce arising from a home that is headed by a single parent. The early experiences of divorce have at most a modest effect on adult adjustment, and the notion that experiencing parental divorce during childhood is an important contributor to later life adjustment derives little support from these representative samples of the American population.

What Can Children Learn From Divorce?

Children can learn that they do not have to stay in unhealthy relationships. They can know that life offers many choices and that it is okay to terminate marriages that are hurtful to the family unit. These children can also learn to become more independent, flexible, and self-reliant. They become familiar with mediation and develop skills along those lines.

Children of divorce can learn to be realistic about adults by accurately assessing their parents' strengths and weaknesses. If they have insight into divorce's effects on the family members, it can lead to a desire to work for changes in their own relationships as adults. Many children of divorce work hard to see that the same histories do not repeat. In living through divorce the children come to find that their parents' opposing views may both be true. Many children of divorce acquire better communication skills, often as an outgrowth of therapies associated with support groups. Children of divorce develop resilience and have greater access to feelings about themselves. They are often more adaptable to change than their two-parent counterparts; and because many of them are brought up in several family groups, they become more familiar with choices about child rearing and differences in life styles. From their acquisition of wisdom about life comes an appreciation of limits and a sense of intact self, and many of these children are more mature than their peers.

Learning to seek counseling is a new skill for survival that awakens a fuller and more realistic self-concept in many. In naming their reality and their pain, children of divorce begin to take responsibility for themselves. As adults, children of divorce may have a greater concern for future generations. They have learned survival skills and become decision makers. When preparing for marriage many years later, they know that divorce is a viable solution to marital problems, especially if provided with a workable model. Their level of self-control is just as developed as that of peers coming from two-parent families, and because they often had to care for their siblings, they may be better caretakers. As adult children, they are able to have intimacies similar to their two-parent family peers. Their academic records are not found to be different from those of "traditional" children, and no differences are found in the quality of parent-child relations when divorce is the key moderator.

Counseling Strategies

Hetherington (1989) concluded that when she first began to study children in divorced families, she had a pathogenic model of divorce. However, after more than two decades of research on marital transitions, she has concluded that in the long run some children are survivors, some are losers, and some are winners, depending on the characteristics of the child, available resources, subsequent life experiences, and, especially, interpersonal relationships. This is a more accurate summary than found in most literature.

Divorce is a complex cultural, social, legal, economic, and psychological process (Kurdek, 1981). Hence, children's divorce-related experiences need to be understood in terms of hierarchically embedded psychological, familial, social, and cultural contexts. Brofenbrenner (1979) has described human development as occurring in an ecological environment composed of such nested contexts. Each system involves a different aspect of the child's environment. The macrosystem involves the cultural beliefs, values, and attitudes surrounding modern family life. The stability of the postdivorce environment and the social support available to the restructured single-parent family make up the ecosystem. The microsystem is the nature of the family interaction during the pre- and postdivorce periods.

According to Fassell (1991), a tendency exists to compare the two-parent family with the one-parent family. She has suggested that there are four forms of one-parent and two-parent families, which include both nonproblem and problem subsets in each category. She has also suggested that comparing children from two-parent and one-parent homes results in an oversimplification of a complex reality. Divorce is a process rather than a static event and should be viewed as such. Because researchers have failed to confirm large negative effects of divorce on children, Baydar (1988) concluded that divorce does not necessarily result in the deterioration of children's well-being and that the divorce process could be viewed as positive or neutral. In other words, pathological versions of the nuclear family as represented in the literature appear to be unfounded in light of the more methodologically sound research. What the literature supports is the notion that parental separation, in and of itself, is not a factor in emotional disorder. Rather myriad variables may account for any children with problems in divorcing families. For example, changes that children experience as a result of divorce—change from a two-parent home to a one-parent home, change in the economic situation (usually a decrease), change in home location (perhaps a move from a house to an apartment), change in school, change in friends—may be the strongest predictive variables. Conversely, many other variables may assist in creating well-adjusted children without problems, despite or because of the divorce process.

Most of the cases coming to the attention of the professional counselor involving children of divorce and their parents are those that have resulted in problems, and these problems should not be minimized. For many, adults and children alike, the divorcing process can be traumatic and seriously painful. However, situations in which children of single-parent households are doing well and perhaps thriving are not necessarily brought to light. As stated earlier, in many school settings the child's family status is only discussed after a problem arises. However, as a review of the literature shows, it becomes more evident that family configuration effects are small and much less pervasive than frequently assumed. As counselors, we need to be aware of the current research findings that will assist us in examining our own biases and in so doing help us empower single-parent families.

The following summary conclusions, based on a thorough review of the research on children of divorce, may be used as guidelines to assist counselors and their clients in achieving the competent divorce:

- **Nonstigmatization of the single parent status and divorce.** The manner in which parents approach divorce affects the way they and their children perceive the divorce. If people significant to them judge the single-parent home and the divorce process as a viable rather than a pathological situation, adults and children do better.
- **Reduced parental conflict.** Parents who are able to reduce their marital conflicts and friction and who have a tendency to get along with each other without turmoil and aggression create better adjustment environments for their children.
- **Family functioning.** Families that provide a sense of sharing and emotional support for one another in a loving manner have better adjusted children. Single-parent families who maintain family rituals around birthdays, holidays, and other special occasions provide a sense of security for the children.

- **Stable, loving relationship with both parents.** Children adjust better if they maintain consistent, predictable, positive relationships with both parents and have regular dependable visiting patterns.
- **Appropriate role allocation.** Single-parent families that have assigned chores and roles appropriate to their children's abilities have better adjusted children.
- **Effective parenting.** Effective parenting is defined as parents who have a good rapport with their children, provide for open communication within the family, have warm parent-child relationships in which discipline is stressed, and provide stable, predictable environments with clearly specified rules.
- **Strong support systems.** Single-parent families do better if they have strong support systems, consisting of regular friendships with relatives, such as grandparents, and peers.
- **Nonadversarial divorce.** Single-parent families do better if they have a nonadversarial postdivorce adjustment and a friendly coparental relationship.
- **Parent's own sense of well-being.** One of the most important predictors of children's postdivorce adjustment is the single parent's sense of well-being. If the single-parent mother or father has adjusted in a healthy way to the divorce, the children will also. This process can be facilitated through counseling and support structures.
- **Economics.** Probably the most important factor involved in the adjustment of the single-parent family, corroborated by recent research, is economics. If single parents have adequate money to support themselves and their families, many of the problems associated with divorce disappear. Given the current laws around child support and the associated problems with the percentage of reneging fathers, it is difficult to ascertain how this problem can be alleviated in the very near future.

Chapter 5
REDEFINING RELATIONSHIPS

Several of the most pertinent differences between the experiences of divorced versus widowed single parents are highlighted in chapters 1 and 2. To work effectively with these clients, the counselor must employ his or her knowledge of these variations in the planning of interventions and strategies. As an extreme example: the widowed are often counseled to visit the grave site as one means of finishing up business with the spouse, but the divorced are unlikely to be directed to return to the court room where the divorce was granted.

This chapter focuses on one factor that widowed and divorced single parents share: before single parents can begin to redefine their relationships with family and friends, or begin to form new adult relationships, they must first come to terms with the loss of the previous spouse. Even while new roles and functions are assigned to the remaining family members, and even while the family struggles for emotional acceptance of its loss, the memories of what used to be persist.

The external reality of single parents is permanently altered: a one-time partner is absent; economic status generally changes; fewer people are available to complete requisite tasks. Relationships with in-laws, with family, with coupled and single friends, are all made different to the degree that they were predicated upon the presence of the now-absent partner. The successful redefinition of these relationships is of central importance to the well-being of the single parent.

The memory of what used to be can create an alternative, subjectively held reality for some single parents. For these persons the maintenance of a relationship with the ghost of the absent partner can become a central counseling issue: living with ghosts while ignoring the living does not represent an adequate adjustment to an altered life style. Redefining relationships with family and friends in the present becomes impossible for those who refuse to acknowledge the differences between then and now.

The maintenance of a past-oriented, subjective reality that is at odds with the external reality is normative to some degree. Every single parent's external definition is changed at a discrete moment in time: at the hour of the death or when the divorce decree is made final. Internal, subjectively held self-definitions take much longer to change, however, than do legal ones. These changes do not happen at a specific point in time, but are better understood in terms of the developmental processes outlined in the previous chapters. Because of this gap in the time when legal and psychological self-definitions change, in some circumstances single parents will think, feel and, behave as if they are single, but at other times their cognitive, affective, and behavioral responses will be more like those of coupled people. In most cases, over time, the two sets of self-definitions become reconciled and external, and internal realities become congruent. Memories of what used to be either fade in importance or become fond recollections of an earlier time that is in no way confused with the present.

The clinical picture is different for those persons who, at the level of the unconscious, refuse to give up the ghosts of the past. For these single parents, the ghost becomes a demon who makes impossible an adequate adjustment to life's reality demands.

The discussion that follows concerning the redefinition of relationships following loss does not always differentiate between widowhood and divorce. The counselor is advised to apply his or her knowledge of these general principles to specific clients' situations.

We do not agree with the position taken by many theorists (e.g., Pollock, 1975) that one of the reasons for studying loss reactions following death is that such study will inform the understanding of reactions to all forms of loss. As Frantz (1984) writes:

> Coping and grieving are things we learn, we are taught, and we develop from the time we are infants. . . . By the time we are adults we've all had a lot of experiences with loss, starting with the rattle in our own crib, up on through our baseball gloves, dolls, teddy bears, high school boy friend or girl friend, graduation from high school or college, moving away from friends, and grandparents dying.

The implication seems to be that a loss, is a loss, is a loss—regardless of whom or what was lost. We believe this to be true in only the most general way: all losses involve the breaking of an attachment bond (Bowlby, 1980). Not all bonds are equally strong; neither are all equally desirable. It seems reasonable, therefore, that loss reactions are moderated by these variables.

The Ghost Versus Reality: Stress Reactions

Mourning is the process through which the subjectively held internal reality of single parents becomes aligned with external reality. The burden of change is upon the mourner:

Those who recover from bereavement do not return to being the same people they had been before their marriages or before their spouses' deaths. Nor do they forget the past and start a new life. Rather, they recognize that change has taken place, accept it, examine how their basic assumptions about themselves and their world must be changed, and go on from there. (Parkes & Weiss, 1983)

Most people do not give up the ghost as easily as may be implied from this citation. Perhaps the most thoroughly researched aspect of adults' reactions to loss concerns its effects as a stressor.

In his review of the literature, Jacobson (1983) cited studies that report adverse health changes and increased mortality among the separated and divorced. Other work cited in this article independently reports findings of increased anxiety, depression, resentfulness, anger, feelings of incompetence, suicidal ideation, death wishes, somatic complaints, weight loss, tiredness, difficulty in concentration, blaming of others, increased rate of smoking and drinking, self-neglect, and sleepiness. After reviewing the literature, Parkes and Weiss (1983) concluded that there is often a deterioration in health following loss as well as an increase in death rate. They did not speculate as to how specifically bereavement influences death, but as a stressor, it seems likely that loss impacts significantly on the immune system.

The review by Hodges (1986) reported that the suicide rate for divorced men is three times greater than for married men. Other stress-related outcomes are that the risk of death by homicide is far greater for the divorced than the married, the death rate by disease is much greater for the divorced, and the widowed and divorced have higher age-adjusted death rates from all causes than married people of equivalent age, sex, and race.

Evidence from the works of Wallerstein and Kelly (1980c), Jacobson (1983), and Garfield (1982) agrees with the position taken in an earlier chapter that emotional resolution of the loss—and its concomitant stress reactions—take a number of years to complete. The ghost often does not leave gently.

The Ghost Versus Reality: Relationship Rules

Some of the most powerful influences over behavior are often covert rules that people co-create to choreograph their interactions. Consider the fictional relationship between two adult couples with children. The tacit rule may be that when all four adults are together it is allowable to complain about the behavior of children but not that of the spouses. When the two wives or the two husbands are alone, however, the rule may be changed to include talk of dissatisfaction within the marriage. Although covert, the effects of rules such as these are enormous.

The process of renegotiating relationship rules following death or divorce can be a difficult one. Changes in rules about the relationships between the newly single parent and his or her family and friends must reflect the change in the marital relationship. At times, it is the single parent, at other times it is the family or friends, but often it is both parties who refuse to renegotiate relationships based on a new reality.

Stacy's status changed from that of a young, happily married mother to that of a widow without warning. She and her husband Bob had been trying to conceive and deliver a child for several years. It had not been easy. As each was less than maximally fertile, the couple had become involved with a lengthy and trying medical regime in order to fulfill their dream of becoming parents. Two conceptions resulted in miscarriages. The losses of these unborn children stressed their marriage, but the bond between Stacy and Bob remained strong. A third pregnancy resulted in the birth of the couple's son Zach.

Stacy and Bob, both in their 30s, were very healthy and health-conscious people. With the exception of their fertility problems, the only real medical problem either had ever faced was Bob's childhood bout with asthma. He had been symptom free for decades.

One Sunday morning, when Zach was 3 months old, Bob complained of feeling run down. When his complaints continued through Wednesday, Stacy, a nurse, insisted that he see a physician. The couple visited the doctor together, and Bob was diagnosed as having a recurrence of his childhood ailment.

Returning home, Bob went to bed and asked that Stacy bring him some soup. While she was preparing the meal, she heard Bob call for her. As Zach and the soup both required her attention at that moment, she did not respond immediately to Bob's call. When she arrived at the bedroom, Bob was unconscious. She began CPR. He was dead in minutes. The doctor had missed the diagnosis; Bob's heart had been invaded by a virus.

Stacy entered therapy 4 months after Bob's death. She was angry and depressed and knew her reactions had to do with her loss. Although her symptoms and the pain they caused were real, they were in no sense pathological. Stacy's relationship with Bob had been good. She could review it realistically. She neither overidealized not bastardized him. She had no psychological need to stay married to the ghost. She was progressing through the mourning process well, but how it hurt!

Anger is a common reaction shortly after loss, and Stacy's anger had a favorite target. Two of her married friends, in an effort to help, had made comments to the effect that they "knew what she was going through" as their husbands were so unhelpful in maintaining the household that they, too, "might as well be widowed." At times, Stacy hated these women. "I used to think that Bob did nothing, too," Stacy stated, "until I had to do all the things I didn't realize he was doing."

One of the things that Bob did was to enforce the rules governing the relationship between the couple and Zach's paternal grandparents. Even before the boy's birth, Bob's parents tended to intrude upon the couple's life. Their efforts to become more involved redoubled after the birth of their grandson.

In therapy, Stacy realized that one of the rules that she and Bob had co-created was that, when necessary, he was as blunt and forceful as required to keep his parents at an appropriate psychological distance. This allowed Stacy to play the "nice-guy" role with her in-laws while Bob became the target of his parents' anger over the ongoing situation.

After Bob's death, the rules had to be changed. Bob's parents called daily and offered unsolicited advice to Stacy in regard to dealing with her situation. If she chose to ignore their advice, they became punitive. She arranged her incredibly busy schedule so that they could see Zach three or four times a week. The grandparents wanted more of the boy, and often dropped in, unannounced, at inopportune times. Clearly, the nice-guy role and the rules around the relationship between Stacy and her in-laws were not working. The status quo was causing her to become angry, agitated, and depressed.

Stacy was able to assume the role of adult with her in-laws and to insist assertively that they respect her boundaries. The changes were not easily accomplished, but they were put into effect. In adopting a new role and in insisting on changes in the relationship rules, Stacy had essentially eliminated a significant source of stress from her life.

The success that Stacy enjoyed in renegotiating with her in-laws derived from the fact that she dealt realistically with the demands of her current situation rather than behaving as if Bob were still alive. To be sure, her fantasy was to have her husband back. The unconscious wish for reunion is completely normal shortly after a loss. Stacy, however, was able to separate from the fantasy. This separation allowed her to function adaptively, with a new set of rules, in the present. Had she instead relied on the old rules, and behaved as though Bob's ghost could continue to protect her from her in-laws, Stacy's growth would have been thwarted.

After several weeks of treatment, Stacy expressed one of her core beliefs: her husband did not have to die. Her widowhood and the burdens of single parenthood could and should have been avoided. She spoke with absolute conviction and with an intense anger that was directed at the attending physician. In her view, the doctor had misdiagnosed the condition. He had done an inadequate assessment of the husband's health status.

He had been overfocused on the history of asthma. He had ignored the subtle manifestations of viral infection. He had based treatment on the faulty diagnosis. He had been the proximal cause of the husband's death, her widowhood, and her son's loss of a father.

Stacy's words impacted on her counselor at several levels. They had both diagnostic and prognostic meanings. Her anger was a predictable and biologically based response to her loss (Bowlby, 1980). The counselor should reassure her of this and, in so doing, help normalize her feelings. The realistic way in which she described the husband and the marital relationship indicated that Stacy's bereavement was not complicated by feelings of extreme ambivalence. The counselor should not, without much more inquiry, jump to the reductionistic conclusion that the anger directed at the physician was "really" meant for the husband. The unexpected and untimely nature of the loss suggested the possibility that Stacy may have been suffering from a posttraumatic stress reaction (Rynearson, 1987). The counselor should factor this into any assessment and intervention decisions. The creation of a story that "explained" her loss served to inoculate her against unrealistic fear of future losses and was indicative of her progress with the work of mourning. The counselor should make no effort, at this time at least, to have Stacy examine the validity of her version of the role played by the doctor. The counselor should, however, vigorously assist her in disputing any belief system that suggested that the death of her husband had rendered her unable to cope with the demands of single parenthood (Beck, Rush, Shaw, & Emery, 1979; Meichenbaum, 1977; Mince, 1992; Rynearson, 1987).

At another level, meta to Stacy's individual story, her words reminded the counselor that an accurate and thorough assessment is as important for therapy clients as it is for medical patients. Thorough assessment is an ongoing and difficult process. The sorts of problems that counselors are asked to help clients deal with often have multiple and interacting causes (Krupp, Genovese, & Krupp, 1986).

Perpetual Divorce and Ambiguous Loss

Not all single parents are as successful as Stacy in redefining relationships. The case of Terese and Fred illustrates a rather common counseling situation: the perpetual divorce.

Although divorced for several years, Terese and Fred managed to keep their dysfunctional relationship alive. Their refusal to give up their anger was manifested through endless unnecessary legal squabbles. Moreover, each was involved in overt attempts to convince the children that the other parent was "to blame."

The paradox is as common as it is interesting: the despised ex-spouse continues to be the person who has greatest control over the other's thoughts, feelings, and actions. The children of parents who are perpetually divorcing often take on a problem. Typically, the children are brought to the counselor's office by the custodial parent who requests help with some behavioral or academic problem. Careful assessment in these cases often leads to the conclusion that the problem does not reside within the children but rather within the unrenegotiated relationship between the ex-spouses.

In most cases of perpetual divorce, the ex-spouse is physically absent from the family but psychologically very much alive within it. Boss (1991) referred to the situation as *ambiguous loss.* When the ex-spouse is simultaneously both in and out of the family, confusion and conflict ensue. Boss labeled this phenomenon as *boundary ambiguity* and pointed out that its purpose often is the denial of loss. The anger and hostility can serve to keep the dysfunctional marital relationship intact to some degree: the relationship with the ghost renders adaptation in the present unattainable.

Although boundary ambiguity often allows for the denial of permanent change in a former relationship, it is much more than an intrapsychic event. The ambiguity frequently is maintained by a complex pattern of interactions among the former spouses, their children, families, and friends. The plot of this play impacts enormously on the thinking, behaving, and feelings of all the actors involved.

> *Prior to the decision to divorce and during the divorce process, Fred could be described as emotionally distant from his children, acting out his sexual and angry impulses without regard to consequences. He was hostile, other-blaming, and without insight into his role in the disintegration of the marriage. Terese, at this time, gave free rein to her hostility by openly attacking Fred in conversations with the children and limiting his access to them. When any of the children manifested a caring or concerned attitude toward their father, Terese responded in a punitive fashion. She was as unaware of her contribution to the problemed situation as Fred.*
>
> *After the divorce, and when each former spouse was temporarily removed from battling ghosts, both made remarkable strides. The details of their growth patterns were different. Fred chose to return to school and transformed himself from an underpaid, underachieving, and unhappy worker into a competent and successful CPA. He was able to form stable, intimate relationships with his family and friends. His new relationships with women showed none of the sexual and angry acting-out behaviors that characterized his relationship with Terese. He became a caring father. Terese, for her part, became highly responsive to her children's needs and was able to separate those needs from her own. Her professional life*

blossomed. Where before she was rather lax in her approach to her work, she now was a highly focused and successful attorney. Her relationships, too, were more mutually satisfying.

Common to the growth of both Terese and Fred was a change in focus from blaming the former spouse to a realization that each was responsible for his or her own life.

As is often the case, however, the ghost has many reincarnations. Fred and Terese seemed to take turns in resurrecting the patterns of their problemed relationship. At times, they became consumed with "righteous" anger at the former spouse and fired off a salvo, usually in the form of some legal maneuver. The salvo initiated anger in the other, and soon the old relationship was alive again: Fred angry and acting out, Teresa, enmeshed with the children, punitive and blaming.

Some instances of boundary ambiguity are characterized and complicated not only by the psychological presence of the former spouse but also by his or her physical presence. These cases are not to be confused with those successful divorces in which both adults have been able to separate their spousal and parental roles well, and are available to one another in the task of raising the children. Rather the boundary ambiguities in question serve to maintain nonadaptive relationships that are emotionally alive but legally dead.

Katlin and Rob provide a stark example of how some people refuse to live in the present. Their boundary ambiguity not only makes the establishment of new relationships difficult for them, as adults, but it also has made adjustment for their children impossible:

After 15 years of marriage, the relationship between Rob and Katlin was dead, and each was aware of it. No longer friends and no longer lovers, neither found satisfaction in the other. For a number of years, however, they had tacitly decided to remain married in order to preserve a "normal" life style for the children. The relationship rule was simple: each was expected and allowed to find personal and sexual intimacy with lovers; these affairs, however, were not to interfere with each partner's functioning as a parent.

For some time the rule seemed to work, although the children showed some relatively minor academic and behavioral problems. Dinner was a nightly family gathering. Both parents attended PTA meetings, the girls' swim meets, and the boy's soccer games. Birthdays and holidays were celebrated. The extended family was unaware of the condition of the marriage.

When one of Katlin's affairs turned into a romance, the relationship rule was broken, and predictably, chaos ensued. Typical of the romantic love phase of a relationship, both Katlin and her lover overidealized each other and conspired to be together as much as possible. As a result, Rob had to assume essentially all of the parental duties. He felt furious and cheated: it was not that Katlin had an affair. As a matter of fact, he continued his own affairs. It was that the facade of a happy, two-parent, functional family unit was exposed for what it truly was. The divorce settlement called for Rob to have sole physical custody of the children. A substantial cash settlement was awarded to Katlin, but there were no spousal support payments. Rob and the children were to reside in the marital home until the youngest completed college.

By the time the divorce was final, Katlin's romance had faded. Her financial need and Rob's need for someone to care for the children combined to allow the former spouses to exponentially compound the boundary ambiguity: Rob hired Katlin to baby-sit for the children. Once again, the children had two parents in the home. Once again, the adults led separate lives. And once again, the fact that each parent had a significant other was kept hidden from the children.

It was almost predictable that the reestablishment of old relationship rules eventually led to a similar outcome. When next Katlin fell in love, she left the children and Rob without warning. The rule had been broken once more, and once more Katlin was cast as villain. The children were devastated: the mourning work was greatly complicated by having lost the same mother twice.

Another case further illustrates boundary ambiguity:

In addition to whatever intrapsychic and interpersonal issues were at work, the boundary ambiguity around Bill and Diane's relationship was compounded by Diane's poverty. She entered treatment as a single parent who was having difficulty with her three children, aged 19, 17, and 15. The situation at home improved dramatically as Diane and her children allowed each other the psychological space necessary to become mutually weaned from each other, which is the central developmental task for families with adolescents. When Bill reentered the family, however, the old patterns reemerged.

Bill and Diane had a 22-year common-law marriage. After the birth of the children, Diane became financially dependent upon Bill. She used her welfare benefits to provide her family with a marginal existence, but she needed Bill's contribution in order to provide the children with a first-class private education. It was her goal that each of the three had the opportunity to graduate from college at her expense.

This dream was at odds with the reality of her life. Diane found Bill to be simultaneously withdrawing and overwhelming. When her dissatisfaction and anxiety concerning the relationship became unbearable, she be-

came overly focused and involved with the children. As the children grew older, they rebeled at Diane's overinvolvement. The anxiety was reduced when Diane threw Bill out of the house. The separations lasted from a few weeks to half a year. Diane at first rejected Bill's pleas to come home. Over time, however, she felt guilty about taking money from Bill and allowed him to return. The process would began anew.

No true gains were made in counseling until the goal of eliminating the boundary ambiguity was attained.

As students of the intricate interplay and mutually influencing behavior among family members, systemic therapists and theorists have created a literature that abounds in examples of how some families endeavor to keep the ghost alive.

Loss and the Family

Some single parents are sure to become withdrawn and depressed at times, as they go through the developmental process of renegotiating past relationships. Garfield (1982) described the process as a complex set of biological and psychological reactions that often involve a withdrawal from life's normal activities. Theorists such as Bowlby (1980), Freud (1952), Parkes and Weiss (1983), Rando (1984), and Sanders (1989) have described developmentally appropriate withdrawal and depressive stages.

What may be developmentally appropriate for a single parent's individual growth may, however, spark abandonment fears in the children. In most cases, father is already gone, and a depressed and withdrawn mother may appear to be unavailable as well. Hoffman (1981) suggested that behavioral problems on the part of children may serve to "bring back" the attention of a depressed mother. Another example is provided by Fulmer (1983), who described the enmeshment between a single mother and her adolescent son, as well as the mother's depression, in terms of the mother's inability to mourn the death of her parents and the loss of her marriage. It is clear from the literature that the renegotiation of the relationship with the former spouse often impacts on the ongoing and evolving relationships between the single parent and many other significant persons.

As most relationships are best understood in terms of the dyadic, and at times triadic, interactions between and among people (Hoffman, 1981), an understanding of systemic factors is invaluable to the counselor in helping single parents renegotiate relationship rules with the important people in their lives. At times, however, a thorough knowledge of the individual's intrapsychic processes is required (Bowlby, 1980; Freud, 1952; Genovese, 1992; Krupp et al., 1986; Rando, 1984). This is especially true for those single parents for whom the loss of the marital relationship recalls thoughts of unresolved relationships that predate the marriage.

Many theoreticians (Bowen, 1978; Kaslow, 1981) have suggested that powerful, unconscious motives may underlie mate selection. Often a partner is selected based upon the unconscious wish for the reparation of old relationship wounds, or in an attempt to make the self whole through union with the other. Rynearson (1987) suggested that the marital relationship can have a large positive impact upon the self-concept of certain individuals. For these persons, distress during the early stages of the separation-individuation process (Mahler, Pine, & Bergman, 1975) has translated into a self-concept characterized by feelings of incompetence, dependency, and self-loathing.

The establishment and development of the attachment bond (Bowlby, 1980) forged between the couple serves to change the self-concept into a "we-concept." The we-concept can be in stark contrast to the self-concept: I am incapable; we can do it. These individuals become dependent upon the marital relationship to ward off the ghosts of problemed relationships from the family of origin.

Thus the loss of the marital bond through death or divorce is a compounded one. Not only is the partner gone, but the positive we-concept is also replaced by the negative self-image. In a sense, these individuals must learn first how to deal with, and then how to bury, two generations of ghosts.

> *Twenty-five-year-old Lynne adored her father, and he doted upon his little girl. She felt that her mother was distant and uncaring but that her father could always make things right. She felt intensely jealous of her sister, and felt the need to compete against her for her father's love. The father, a gangster of sorts, was murdered when Lynne was 5 years old. She has been searching for him ever since.*
>
> *During her early and middle adolescence, Lynne's depression, lack of self-esteem, and need for her father took a self-destructive turn. She became sexually involved with a large number of much older men, all of whom operated at the fringes of society. They introduced her to drugs and alcohol, and she became an abuser of these substances. One of these relationships resulted in an unplanned pregnancy. Lynne married her son's father, but the marriage lasted only a short while. She divorced the man to be with Jack.*
>
> *Five years ago, when she was 20, Lynne fell in love with Jack. Her search for her father seemed completed. Jack, a mobster as was her father, was also in his 40s.*

Through the machinations of projective identification (Krupp et al., 1986) and family projective process (Bowen, 1978), Lynne and Jack recreated her childhood. The relationship was "ideal" so long as Lynne played the incompetent, all-loving little girl and Jack the paternal hero. However, as is often the case in relationships, what is desired in fantasy is unbearable in reality.

> *Over time, Lynne began to feel stifled by her relationship with Jack. Her increasing need for autonomy resulted in a straining of the relationship. Their frequent arguments and fights were a sort of angry negotiation for autonomy within the context of the relationship.*
>
> *This battle in the here-and-now was complicated by the ghost of Lynne's father. When the psychological distance from Jack became too great, threatening the continuance of the bond, Lynne became panic stricken. She lost control, threw temper tantrums (as well as pots and pans), became insanely jealous, and lost interest in her children. She, in fact, became a child who needed her Daddy's guidance. The patterns were reestablished.*

The Role of the Professional Counselor

Whatever the counselor's particular theoretical orientation may be, the establishment of an open, honest, caring, accepting and, empathetic relationship (Minuchin, 1974; Rogers, 1951) with the single parent is a prerequisite if treatment is to result in growth.

To be empathic, however, is not to accept completely the client's view of his or her own reality. Much of society and many single parents themselves relate to single parenthood as if it were a diagnostic entity—a pathological state—that explains behavior, emotions, and cognitions. Teachers often attribute a child's poor academic performance to the fact that "she is from a broken home." Single parents often attribute their depression, anxiety, and anger to their single-parent status.

One important role of the professional counselor is to help the single parent dispute the validity of the assertion that single parenthood "causes" anything. To be sure, the loss of a marital partner is a nodal event in an individual's life. To be sure, nodal events are anxiety producing in that they demand that changes must be made. However, the role of the counselor is to help the client reframe single parenthood from that of a toxic state dictating the direction of life to that of a developmental phase in the individual's and the family's life cycle. As in all developmental phases, there are clear tasks to be accomplished.

Walsh and McGoldrick (1991) posited that the three primary tasks to be accomplished are the reorganization of the roles of the remaining members of the family in order to accomplish necessary tasks, the shared acknowledgment of the loss, and the reinvestment of energy into new relationships and activities. The counselor must help the client focus on the necessary family structural changes and create an atmosphere in which the single parent and children are free to express openly any and all feelings of loss, and are open to the possibility of new satisfactions.

The counselor must be aware that many of the most powerful behavior-directing relationship rules are covert and below the level of the client's consciousness. The counselor must help the client make the covert overt.

The counselor serves an educational function when he or she is able to take what is known from theory (Bowlby, 1980; Parkes & Weiss, 1983) and apply it to the client's experience. In so doing, the counselor not only normalizes the single parent's experience but also provides a unifying theme for the many disparate and distressing manifestations of loss.

In adopting a developmental stance with regard to single parenthood, the counselor helps the client become aware of the possibility of new and satisfying relationships in the present and in the future.

In helping the client renegotiate old relationships and establish new ones, the counselor is aware of the dyadic nature of relationships. In taking this position, the counselor helps the client explore the renegotiation from a systemic as well as from an individual perspective. The counselor thus remains open to the possibility and desirability of conjoint sessions with the single parent and the children, or with extended family members and friends.

The counselor is aware that the impact of the dissolution of the marital bond in the present may be exacerbated by whatever family-of-origin legacies the single parent brings to his or her own situation. Is divorce shameful? Does it represent failure? Is it an act of selfishness? Does the death of a spouse rekindle previous unresolved loss? The counselor helps the client understand these historical issues not only through insight-oriented counseling but also through the use of sessions with the client's family of origin (Framo, 1992).

The counselor is aware that one very important effect of single parent-hood often is a greatly reduced income (McLanhan, Garfinkel, & Ooms, 1987). He or she must be knowledgeable of the workings of social service agencies and school systems, and must help the client to negotiate any dealings with such organizations.

Counseling Strategies

Not all single parents who enter counseling need help with adjusting to the loss of the marital partner, but nearly all need to effect significant changes in the way their families work. The number of tasks that need to be completed does not diminish after the family is transformed from a two-parent to a one-parent system. There are simply fewer hands available to accomplish what must be done.

Working a full-time job, nurturing and tending to young Zach's needs, and reestablishing and redefining her relationship with her in-laws as well as gardening, painting the garage, taking out the trash, and doing myriad other things that Bob used to do meant that Stacy's usual condition was one of near exhaustion.

What has to be done, and who is responsible, varies over the course of a family's life cycle (Carter & McGoldrick, 1980). The degree of family restructuring required following death or divorce is also a function of when it occurs in the family's history: the divorce of a married couple both 65 years of age with grown children requires less restructuring than the divorce of two 43 year olds with adolescent children.

In single-parent families, children commonly must take on roles and responsibilities at a younger age than their peers who live in two-parent families. Their status is reflected in the nature and direction of the communication flow between the children and the single parent. These children are often consulted and have input into decisions as mundane as when the dinner hour should be and as special as where the family should vacation. To a greater degree than others their age, these children are more important to the family's functioning and have a greater amount of power in negotiating family decisions.

In and of itself, this is not a pathological situation. Rather, it represents an insightful and artful solution to a difficult problem. Taken to an extreme, however, this particular family structure can engender more anxiety and nonadaptive behavior than it solves.

The works of Minuchin (1974) and Minuchin and Fishman (1981) have stated that to function effectively the boundaries between the generations and the structure of the power hierarchy must be clear to all family members. The use of family maps (Minuchin & Fishman, 1981), a schematic depicting the boundaries among the family's subsystems, its coalitions and alliances, and its power hierarchy, is a useful counseling tool. It provides not only an assessment of the family's structure but also suggests in-session maneuvers and between-session tasks designed to clarify boundaries and hierarchies.

Among the many structural moves described by Minuchin and Fishman are seating the family in groups based on age, and having the children solve problems alone. For example, the counselor might suggest to the single parent that the children may be able to solve some problem—getting ready for school in the morning perhaps—as they may have insights not available to the adults. The adults observe as the children wrestle with the problem. Then the single parent takes what is valuable from the children's solution and modifies it from the adult perspective. This strategy strengthens generational boundaries and reinforces the single parent's position at the apex of the power hierarchy. The counselor may also employ Madanes' (1981) technique of blocking any parent-talk or children-talk that implies that the children have either parity or superiority in making family decisions.

Sherman and Fredman (1986) listed many structural moves designed to reinforce generational boundaries. Important for the single parent are those aimed at ensuring the privacy of the parent and the children, and those that enable the parent to enjoy activities unrelated to the children.

Herz Brown (1988) made an observation that can be of great value to the counselor. Adolescents in single-parent families are often more closely tied to the family than are their age peers. Again, this is a function of the increased responsibility these young people have for the functioning of the family. The primary developmental task at this point in the life cycle—the mutual weaning of parent and children—can be made more difficult by the structure of single-parent families. It is as if the adolescents' developmental needs are in conflict with the family's need for cohesion. Often the usual rebellion and extrafamilial focus employed to effect adolescent-parent weaning are unavailable. The counselor must strive to make these processes overt.

Restructuring techniques can also be useful in the renegotiation of relationships between the single parent and various members of the extended family and friends. The counselor must be open to the use of conjoint sessions, however, if the restructuring is to be most effective.

The counseling goal is the formation of clear boundaries and power parity among adult peers. Renegotiation to peerhood with the single parent's own parents may be met with resistance: often the relationship rules between parents and adult children disallow peerhood. The use of tracking, a sort of multiperson functional analysis of repetitive behavioral sequences described in detail by Sherman and Fredman (1986), is a highly effective technique of making overt the covert relationship rules that govern interactions and define relationships. Tracking can be used in any conjoint sessions regardless of whom is in attendance.

Delving into the family legacies with regard to death and divorce can be accomplished in conjoint sessions with the single parent and his or her own parents. Such inquiry is made easier if the genogram—an extended family tree—is employed. The use of the genogram is explained fully by Carter and McGoldrick (1980).

One of the primary goals in working individually with single parents is to change their stance from passive pawns to active problem solvers. The adoption by the therapist of a developmental view of single parenthood aids in this conceptual shift. The cognitive restructuring techniques of Ellis's (1962) rational emotive therapy are well suited to attack irrationally held beliefs about powerlessness in changing nonadaptive behavior patterns. These same techniques are useful in undermining any beliefs that suggest that the single parent, children, former spouse, former spouse's ghost, members of the extended family, friends, co-workers, or new partners must, should, or have to behave in some specified way in order for the single parent to feel well and happy.

The cognitive techniques of Beck et al. (1979) can be employed in dealing with any depression brought about by the loss of the marital partner, as can inquiry into the nature of the ambivalence in the relationship with the former spouse (Krupp et al., 1986). Normalizing the negative aspect of the ambivalence can bring relief to inappropriate guilt feelings around the relationship with the former spouse.

The goal of having the single parent reinvest in new relationships and activities can be made difficult by the stress produced in meeting new people. In instances such as these, Meichenbaum's (1977) stress-inoculation procedure can be employed. The first phase of this treatment is to convince the single parent that much anxiety is generated not by the situation per se but by the client's interpretation of the situation and the nature of the internal dialogue generated by that interpretation. In the second step, the single parent practices stress-reducing dialogue in the counselor's office. Anxiety generated by an imagined social situation is labeled as a result of nonadaptive internal dialogue and is used to signal more adaptive self-talk. In the final phase, the single parent creates situations that allow for practice in vivo.

To address the problem of boundary ambiguity, Sherman, Oresky, and Rountree (1992) offered the empty-chair technique, which they referred to as a real "ghostbuster." In this procedure, family members speak to an empty chair as if the missing spouse were there. They take turns role playing responses likely to have come from the person represented by the chair. The technique serves to diminish the incongruity between psychological presence and physical absence. It serves further to externalize the problem. Once externalized, each family member can be helped to explore his or her relationship with the problem (Epston & White, 1990; White & Epston, 1990).

For those single-parent families who need help in dealing with the ghost of past relationships, McGoldrick (1988) placed great emphasis on the open flow of information among family members. In the relationship review technique, each member tells the story of his or her own relationship with the former spouse. The review begins with each individual's first memory of the relationship. Ghost-related issues are often highlighted by an unrealistic view of the person: the former spouse is often seen either as an angel or as a demon. The open expression of these misrepresentations allows family members to serve as reality checks for one another, and to dispute irrational beliefs. Asking the family very specific questions concerning the details surrounding the loss to open up the system is suggested. In the case of the death of a parent, visiting the cemetery, writing letters to the deceased, making picture albums, and keeping a journal of memories and feelings are also suggested.

Rynearson's (1987) work indicated that the choice of intervention employed with single parents should be predicated upon the type of loss involved. In cases of untimely or unexpected loss, he suggested the use of posttraumatic shock techniques. Weiss (1975), Wallerstein and Kelly (1980c), and Peck and Manocherian (1988) all referred to the differences between the reactions of the spouse who makes the decision to divorce and those of the one who has been left. Perhaps, in working with single parents who were left, counselors might also at times employ posttraumatic shock procedures. In cases in which the single parent had a highly dependent relationship with the former spouse, Rynearson (1987) suggested the use of cognitive restructuring techniques to attack any self-images characterized by feelings of weakness and incompetence. Rynearson believed insight-oriented psychodynamic therapy to be the treatment of choice in dealing with single parents whose previous relationship was highly conflicted. The counselor should strive to ensure that the client gains insight into his or her own contribution to the dysfunctional relationship.

Parkes and Weiss (1983) separated the process of recovery from loss into three phases. The goal of the first is *intellectual recognition*. During this phase, the counselor helps the single parent formulate a story that settles the question of why the loss occurred. Without such an account, the ability to reinvest in new relationships is diminished. If people do not know why they have suffered a painful loss, they will be loathe to form new attachment bonds that may again, for no reason, be taken from them.

The goal of the second phase is *emotional acceptance*. Operationally, emotional acceptance implies a diminished fear of being overwhelmed by grief, pain, or remorse. Part of the recovery process involves the working through of what Parkes and Weiss (1983) referred to as the obsessive review: the painful and time-consuming task of dealing with each and every memory trace of the former relationship, grieving over it, and, ultimately, neutralizing it. No change in the content of the review is contraindicative of growth.

In the third phase, *identity transformation*, the single parent creates new self-definitions that are not predicated on the previous relationship. A single parent may sound wistful when he or she reports, "I don't feel married any more," but the counselor sees the meaning behind the words: the ghost has been exorcised.

PART II

SEXUAL EXPERIENCES OF THOSE WHO ARE SINGLE AGAIN

Chapter 6

RELATIONAL AND SEXUAL CONCERNS AND CONSIDERATIONS AFTER DIVORCE

Few human activities have as many facets as sex. Sex can be the height of sharing and the extreme of selfishness. Most of all, sex can be many things at once—animalistic and spiritual, honorable and despicable, tender and brutal.

It is a human activity that has kept moralists, philosophers, politicians, and poets busy for centuries. The opinions about sex waver, the meanings change, the values shift, but the puzzle of sex remains.

Sexually Single Again

The puzzle of sex is especially troublesome to the growing number in our society who become sexually single again through divorce and widowhood. Perhaps it was always so for the widowed. But in a culture that gives lip service to the goodness of sex, it has now become doubly difficult to deal with, given the pervasive though elusive presence of the AIDS virus. Mary is a case in point.

She had just turned 50 when the separation shock took place. Her husband left her for a younger woman—again! They had been separated two times before for the same reason. So this was the end, and they obtained a divorce exactly 1 year after the separation. At first Mary's rage consumed her. From morning to night she was angry, furious. "What's a woman at my age going to do? Where will I find a partner? Not that I want one now. But I don't want to be alone either." Her two children were teenagers on the way to adulthood. They had adjusted, and their father was providing for their financial needs. Mary, however, could not survive with the court-mandated money he sent her every other week. So she went back to teaching, the career she had interrupted 18 years earlier. It was tough to get up before dawn every day, fight the traffic for a whole hour, face the unmotivated and undisciplined students, come back home again in the middle of heavy traffic, exhausted, only to take care of the house chores, watch some television, and go to bed early just to start the same routine all over again the next day. And it was lonely. Her life had changed. Her neighbors, friends (the ones that were left after the divorce), even relatives treated her differently. It was very lonely. But, thank heaven, all this happened nearly 3 years ago.

Now there was Joe who started to show interest in her. She liked him too, but she felt so insecure, so full of doubts. She couldn't believe it. The fear of being hurt was very real, and the whole sexual side of the situation scared her silly. That was the real problem, sex. Nothing had happened yet, but Mary felt so uncomfortable and self-conscious. She felt inadequate, full of questions, childish. Yes, that was it, she felt like a young teenager! She had never been sexually involved with any other person besides her husband. Now the mere thought of sex with Joe reopened areas of sensitivity from her marriage. In spite of all of this, she knew that she wanted the physical closeness with Joe. "But how will he react if she agreed to it?" All the old prejudices were still there. And she thought she had grown up, finally! The thoughts kept coming. "All a man wants is sex. Once he gets it, forget it. Will he then lose interest in her? Will he think less of her? And what about infection?" The word infuriated her, but it kept sticking to her brain. Joe had been widowed for over 6 years with no children. He was religious and had traditional and rather conservative values, she knew that. "But who knows for sure? Infection! If he had been sexually involved, maybe even a prostitute . . ." She felt ashamed of her own thoughts. She was getting angry at herself. This whole thing was becoming so complicated and stressful.

For months Mary felt like a fool every time physical closeness was a possibility. She and Joe got along very well, enjoyed each other's company, and had similar tastes and interests. He was attentive to her, considerate and cheerful, and secure in himself. Joe also got along well with her children. All in all she really liked him but she started to dread the moments of intimacy. In 5 months they had not yet been completely naked in each other's presence, let alone had sexual intercourse. One day, a weekend they had planned to stay in his house while her children were both out of town visiting friends, they had come back from a wonderful evening: theater, dinner, a relaxed stroll on a glorious autumn night in Manhattan. Neither was really tired when they finally got home. Mary was happy and grateful for the evening. She hugged him tenderly, and he responded in kind. The sexual stirring was instantaneous. Their caresses became more intimate. She followed the flow of passion while he undressed her and she undressed him on the way to his bedroom. But all of a sudden, with the same unexpected

*speed that her sexuality had been kindled a few moments before, she pan-
icked. She just froze and started to cry begging him to stop. Next day, after a
rather quiet breakfast, she returned home, as they had planned. But he
changed toward her from that day on. He was friendly and polite but never
invited her out again, and the relationship came to a gradual and unevent-
ful end.*

The case of Mary is not unique. She was not more "abnormal" or
pathological than any other woman in her circumstances. What happened
to Mary happens also to many men. To be sexually single again brings about
many real problems to adults who otherwise handle their lives very adequately. In the area of intimacy, those who are sexually single again, men or
women, often are surprised to experience a form of emotional regression,
as Mary did: a conflict of feelings they have not had since young adolescence. The sexually single again, like Mary, need information, reassurance,
and guidance. They have to be clear about their own sexuality. They need
to know concrete facts about this new and unexpected chapter in their lives
because no one can afford not to know about sexuality in the age of AIDS.
Whether we like it or not, ignorance can literally kill us.

However, human sexuality cannot be dealt with in the abstract or as a
set of rules to follow, as the story of Mary and Joe shows. Human beings have
their questions and doubts, their suffering, hopes, dreams, fears, joys, disappointments, pettinesses, and heroism. But life is now being threatened as
never before by a mysterious virus, in addition to the threats to life and
happiness that humans impose on themselves through their prejudices and
the mental tricks they play on themselves.

Sex in itself—the act—is interesting acrobatics: a smooth fitting of
parts marvelously engineered for each other. But sex, beyond the pleasures
of the flesh, involves emotions, meaning systems, and spirituality. Most
humans, at least in our culture, do not just copulate. They make love. They
express feelings through bodily interaction. The attraction for each other,
the need, desire, emotion, love, and passion are all expressed through
fingers, lips, tongue, skin, mucosa, bodily orifices, genitalia. Communion of
the flesh reflects communion of the spirit, and this mingling of flesh and
spirit is what makes sex so complicated. Our own culture has been obsessed
with sex for a long time. The obsession appears in the form of the multimil-
lion-dollar pornography industry and of the moral and religious watchdogs.
It is either sex without spirit or sex without playfulness and fun: the rootless,
dehumanized, pornographer caught up in the mechanics of sex, or the
joyless, dehumanized, fanatic concerned with the "sinfulness" of sex. Both
miss the true complexity of human sexuality and are both are equally
deficient.

The Principle of Autonomy

The balance of sex between flesh and spirit is delicate. Neither beasts nor angels, humans have to strike a unique compromise, oppositional to the pornographer and to the watchdog alike. Because sex is neither beneath nor above human nature, it is a constant challenge. The issue for those who are single again, as for all, is not "to sex or not to sex." The issue is not to miss the joy and enrichment of human sexuality. In this respect, we subscribe to what can be called the principle of autonomy: **anything sexual is acceptable among consenting adults that is not harmful to them or to third parties either physically or emotionally**.

A consequence of the autonomy principle at this point in history is that sexual activities before considered normal, such as copulation, may be harmful if one party is infected with the AIDS virus. Similarly, other sexual activities that in previous times have been considered less than normal, like sexual arousal without copulation, may now be acceptable due to the AIDS epidemic.

Voluntary Abstention

Another issue for those who are single again is that of voluntary sexual abstention. From time immemorial, sexual abstinence, at least temporary abstinence, has been valued for its spiritual enrichment, especially in religious contexts. That celibacy, like fasting, can be salubrious is not difficult to see if it is a temporary condition. Buddhist and Christian monks, among the best known cases, have recognized its advantages. The difficulty—practical, philosophical, and physiological—comes when this state of sexual abstention is made permanent. In our research we found many people in the sexually single again category who had welcomed celibacy as a period of self-reevaluation and reflection that actually strengthened their sexual nature. Their solitude became an experience of being alone, at peace with themselves, in touch with the mystery of their existence in the world. "If a man can't be alone," said the American monk Thomas Merton (Lentfoehr, 1979), "he doesn't know who he is." Or as Dag Hammarskjold (1966) put it, "Your loneliness may spur you into finding someone to live for, great enough to die for." Rollo May (1969) added that without solitude modern persons, bombarded constantly by television and radio, increasingly interacting with computers, find it "exceedingly difficult to let insights from unconscious depths break through."

Bob, whose wife fell in love with a woman friend and left him with the children in order to live with her, confirms such sentiments. "Her lesbianism came as a total surprise to me. After 12 years of marriage and three children, with all that we had gone through together, I was convinced that

I knew Ellen. Her decision crushed me. I thought I was less of a man because . . . I don't know why. Fortunately my sister was able to help me out with the children. She had always been a second mother to them, especially since her only child died of leukemia. She lives only one block away. The kids love her and do not mind spending more time at her house. She also spends much time at our house with them.

"During the first 3 or 4 months after Ellen left me, I was in a state of shock, as I said before. Work was my only medicine. I'd put 70 to 90 hours in a week. Then I 'retaliated,' went out with—went to bed with—sought out any available woman for about 6 or 7 months. But after that, the futility of the sexual conquests hit me. I stopped dating all together. For about a year I became a celibate. Didn't even think about sex much. I reflected a lot, I read, I listened to music, I visited museums, I took long walks in the woods. I enjoyed doing all this alone. I looked forward to my moments of solitude. That year without women—without sex—is one of the most enriching experiences I've ever had. By the end of 1986—exactly 2 years and 3 months since Ellen took off—we became divorced and I felt that I had been reborn. I attribute this sense of freedom to my year of solitude and celibacy. I was ready to start again and was very lucky to meet Sally, my present wife of almost 2 years. One thing I want to emphasize is that I found myself gravitating toward this solitude and lack of sex. I hadn't planned on it, but it started to feel right when I got into it. And, really, it was very good for me. I recommend it!"

Many people who become sexually single again report experiences similar to Bob's. Two points are interesting to note. The first is that their choice of celibacy is always voluntary, out of the felt need to be in touch with themselves and to reach a higher level of honesty and genuineness. The second is that all these people evaluate their period of sexual abstention very positively: it helped them settle down and make a satisfying commitment to another person. Only one of the subjects, married 2 years and without children, whose wife had died of cancer, moved on to prolonged celibacy by becoming a Roman Catholic priest.

The Cognitive Elements

One additional issue of sexuality needs to be mentioned here: the cognitive elements of human sex (Araoz, 1982).

Thought and imagination—cognitive elements or processes—make human actions different from those of other animals on this planet. Thought and imagination make art—one of the activities that distinguishes humans and makes them unique among all other living things—possible. Art is the creative expression of human imagination: it transforms nature, either in what is called artistic expression or through technology, another type of artistic expression. The transformation of nature is especially true of sex. In humans the predictable stages of animals leading to copulation become highly sophisticated. Thought and imagination transform sex, and sex becomes art. The evidence is overwhelming. From the few erotic engravings of the Stone Age (see Tannahill, 1982) to the delicate sexual portrayals on Egyptian and Greek plates, vases, and murals, sex is depicted as varied, playful, and far from predictable and monotonous. From the explicit sexual scenes in many objects preserved from pre-Columbian South and Central America, or from Islam, India, China, or Japan to our modern-age erotic art in paintings, much more than mere "instinct" makes human sex always new.

In studying those who become sexually single again, we realized the important role of these cognitive factors in sexual behavior. What people think about sex either enhances or damages their sexuality. What people think and believe about their bodies, their physical needs, pleasure, and sensuality, their own attractiveness and their self-esteem, makes a significant difference in how they act sexually. In counseling these people we found ourselves often helping them question their "cognitions" in these areas. By this process of self-questioning, people come to realize that many of the things about sex that people believe to be "normal" and "right" are purely cultural and have changed in different societies at different points in history. This realization frequently helps people to be more tolerant and more understanding of differences. The sociocultural beliefs people accept serve to establish a common meaning system from which structure and behavioral scripts flow. Because all human beings are culture-bound, these injunctions serve a positive function not to be dismissed lightly. However, they may also restrict and inhibit freedom of action and choice, often confusing what is "natural" with what is cultural. Homosexuality is a good example of what has been considered right or wrong sexually, based not on nature but on culture. Only in the last two decades have people in this country slowly come to recognize homosexuality as part of the social structure and tentatively to accept it. There is still a long way to go, to be sure, before homosexuals are granted full social and human rights, but the change that is taking place cannot be questioned.

Prostitution is another area of sexual behavior in which there is much confusion. Is it against the nature of humans or is it a cultural taboo? Prostitution has existed universally since time immemorial, which leads us to believe that it fulfills some important role for humans. However, people in America officially refuse to accept prostitution, except for a few notable exceptions, depriving it from the controls that could prevent children and other nonconsenting adults from being exploited. By ignoring prostitution, the rights of innocent persons are neglected. Venereal disease continues to spread at a crucial epidemiological time, endangering the health of the population in general. Finally, by not accepting it, government revenues from regulating this sexual activity are missed. Society embarks on a negative course of action proclaiming prostitution to be wrong. The attitudes about prostitution are socially created. Is it wrong in itself or do beliefs about it make it wrong? This is another example of one of the many sexual activities that become what cognitions make them to be. Other sexual behaviors that are given ethical value by social and psychological meaning systems are, for instance, oral sex, anal sex, polygamy, and active forms of sex education for adolescents.

Moving away from sociosexual issues, the positive side of cognitions in individual sexual behavior needs to be stressed. When people start questioning and challenging their own belief systems and convictions, they find a new freedom, not necessarily to act differently but to accept and respect other forms of sexual behavior. Prejudice is hard to change in general. When it comes to sex, it is usually a prejudgment that comes from childhood and has been accepted without examination or criticism. For instance, not a few of the sexually single again have conflicts with masturbation. In counseling, we never encourage people to act one way or another. We do help them examine the benefits and harm they experience in their activity. We found that most people who have difficulty with masturbation allow the old, unexamined injunction of childhood to continue to be operative. When they explore it in counseling and evaluate masturbation as adults, they begin to question the prejudice that they took for granted as being "the truth." People may change their behavior by forceful means and violence, but when they change themselves, willingly, a cognitive restructuring has always preceded the external—behavioral—change. However, this cognitive change may be neither conscious nor necessarily based on objective truth. For example, the recovering drug addict who "believes" that he or she cannot live without the drug and gives into it again has made a behavioral change coming from a false belief. The cognitive change leads him or her to discontinue the recovery program and return to the drug. Consciously he or she believes that he or she cannot do otherwise. What he or she does not know is that he or she is deceiving him- or herself and giving up on the opportunity to recover and lead a good life (Araoz, 1982).

One of our clients, Olaf, experienced that cognitive-behavioral change regarding masturbation.

As a child, Olaf had been severely punished for "touching himself." This behavior had so effectively inhibited him that he never masturbated during adolescence. Then he got married. Sexual intercourse was frequent during the marriage, and so he did not masturbate in 16 years of marriage either. After his divorce, not being able to establish a steady sexual relationship with a woman and tired of the complications of "touch and go sex," as he called it, as well as of the health dangers of paid sex, he found himself "using morning erections to masturbate in a half-sleep state," as he put it, feeling very guilty and ashamed of himself. However, Olaf had the courage to question and examine his beliefs about masturbation and to change his cognitions. From then on he was able to enjoy this activity without giving it undue importance. Eventually he found a woman who became his steady partner. He told us, about a year later, that he still enjoyed, without any guilt, occasional self-pleasuring, as he now called masturbation.

In sexual behavior the cognitive elements are always at work. If we believe that something is real, it is real in its consequences. What we believe becomes real for us. Because this is so, we encourage people who have difficulties with their new sexual status after having become single again to (1) become aware of their hidden sexual beliefs, (2) question and examine them because they might be creating the problem, (3) change perceptions and beliefs accordingly, and (4) change their behavior, if change is in accordance with their adult self-interest.

The general principle is that positive thoughts stop negative ones but that negative thoughts crowd out positive ones (Araoz, 1982). This, when specifically applied to sex, improves the situation greatly. For those who have become sexually single again, learning to use their thoughts for their own benefit, not against themselves, gives them a new sense of inner liberation and of being in control of their lives. The cognitive elements in human sexuality can never be ignored, and especially should not be ignored when a person has become sexually single again.

Sex is a complicated aspect of human existence because it is right there on the thin border between body and soul. Like a Greek tragedy, sex is an eternal puzzle that keeps humans humble in the recognition of their lack of satisfying answers in such a basic area of living. But humans have been given the marvelous gift of imagination. If people use it positively, it can become a tool to enjoy sex more and thus to live richer and happier lives whether sexually single again or not.

Sexual Practices of the Single Again

A thorough review of the literature with regard to sexual practices of the single parent (or sexual practices of the American people in general) showed no current methodologically sound studies. Although there are several current studies on human sexuality, they suffer from severe methodological difficulties, such as restricted geographic location or population, poor response rate, or nonrandom or nonrepresentative sample. Researchers of sexual conduct found the same problem when they looked to current research on sexuality in order to predict the spread of AIDS in the American public. Not knowing the sexual practices of the American people meant not being able to predict how quickly the disease might spread or into which population. To date, the Kinsey (1948, 1953) studies are the best available. (For a description of the methodological flaws in the available studies on human sexuality or the problems with sex research in general, see Atwood, 1987.)

In any case, making the transition from constructed marital definitions of themselves as sexual persons to postmarital constructions about sexual relationships often presents many challenges to divorced individuals. Along with these challenges, the newly divorced person may also experience considerable ambivalence about sexuality in general as well as fears of intimacy. Feelings of anger, rejection, or fear remaining from the problems of the divorcing process may inhibit the sexual desire of some persons, preventing them initially from reentering intimate relationships. Some individuals, in order to protect themselves from emotional vulnerability, may withdraw completely from potential sexual relationships. Others may react by seeking numerous superficial sexual encounters. This section examines the sexual practices—the available sexual outlets and the actual reported sexual behavior—of those individuals who are sexually single again.

Sexual Outlets

For separated and divorced men and women, there appear to be four main outlets of sexual behavior: interaction with the ex-spouse, masturbation, short-term partners, and ongoing monogamous partners. These outlets are not mutually exclusive, and at any given time any individual may choose one or more.

Sexual interaction with the ex-spouse. It is not unusual for separated or divorced couples to engage in sexual relations with each other. Individuals may be reluctant to discuss or report this behavior in counseling because in many states it is legally defined as "contamination" and may hinder or deem null and void the legal process of the divorce. However, in clinical settings individuals often report engaging in intercourse with their divorcing or former spouse. Usually it occurs while the couple is in the midst of the divorcing process and typically discontinues once one of the individuals begins dating. When it does occur, many individuals report feeling confused as to what it means. Some people feel that it must mean that there is "hope" for the marriage. In other words, it rekindles caring feelings or feelings of attraction for the former spouse. For others, it reinforces feelings of having made the right decision to separate. For yet others it serves as a temporary sexual outlet until one or the other enters into a new relationship. Having sex with an ex-spouse typically complicates the divorcing process and is frequently a cause of concern for the participating individuals. Mary P. typifies this situation.

Mary was a 34-year-old bakery manager. She was a single parent for about 3 years and was having a hard time coping with her children and her single life in general. The main reason Mary gave for the divorce was infidelity on the part of her husband Roy, who was having an ongoing affair with his co-worker. After the divorce, Mary, feeling lonely on several occasions had sex with Roy. Although she enjoyed the sexual release and the emotional comfort, afterwards she often felt guilty. It always made her think about the good times in their marriage, and she then spent weeks questioning her decision to divorce, even though, as Mary stated at other times, under the best of circumstances, the marriage was unfulfilling to her. After these sexual encounters with Roy, she usually felt ambiguous about her decision.

Mary was an attractive woman and began dating shortly after the divorce. This also created many problems for her: on the one hand, she enjoyed sex and often wanted to sleep with the man she was seeing. On the other hand, she felt that it would only confuse her children. There were times when she allowed a boyfriend to sleep over, but only if he promised to leave by 4 a.m. She believed the children would not know the person had slept over. In these cases, she then worried about whether or not the neighbors had seen the man leaving the house. If she slept overnight at a boyfriend's house, she felt she had to be home by 4 a.m. so that her boys and the baby-sitter would not know that she was out all night.

Aside from trying to arrange the logistics of sex, Mary also had many mixed feelings about it. Raised in an upper-middle-class home where she was taught that "nice" women only had sex with their husbands, she often said she felt torn between her intellectual self and her emotional self. Although her intellectual self felt that standards of sexual behavior had changed since she was a girl, her emotional self felt guilty every time she had sex with anyone other than her husband. Aside from these emotions, Mary at times also did not know how to respond to the men she was dating. She often asked questions regarding what was appropriate sexual behavior for a woman in her status. She was unsure of the part that sexuality played in her new role as a single parent. It was at this point that Mary came for counseling.

Masturbation. Masturbation is another outlet of sexual behavior used by separated and divorced individuals. Masturbation is more commonly reported by men, but women also report engaging in this form of sexual activity (Kinsey, Pomeroy, & Martin, 1948; Kinsey, Pomeroy, Martin, & Gebhard, 1953; Atwood & Gagnon, 1987). Divorced women also report having erotic dreams that result in orgasm (Kinsey et al., 1953). It is probably true that no other sexual behavior elicits as much guilt as masturbation; yet we know from Kinsey that the majority of people do engage in masturbatory activity at some point during their lives. If individuals feel guilty about masturbating, it is important for them to obtain accurate information regarding the widespread use of the activity as a sexual outlet and to explore some of the underlying motivational reasons for their guilt. Most counselors believe that masturbation is a legitimate form of sexual expression, but for those who have emotional reactions around this behavior, a motivational self-exploration may be useful. It is helpful for some people to prioritize their sexual outlets and options. For some, developing autoerotic patterns of sexual expression can help them define themselves as being sexually independent. For others, it can be avoidance behavior around a fear of intimacy.

> *Dorothy entered therapy because she felt she was obsessing on depressing thoughts. Recently divorced, she lived alone with her 13-year-old son. She was preoccupied with his life, at times being intrusive (as defined by him). For example, she cleaned out his bedroom drawers once a week, allowing him little privacy. She increasingly became more and more focused on his diet, worrying that everything he ate had some kind of unhealthy chemical in it. She had many friends and was quite outgoing and gregarious. Yet she seemed to have ambivalent feelings about dating. On the one hand, she spoke of her desire to date, reporting that she felt sexually deprived. She had many opportunities to date because she worked in a large corporation where there were many available men. On the other hand, every time she was approached, she rejected the person.*
>
> *After exploring the nature of her fears in therapy, she stated that although she seemed to want to date she was really afraid of men. She reported that every time she came in contact with a man, she felt nervous, shaky, and afraid. Her father had been a stern, controlling force in her life, leaving her with the impression that men were dominant and controlling.*
>
> *As far as her sexual needs, she masturbated frequently, stating that there really was no reason for her to go out on a date or to become sexually active because she had her "trusty vibrator."*

In this case, Dorothy was avoiding sexual contact out of a fear of men, which then became the focus of therapy.

Short-term partners. For many divorced men and women, dating several partners is crucial because in so doing they affirm their sense of attractiveness to the opposite sex. In these cases, individuals typically engage in short-term uncommitted sexual encounters and relationships. Ultimately, most individuals report that they prefer to be in a long-term relationship and that sex with many partners feels shallow. This type of sexuality is more frequently practiced by men than by women. Women tend to prefer sexuality within the context of a relationship that may establish a new long-term intimate union. Generally, individuals report that they feel guilty when they engage in what they define as meaningless sexual activity. In such cases, it may be useful for them to deal with their feelings, attempt to set boundaries around their behavior, and mobilize their will power. In other words, they can begin to make personal choices concerning sexual issues and then take responsibility for their choices. This type of sexual activity—having short-term partners—is recently reported by divorced individuals as being less of an option than it once was because of the fear of contracting AIDS.

Ongoing monogamous partners.   Some men and women are involved in a long-term monogamous relationship that began prior to the divorce. In these cases the divorcing individual's sexual needs are typically met within the context of this relationship. In other situations individuals satisfy their sexual needs in a long-term monogamous relationship that began subsequent to the divorce. The great majority of men and women report that finding an ongoing relationship is their goal.

Incidence and Frequency of Sexual Intercourse

With regard to the actual incidence of sexual intercourse among the divorced, Kinsey et al. (1948, 1953) found that divorced males and females were engaging in less sexual activity than were married men and women of comparable ages. However, Hunt (1974) found a very different picture 25 years later. He found that 100% of the men under age 55 and 90% of the women in his divorced sample had engaged in sexual intercourse in the year prior to the survey. In a later study involving a national questionnaire given to 984 separated and divorced persons and 113 widowed persons, Hunt and Hunt (1977) reported that a great majority of the formerly married became sexually active within 1 year after their divorce. Only 1 man in 20 and 1 woman in 14 reported that they had not engaged in intercourse. In an even later study, Zeiss and Zeiss (1979) found that 50% of the divorced persons they studied began having intercourse within 1 month after their marital separation, and 81% had done so within 1 year. From these findings, it appears that sexual activity among the divorced is quite a bit higher than previous measures had shown.

With regard to the frequency of intercourse, Hunt (1974) found that the typical frequency of intercourse for divorced individuals was twice per week. Zeiss and Zeiss (1979) found that their divorced respondents averaged intercourse once every other day. In Cargan's (1981) research, 36% of the divorced reported that they engaged in intercourse three or more times per week. Even among divorced singles, however, this level of coital activity is characteristic of a minority. Although divorced individuals report the greatest frequency of sexual activity among all the singles, they still report that they preferred to have even more frequent sex than they actually have (Zeiss & Zeiss, 1979), indicating on some level a dissatisfaction with their sexual lives. This finding cannot be taken to mean that divorced singles are frantically hopping from one bed to another in the search for sexual ecstasy. Despite the possibility of an initial flurry of postdivorce sexual activity, divorced individuals tended to have sex less often on the average than most married people. These researchers also found that at any one time the divorced people in their sample were dating only one person and that sexual selectivity was the rule rather than the exception. Many singles in fact find that sexual and dating exclusivity sometimes is problematic because even though the opportunities and attractions may be available, many single people do not feel comfortable about being sexually active with more than one person (Stein, 1976). American society is a traditionally monogamous society, especially in light of the AIDS epidemic.

Number of Partners

From the time of Kinsey's surveys to the present, there has been a definite increase in the number of partners. In the Kinsey studies (1948, 1953), the typical man reported four partners in a year while the average woman reported two partners. In a later study, divorced men had a median of eight partners over the year prior to the survey, and women reported a median of four partners (Hunt, 1974). More recently about one third of divorced individuals reported more than 10 sexual partners in a year (Cargan & Melko, 1982). It is difficult to assess the actual incidences and frequencies of sexual behavior in the general population, let alone in the divorced population. There has been no national sample of human sexuality since the Kinsey studies in 1948 and 1953. (The data for these studies were gathered in the late 1930s and early 1940s). The studies done since then have suffered from serious methodological problems and have been subject to much criticism from academic researchers. The fact that there is still so much hesitation about researching human sexuality in the United Sates does not go unnoticed in terms of attitudes and values toward sexuality; however, even more importantly, this ignorance has profound implications for the society in terms of the spread of AIDS. Not only is little known about the sexual behavior of the American people but also the direction the AIDS virus will follow can not be predicted. However, in spite of the fact that most of the studies reported in this chapter are old, the data confirm our clinical experience of those individuals who are sexually single again.

A count of the sexual partners of divorced people may not accurately reflect their sexual activity. For example, many divorced people go through a variety of sexual partners during the first year after their divorce. This stage of sexual experimentation may be motivated by the feeling of having escaped from a sexually restrictive marriage, by a search for intimacy with someone new, by a wish to avoid commitment in another intimate relationship, or by an attempt to ascertain their attractiveness to the opposite sex. The divorced person's sense of new freedom may quickly wane, however, because before long, most men are looking for "meaningful relationships," and most women are complaining that casual sex lowers their self-esteem and leads to feelings of depression and even desperation (Hetherington, Cox, & Cox, 1976).

Initiating Sex

Not all sex appears to be male initiated. Approximately two thirds of the men and one fifth of the women reported that sometimes sex is female initiated (Hunt & Hunt, 1977). How quickly does sex occurs after it is attempted? Only one in five women stated that they accepted sex the first time, whereas four fifths of the men claimed that women accept their advances on the first attempt. It is difficult to ascertain what the disparity in male and female reports means. It is possible that because of the gender stereotypes regarding male and female sexuality that the men in the sample were inflating their sexual desirability while the women in the sample were hesitant to express their sexual aggressiveness.

Quality of Sex

The divorced group in Hunt's (1974) study indicated that some of the qualitative dimensions of their sexual lives were better than their marital sexual experiences. Divorced men and women both reported greater variety of sexual arousal techniques and sexual positions, and the women reported higher orgasm rates. Although orgasm is not necessarily an indicator of the quality of sex, women often reported more orgasms in postmarital relationships than in their former marriages, and they also reported higher orgasm rates than wives of the same age (Gebhard, 1970). Almost all of the divorced persons rated their current sex lives as *very pleasurable* or *mostly pleasurable*. However, even though they rated their current sexual pleasure as higher than their experiences in marriage, it should be remembered that they were probably comparing their present sexual situation with disintegrating marriages in which they may have experienced numerous sexual and other problems, including feelings of inadequacy, lack of communication, and financial stress. Getting a divorce may resolve some of these issues and thereby allow the person to engage in a fuller sex life. Of course, the opposite can occur. In these cases, the trauma of the divorce leads to feelings of sexual inadequacy, doubt, and dysfunction (Gebhard, 1968). In a later study, Cargan and Melko (1982) found that the divorced individuals in their sample reported that they were more dissatisfied with their sex lives than the married, the never married, or the remarried. They found that married individuals were the most satisfied with their sex lives, followed by divorced persons, followed by the never married. In their study this same pattern was somewhat evident when individuals who were divorced compared their present sexual life with that of the period when they were married. Marital sex still held a slight edge. Thus the findings are somewhat inconclusive, but the data do support the notion that there is much variation and a great deal of ambiguity on the part of those who are sexually single again.

Divorced women have been falsely depicted as lonely and sexually deprived; divorced men have been incorrectly portrayed as having full sex lives with scores of partners. Hunt and Hunt (1977) indicated that the formerly married are much more open and liberal about sex with new partners than their counterparts were a generation ago. Years ago, sneaking around, particularly if there were children involved, was the norm. But in contemporary society, at least some divorced individuals appear to be more eager and spontaneous about sexual encounters, and fewer report that they hide their activities from their children (Hunt & Hunt, 1977).

> *Linda's postseparation experience portrayed the ambivalent feelings women often experience at this time. Initially, when she first began dating, she was unsure of herself. She didn't know if men would find her attractive; she thought she was too fat; and she felt she didn't know how to behave. She had never had sex with anyone but her husband and felt strange about the prospect of "being with" another man. She felt so unsure that after her first date, she asked her therapist if perhaps she "should" have slept with him because he had bought her dinner. She was insecure in her role as a newly single person. She had entered marriage at a young age, and now many years later she felt cast out into the single scene unprepared.*

Immediately following a divorce some divorced men and women may engage in a short period of increased sexual experimentation, but in most cases, they soon settle down to a more stable sexual style within the context of a longer term relationship. In some situations, this increased sexual activity enables persons to construct a reality that includes far less emotional attachment and commitment to their sexual relationships. The interviewees reported confusion about and difficulty with suddenly finding themselves required to date and engage in various types of courtship behaviors after years of being in a monogamous situation. They reported that they often did not know the current appropriate behavior in dating situations and frequently felt insecure with members of the opposite sex. They were also often unsure of themselves and felt value conflicts about their actions. It was not unusual for men to experience occasions of erectile dysfunction as they tried to have intercourse with new partners whom they perceived as being sexually more demanding and aggressive than their former wives. For some men and women, these anxieties and insecurities led to postmarital sexual problems.

After divorce many individuals seem wary of another involvement. They may feel lonely, rejected, and sexually unsatisfied. A typical reaction, although occurring less frequently because of the AIDS epidemic, is to have casual and friendly sexual relationships with little commitment. These new relationships can serve an important psychological function, however, for they can heal a sensitive ego and encourage people to involve themselves in an intimate relationship again. And, for some, they can even result in more satisfying sexual expression.

Sex and Single Parents

Many of these divorced individuals are single parents. If there are children involved, even if an individual is not the primary caretaker of the children after a divorce, there are times when he or she is. Census experts estimate that about 45% of children born in 1978 will live with one parent for at least a while before they are 18. In 1980, 20% of children under the age of 18 lived with only one parent. About 17% of all living arrangements including a child under 18 are with the mother only, with about 1.6% living with the father (Glick & Norton, 1979). Approximately 90% of single-parent mothers are custodians of their children. Thus for the most part, when we speak about single parents we are speaking about women as heads of households.

The Single Mother

Because mothers are more likely to be given custody of their children in cases of separation or divorce, and because mothers are more likely to be widowed, it is not surprising that most children in single-parent homes live with their mothers. Over 8 million children in this country live with their mothers alone while 800,000 live with their fathers.

Money is an especially critical problem for single parents. One-parent families in general have considerably lower income than two-parent families, and their problems are often tied to economics. Not surprisingly, single working mothers make less than half of what single fathers make, and because child care must often be arranged and paid for, single mothers are constantly fraught with financial worries. It is no wonder that some writers speak of the feminization of poverty. Because of these very real economic pressures, the single mother may find it difficult to go out to social events where she may meet someone. She may be unable to buy new attractive clothing, or she may not have extra money for a baby-sitter. These factors may restrict the likelihood of her entering dating situations. She may feel uncomfortable about bringing new men to her home to meet her children.

> *When she first started dating, Linda felt compelled to meet her dates at shopping malls or parking lots. She didn't want her children to see her dating different men. She thought they would lose respect for her, and she didn't want her children to see her with "one man after another."*

The Single Father

Relatively few (less than 10%) of one-parent families are headed by men. When they do exist, they usually arise because the mother has died. In these cases, the widower experiences many of the same psychological and emotional problems faced by widowed mothers, such as loneliness, sorrow, bitterness, and a sense of being overwhelmed by the full responsibility of child care. Most motherless families have fewer economic problems than fatherless families. However, if many single mothers are at least initially unprepared for the work role, many single fathers are unprepared for child-care responsibilities and home management tasks such as shopping, cooking, doing laundry, and cleaning house—tasks formerly done by their wives. Some men do these chores themselves, but others rely on relatives or friends for help or else they hire outside workers. Even with the additional responsibilities a single-parent father takes on, it is often less difficult for him than for the single-parent mothers because there is often not as much of a financial decrease (if any) for the single-parent father, and there generally are many women available for him for caretaking services. The single-parent woman is often devalued in our society, and many women fuss over a single-parent father.

> *Larry's wife left him after 12 years of marriage. He became the custodian of their two sons, David, age 11, and Christian, age 9. The women in the neighborhood, believing that Larry could not possibly handle all the responsibilities of a job and the children, took turns cooking supper for them and doing the laundry. They also introduced him to many available women.*

But many women ignore the single-parent mother. Sisterhood is not very powerful in these cases.

> *Barbara's husband Clint left her with two young children, ages 4 and 5, for a younger woman. Barbara, devastated by her feelings of abandon-*

ment, was forced back into the labor force in order to provide for herself and the children. The women in the neighborhood were threatened by Barbara's attractiveness, and even her close friends were hesitant to allow their husbands to help Barbara out if her car broke down. Occasionally they baby-sat for the children if Barbara had a date, but they were reluctant to interact with her, and as time passed she saw less and less of her once good friends. Eventually she moved out of the neighborhood and bought a condominium where many singles lived.

As noted in chapter 3, a teenage daughter or son is sometimes put in the role of "little mother" or the parental child and given considerable responsibility for the house and the younger siblings (George & Wilding, 1972). In such cases, there is often resentment on the part of this child because he or she is unable to enjoy childhood activities and often feels overburdened by feelings of responsibility for the emotional well-being of the parent. Other children in the family system may also feel resentment toward the parental child because they believe that he or she holds a special favored position in the parent's eyes. The father may come to rely on the company of this child, and in some cases, this may prevent him from seeking out appropriate social partners of the opposite sex. This is typified by the case of Ron, a 47-year-old construction worker.

Ron's wife left him with two children, a boy and a girl, ages 13 and 10. Initially, he was lost, unfamiliar with their physical and emotional needs. Gradually, though, with the aid of a cleaning person, he learned how to manage the children and the household tasks. All his extra time was spent with the children. He planned weekend activities with them, took them on vacations, and monitored their lives. When he visited relatives, all he spoke about was his involvement with them. Gradually, his friends dwindled, and his adult activities virtually ceased. Two years later, he wound up in therapy for depression.

Meeting sexual and intimacy needs while taking care of children without a partner may be fraught with problems of privacy, energy, and time. In an interview study with 38 single parents, Greenberg (1979) reported that most of her sample believed that their sexual activity should not be known to their children. The double standard was evident because more men than women accepted sex among single parents even if it was apparent to their children. In a study of 127 separated or divorced fathers with full or joint custody of their children, Rosenthal and Keshet (1978) found that when the father dated a new woman and stayed overnight, it was more typically at her home rather than his. The women involved in the sample reported that they felt more comfortable and more romantic in their own homes or apartments. They reported that they did not have to worry about their date's children in their own homes. If after a while a serious relationship developed, then a sense of a new couple emerged. Eventually, 75% of the single fathers asked their new partners to sleep over (Rosenthal & Keshet, 1979), although they reported that this was initially very difficult for them to do. Single fathers also reported that they were generally uncomfortable about having a female sleep over when the children were present. They reported that they worried that their children might feel that sex should be totally uncommitted and free. This idea was uncomfortable for them (Rosenthal & Keshet, 1979) and is typified by the situation in the movie *Kramer vs. Kramer* when Dustin Hoffman's naked female friend encountered his 4-year-old son in the hall.

It may be especially important for the single father that whomever he becomes involved with get along with his children. If the relationship leads to a traditional marriage, the woman may be expected to assume much of the responsibility for managing the household and caring for the children. Single mothers, however, may consider financial security more important in their mate selection. Women who are not working and who rely solely on their former partners for support might consider the possibility that the children's biological father could renege on support payments, thereby making the stepparent more responsible for the children's welfare. In this sense, for these single mothers financial security of the future mate is an important variable, but for single fathers the person's ability to assume responsibility for child care and household maintenance might be more important considerations. In more modern arrangements based on convenience and partnership, these considerations become minimal as more and more androgynous role taking is the norm, with child care and household chore allocation beginning to approach equality (though not yet equal—remember the "super moms").

Counseling Strategies

In general, the single parent must confront several issues regarding dating and sexuality. First are *time considerations*. The decision to begin dating may lead to guilt feelings concerning the children. If the single parent works and his or her children are in child care all day or in school, he or she is faced with the decision of either going out on a date or spending time with the children.

Second are *potential parent considerations*. The single parent generally looks at the men or women he or she meets not only as potential marital partners but also as potential parents. A new criterion then enters the process by which the single parent evaluates the parental capabilities of the person. The individual may be fun to be with, but he or she may not be interested in assuming parental responsibilities. This type of relationship is probably time limited. In another situation an individual may be willing to assume parental responsibilities, but the children may be so threatened by his or her presence that they may sabotage the relationship between him or her and their parent, attempting to maintain the status quo. One parent reported that as her boyfriend was leaving the house after a date, he walked over to her darling 5 year old to say goodbye and to shake hands. Her gracious son smiled devilishly and looking up with big blue eyes shouted, "Penis breath!!"

Third are *financial and fatigue considerations.* Aside from the other dilemmas are all the practicalities of dating to worry about, including the costs in time, energy, and money. If the children are small, dating requires finding and paying a baby-sitter. Both men and women need to have up-to-date clothes in good order. If finances are limited, there may be competition between these needs and the needs of the children. Going out also imposes a cost in fatigue. It means less time to get other things done and less time to sleep and rest. It also means less time for the children. Single parents who work may feel that they spend too little time as it is with their children. Dating means that the children will be left once again with a baby-sitter. This can create a great deal of guilt in the parent who opts to leave the children with a baby-sitter and can also create much conflict when he or she attempts to decide whether or not to date in the first place.

Fourth are *reputational considerations.* Some individuals, especially those from very traditional families who live in traditional neighborhoods, may worry about their reputations. In family neighborhoods there are neighbors and what they might think to worry about, and the consequential repercussions on the children. It is also possible that the single parent fears that the former spouse could use the parent's dating to malign the parent to the children or to argue in court for renegotiation of support or custody. Most single parents also worry about their children's reactions as they begin to date. They are likely to be aware that their children will now see them as having sexual needs, and they may be concerned about their children's reactions to the people they date. The children may actively discourage parents who are already uncertain about entering into dating. Children may cause immediate problems, either by being negative to anyone they see as possibly taking their mother's or father's place, or by being excessively positive and frightening others off immediately by asking, "Are you going to be my new Daddy?" And although parents may feel it a relinquishing of their rights as independent adults to permit their children to control their personal lives, their childrens' objectives may in fact affect their dating behavior.

Fifth are *personal considerations.* Single parents further recognize that not only has society changed but so also have they. They are older. They may feel less attractive. They may worry about the condition of their bodies. Women may be concerned about sagging breasts and stretchmarks. Men may worry about pot bellies, thinning hair, and impotence. And now they are parents. They come as a package deal: adult with children. The person with children is likely to feel him- or herself less "marriageable" because many prospective partners are hesitant to take on the added responsibility of parenthood with someone else's children.

Sixth are *considerations of a social-sexual nature.* Meeting "eligible" mates can be difficult. Many single parents do not know where to go to meet eligible persons. Many detest the "bar scene" and are leery of the personals. Often single parents despair of meeting the right person and feel there is "no one out there for me." Furthermore, when they do meet someone they must decide whether to permit a date or a lover to spend the night when the children are present. To allow someone to spend the night who is not the children's mother or father is often an important symbolic act for the parent. For one thing, it generally involves the children in the relationship with the person. If there is no commitment to the person, the parent may fear that the children will become emotionally involved with the person, and if the relationship then ends, the parent will have to deal not only with his or her own feelings about the break up but also with the children's feelings. Allowing a date or a lover to sleep over also reveals to the children that their parent is a sexual person. This, in many cases, may make the parent feel somewhat uncomfortable for he or she may feel that the children are passing moral judgment. And they very well might be.

Last are *"right person" considerations.* Single parents, both men and women, can easily despair of finding the right person. Single fathers may have an easier time meeting someone. But they may complain that those they meet are too young, or, if older and never married, then too involved with their careers or too "prudish." If they are divorced, men report that many feel bitter toward men. If the woman is a widow, she may idealize her former husband, creating an unrealistic ideal person for her date to compete with. Single mothers who are themselves in their 30s or 40s espouse similar complaints. There may be men around, they report, but not the right type. If the men have never been married, then it is probably because something is wrong with them and no one else wants them: they are unwilling to settle down, or perhaps they are still tied to their mothers, or else they may be homosexual. If the men have been married, then they are likely still to have responsibilities to their former families, still to have wives to whom they must furnish child support and children whom they must see. Then there is also the phenomenon called the "mating gradient," which refers to the fact that because men usually marry women younger than they and generally slightly less educated, there remain two pools of eligibles: a group of educated, successful women who remain at the top of the gradient and a group of socially unfortunate men who remain at the bottom. Many single parents, male or female, feel themselves drawn to the conclusion, "Why bother?"

All single parents experience at times the difficulties of providing for the physical, social, and emotional needs of themselves and their children. There are problems of fatigue and role overload irrespective of the family's financial situation, though surely those with financial difficulties are more likely to experience such problems. The pressure of family responsibilities can prevent the single parent from arranging long periods of time with members of the opposite sex in order to get to know them better. Many single parents will not have a date or lover sleep over because they believe that their children should not be exposed to their sexual lives in this way. They may not be able to spend the night at another's home because they may not have a baby-sitter. Similar child care problems make the chance of going away for an evening, weekend, or vacation with someone of the opposite sex slim. There is lesser movement into marriage from the world of single parents than from some of the other unmarried populations. Some of these structural impediments certainly add to, and account for, the general lack of desire for remarriage of many of these single parents. However, many single parents feel good about their new-found freedom and look forward to dating and meeting new people with positive anticipation.

Thus on the one hand are emotional, physical, and social needs pressing the single parent toward finding a new partner, but on the other hand are very real reasons for hesitancy, including the costs of dating and concerns about dignity and self-respect. This adds to the notion that there is not one model of single parenting that can account for the concept of single parent. Just as there are many types of two-parent households holding many different value systems, economic levels, and educational achievements, so too are there differences among single-parent families, and these differences also manifest in the sexual arena.

Chapter 7
RELATIONAL AND SEXUAL CONCERNS AND CONSIDERATIONS AFTER WIDOWHOOD

Where do widowed persons seek companionship? How do they live if they are unwilling to search for a husband or wife or unable to find one? It is helpful for counselors to explore the sexual concerns of widows and widowers.

People who are widowed may have very different responses from the divorced or separated. Their marriages ended through death rather than choice, and this loss invariably produces trauma or conflicting emotions. They are likely to fear or resent experiences that might devalue memories of their partner. They may retain a sense that the dead partner is still present—almost like a conscience—inhibiting them from sexual involvement. Questions about the meaning of life and the significance of the passage of time can lead some surviving spouses to shut off from sexual activities, sometimes temporarily, sometimes forever. Others may view a new marriage or relationship as cheating on their dead spouse. (This also occurs in the divorced group but to a lesser degree.) In addition, many elderly men and women are inclined to adhere to the customs of their youth—no sex outside of marriage—and are therefore forced into celibacy regardless of personal inclination. Consequently, widowed persons have fewer postmarital experiences than their divorced peers of any age group.

As already noted, the world of the widowed is largely female. Because widowed persons have a median age of 67.8, they are profoundly affected by age and sex stereotypes concerning sexuality. Widows in particular are affected. The double standard of aging makes it more difficult for aged women to find partners. Not only are they considered less attractive and erotic than younger women, but the pool of older men is also considerably smaller because men die younger than women. Virtually all widowed men return to an active sex life, but substantially fewer widowed women engage in postmarital sex (Gebhard, 1968).

111

Because widowed persons tend to be elderly, the death of their partner often means an end to their sexuality. The availability of a marriage partner and good health are the primary determinants of an active sex life in old age. But what older people generally miss with their partner's death is not the sexuality but the companionship and comfort of their mate.

When the factors related to sexual activity in older persons are examined, an important difference between males and females is found. For males, the variable most strongly related to sexual activity is age. Among females, the most important variable is marital status. The reason for this difference between males and females is a socially constructed: marital status, especially for women, still means the presence or absence of a socially approved sexual partner. For women, if there is a socially approved sexual partner (a husband), sexual activity is likely to continue. If the woman does not have a socially approved sexual partner, her sexual activity is most likely to cease. For males, the existence of a socially approved sexual partner (a wife) is much less important for the continuation of sexual activity (Persson, 1980; Pfeiffer & Davis, 1972).

These socially constructed definitions of appropriate sexuality for older men and women are especially important because a married woman in the United States today can expect her husband to die approximately 13 years before she does. Consequently, it is possible that she will spend a considerable portion of her life as a nonsexually active person if she follows the traditional sexual script.

Most widows are aware of unmet sexual needs after the death of their husbands (Barrett, 1981). The social construction of female sexuality in American society tends, especially for older women, to make it very difficult for most widows to come in contact with a socially approved sexual partner. Because women learn via social definitions to connect sex and interpersonal relationships strongly, and a person who has been married for 40 years may find it difficult to see herself with anyone else, more widows are unlikely to seek out another socially approved sexual partner. Clayton and Bornstein (1976) studied a sample of widows with an average age of 60. They found that 13 months after the death of the husband only 7% had dated and only 2% had engaged in intercourse. Gebhard (1970) found that only about half as many widows had engaged in intercourse as had divorced women, and that of those widows who had, the frequency was low. As Gebhard pointed out, in-laws and married friends of the widow are comforting but also stifling in terms of maintaining the same patterns of behavior as when her husband was alive. A lack of sexual activity is further supported by the romantic ideal of "being loyal to the memory" of her husband (Gebhard, 1970). For males, the widower status has much less impact on sexual activity (Persson, 1980). However, in a study reported by Newman and

Nichols (1960), only 7 of the 101 single, divorced, or widowed men over 60 reported any sexual activity.

Even before her husband's death, the older woman is faced with a lack of sexual opportunity not of her own choosing. Research repeatedly finds that when sexual activity in marriage ceases in the later years, the cessation is due to the husband, not the wife. For example, Pfeiffer and Davis (1972) found that of elderly married men and women who no longer engaged in intercourse, 86% of the women and only 42% of the men attributed the cessation of sex to their spouse. In another study by these researchers, 6% of the men said they were no longer engaged in coitus because of their wife, but 40% said the cessation was due to their own lack of ability.

Pfeiffer and Davis (1972) also noted that there is a rapid decline in sexual interest on the part of older married women. The researchers argued that this is a protective mechanism. It is adaptive for a woman to lose interest in sex as she ages because the odds are that she will be without a socially approved sexual partner for a considerable period of her life. If her husband does live as long as she does, it is highly probable that their sexual activity level will drastically decline or stop altogether through no fault of hers.

Projections for the 1990s are that there will be 67.5 males to every 100 females for people over 65 and that the ratio will decrease to 57.8 men for every 100 women at age 75. For the widowed, single life often comes as a shock. Adjusting to a single life style can be a formidable task over age 60. Most traditional older women never developed the social skills necessary for their new existence, so they must invent them. How do they enter the dating scene at 72 when they were married at 18 in a different era? Widows quickly learn that available men are few and the competition fierce.

According to the Duke studies (Pfeiffer, Verwoerdt, & Davis, 1972), the sex lives of women born 60 to 80 years ago depend heavily upon the availability of a partner who is socially approved and sexually capable—that is, a husband who is still alive and sexually interested. Because women tend to marry men several years older and then outlive them by 10 or more years, many older women are widows. Because they have no husbands, they are sexually inactive. The starkness of this issue can be shown by the unequal sex ratio of persons over 65: 146 women for every 100 men. There are 14 million older women to 9.5 million older men. If socially constructed notions about the acceptability of singles and extrarelationship sex were to change, women who wished to do so could realize much more of their sexual potential.

Sexual needs are similar for the divorced and the widowed, who have been conditioned by years of marriage to expect and desire both the physical release and emotional closeness of a continuing sexual relationship. However, although their needs may be similar, there are important differences between the widowed and the divorced with respect to their social situation.

During the last months or years of a marriage that ends in divorce, sexual relations usually deteriorate or are terminated. The recently divorced person has therefore often gone through a period of relative sexual deprivation (Waller, 1967). In addition, although changing, many people are left after a divorce with a sense of having failed in an interpersonal relationship. Divorced people may compensate for both their recent sexual deprivation and their sensitive ego by seeking sexual encounters.

Recently, widowed people are in a somewhat different situation. Unless their spouse was ill for a long time, they typically have not experienced a deterioration of their marital relationship just prior to their spouse's death and, consequently, do not have a sense of having failed in their most important sexual relationship.

Another factor that may affect the sexual adjustment of the widowed and the divorced differently is the quality of the emotional tie to the absent mate. Widowed people seldom feel hostile toward their deceased mate and, in fact, may retain strong emotional ties with his or her memory. Over time, the survivor may exaggerate the good qualities of the deceased and selectively forget all the shortcomings. This memory can be a deterrent to the establishment of new relationships, sexual or otherwise, because no living person can possibly equal the exalted image of the deceased.

The friends and family of the widowed often exert a subtle pressure to remain faithful to the deceased because many feel that a new love would be disloyal and (for some) even sexually immoral. The widowed person, more often than the divorced one, will have a supportive group of in-laws and married friends who encourage maintenance of previous patterns of behavior. Although possibly not intending to do so, well-meaning friends and relatives by their moral support lessen the chances that a widow or widower will seek new relationships.

Men are already largely free from narrow ideas about acceptable sex partners. Whereas 90% of the women in the Duke studies cited spouse-oriented reasons for stopping sexual activity (death of spouse, divorce from spouse, illness of spouse, spouse unable to engage in sex, spouse lost interest), only 29% of the men noted spouse-oriented reasons for stopping. Instead they emphasized three things about their own incapacity for sex: 14% cited personal loss of interest, 17% cited their own illness, and 40% thought they were unable to perform sexually (Pfeiffer et al., 1972).

Even though people's close ties to someone now dead can be transcended, either personally or socially, reaching out, especially sexually to a "new" person, can evoke guilty feelings of cheating on the deceased lover. This reaction prompts reticence and perhaps impotence and makes reentry into social life with others difficult. As the tears and years pass, people may feel increasingly awkward about sex, as though it were a skill and they had forgotten how to do it (Kohn & Kohn, 1978).

In addition to their own hesitations about getting sexually involved again, widowed people may be treated as outcasts if their social world consists only of paired couples. Some widowed people report feeling awkward because they are always thought of as the widowed person—part of a couple—not as a single person. In addition, widows may remind friends too vividly of the nearness of their own husband's death and their own possible singlehood and they may be politely shunned.

Gender Issues

Both widows and widowers complain that society does not provide suitable outlets for them to express sexual needs relevant to old age and widowhood. Counselors need to keep in mind that although widows and widowers face many problems in their attempts to find sexual happiness in their later years many remain vigorous and unwilling to forgo a meaningful relationship with someone of the opposite sex. Nevertheless, many authors who write about widowhood must assume that most widows and widowers have relinquished all sexual interests because there are many books on the subject without a word concerning sex.

A notable exception are Kreis and Pattie (1969), two widows who worked as a team collecting data on sexual problems during widowhood. They noted that once the initial shock, grief, and suffering are over, the sexual appetite of healthy men and women rekindled. Many examples showing how widows and widowers handle their feelings about sex during and after bereavement are provided. Some are plagued with feelings of guilt when attempting to separate sex from marriage, whereas others, particularly widowers, can work out their problem without entering into another permanent relationship. Women who establish a new sexual relationship after a period of mourning are likely to either remarry or form a new stable partnership with a man they consider a boyfriend (Clayton & Bornstein, 1976).

The double standard of aging is also apparent in the differential options available for widowed men and women. Socially constructed definitions clearly depict remarriage or a continued sex life in some other arrangement more favorably for widowers than for widows. The widowed man, although not without problems, appears to have distinct advantages. Because widows outnumber widowers considerably, the widower is, in effect, in a buyer's market. Socially the widower is an asset; the widowed woman is a liability. For him there are many possible partners. For her the pool of available men to marry shrinks continuously. Particularly for women over

60, the sex differential in mortality rates may create a severe shortage of partners.

Even the Social Security system used to favor widowers over widows because it was the widow who was forced to give up her husband's benefits when she remarried. Thus there were economic incentives for the widow to live with her partner, rather than marry him, in what was described as "Social Security sin." Fortunately, the problem was recently recognized by Congress, and legislation was passed allowing a widow to retain her previous pension or choose her new husband's benefits, whichever is greater.

In addition to having more opportunities to remarry, widowers can choose nonmarital affairs, sexual fantasies, or masturbation. Most of these expressions of sexual interests are socially disapproved of for widows, who are expected to devote themselves to their children or grandchildren, volunteer services in the community, and memories of their husbands. Further, many assume that the elderly widowed man needs a woman to look after him, but this assumption is no longer valid in the case of the elderly widow.

There are few current data on the sexual life of the widowed. One study of divorced and widowed women interviewed between 1939 and 1956 found that widowed women were slower than divorced women of the same age to resume an active sex life after losing their spouse. Eighty-two percent of divorced women had postmarital coitus while 43% of widowed women did. As noted earlier, the lower incidence of postmarital sex among widows is due in part to the fact that widows are, on the average, older than divorced women; but even when matched for age, widows are still less likely to engage in postmarital sex. Among the reasons for this may be that widows are more likely to be financially secure than divorced women and therefore have less motivation for engaging in sex as a prelude to remarriage, and that they have the continuing social support system of in-laws and friends and so are less motivated to seek new friendships. In addition, there is also a belief that a widow should be loyal to her dead husband. Thus many widows believe that having a sexual relationship with another man is disloyal, and they may also tell themselves that they will never find another one like their dead spouse.

Most widowed women who have postmarital sex begin such relationships about a year after the death. Gebhard (1968) found that 16% of the widowed had postmarital sex with more than one partner. More widowed than divorced women in all age ranges remained celibate. When widowed women did resume coitus, their frequency of intercourse was lower than that of divorced women of the same age. Widows, however, were equally as likely as divorced women to reach orgasm in their postmarital sexual intercourse (Gebhard, 1970).

Comparable data for divorced and widowed men are not available, but it can be assumed that the percentage who have postmarital coitus, the frequency of postmarital coitus, and the speed with which postmarital coitus is begun after the end of the marriage are all higher than the comparable figures for widowed men. This assumption is based on three facts: One is that sexual aggressiveness in our society is more acceptable in men than in women; hence a widower is less likely to be criticized for pursuing new partners than a widow. A second fact is that the higher male death rate means there are more women than men in the middle and later years. A widow might have more difficulty than a widower in finding a new partner because of the scarcity of men in her age range. There are almost five widows for every widower (Clayton & Bornstein, 1976, p. 31.)

For some older women and men, masturbation can become or continue to a major alternative to gain sexual release and expression. A study of more than 800 people between the ages of 60 and 91 years of age reported that older women are becoming more accepting of masturbation as a means of sexual expression (Starr & Weiner, 1981), although many older men and women reflect outdated beliefs because of social definitions and feel that is is wrong for people of their age to engage in this practice.

Older people may redefine their sexual and affectional relationships. Nonsexual friendships with either sex can offer affectionate physical contact, emotional closeness, intellectual stimulation, and opportunities for socializing. People of two or more generations may live together or an unmarried couple may share a household. Although probably rare because of the traditionally negative social definitions, sexual relationships with same-sex partners may be explored. Remarriage may also be an option; each year there are more than 35,000 marriages in the United States in which one of the partners is 65 or older (Vinick, 1978).

A third fact on which the assumption is based is that it is socially acceptable for a man to date a younger woman, but (although changing) not as acceptable for an older woman to date a younger man. The widow of middle age or older is thus less likely than the widower to find an acceptable mate because the few men in her age range may seek younger women. Often the choices of the single woman in the middle or later years are limited to men who are much older than she is. A widow may feel reluctant to become involved with an older man who is likely to become senile and ill and to die much before she does. Once widowed, a woman may hesitate to risk being widowed again. For a number of reasons, one being the reduction in Social Security benefits that formerly occurred when retired people married, the elderly have sometimes engaged in what geriatric counselors refer to as *unmarriages of convenience.* These are companionable, sexual relationships not formalized by license or ceremony. The Social Security law was changed in 1977 so that newlyweds who are 60 or over now lose none of their benefits. Certain older people, especially men, still confess to enjoying the secretive swinging–singles experience of living together without the benefit of clergy. But most elderly couples are not swingers and elect to marry rather than face the censure of conventional society and their own consciences.

The proliferation of retirement communities may be one answer to the segregation of single older women. In these communities single women may find some wholesome associations with men (even though married) in educational classes, volunteer work, social activities, and recreational activities. Although an occasional swim, dance, or card game with a married man is not the equivalent of living with him, this nevertheless does provide contact and companionship. In many of these communities such men are perfectly willing to act as a kind of surrogate handyman and fix water sprinklers or the fence for their widowed female neighbors. This kind of friendship is not at all sexual, but it does provide the basis for emotional support. In cases in which a married couple has had a long stormy history, the husband may find comfort in the arms of another woman. A few have tried communal living; some like it and some do not.

There have been no direct studies of the postmarital sexual adjustment of widows and widowers. This does not mean that they do not have sexual problems. In fact, their problems may be far more complex than those of younger people. It does, however, reflect the socially constructed view that older people should be nonsexual and that any sexual interest among the older population is unnatural. Researchers of sexuality also appear to have accepted this view, at least as evidenced by their historical lack of attention to this group. With the increased awareness that sexual interest and activity can continue indefinitely, perhaps there will be greater concern about and interest in the special problems of widowed individuals as they face postmarital sexual adjustment.

Case Histories

A large percentage of the single population is composed of the divorced and widowed of both sexes. Singlehood is often thrust upon them by circumstances and is not a chosen lifestyle. These people have often been involved in exclusive relationships for many years. Suddenly they find themselves in the arena of dating and courtship. Because socially constructed values have changed so radically since they were a part of the dating scene, this can be a particularly difficult transition. The inability to cope with the demands of dating today often leave the older divorced or widowed person in a state of confusion. Some retreat into a celibate single life, unable to cope with the pressures of dating in present day society.

Widows and widowers clearly face different situations than those single again because of divorce. However, they also may face the social, psychological, and sexual life style adjustments and the grieving process described in our discussion of divorce—and often to a greater degree.

Harry (whom we met in chapter 2) said that with his first wife sex was a very important part of their lives, but after her death, for the whole 6 or so months that he was mourning her, he lost all sexual interest. "Toward the end of those 6 months I started to get a bit concerned," he said with a smile, "because I had even lost my normal sensations in the sexual area. It was as if my sexuality was dead. I didn't think of sex, I didn't feel anything sexual, I didn't even think of the great sexual moments Odile and I had for so many years."

Then, slowly, as he started to meet old friends and new people, he realized that his sexuality was far from dead. His general energy and vitality extended to his sexuality. Before he settle down with Connie and accepted her as his new companion and lover, he had dated other women and had gone to bed with a few of them. Initially he was surprised that he had responded so well in these encounters after the lack of sexual feeling in the period of mourning. Then, when Connie became his new love, sex was again an essential part of the relationship.

Connie, who was 24 years younger than Harry's 76, talked very positively of their sex life. They made love regularly, up to five times a week, and they spent a long time "playing with each other sexually," as she described it. We inquired whether Harry had difficulties functioning sexually at his age. Her response was a spontaneous laugh: "Are you kidding? He is more vital than other men I have been with who were 20 years younger. He's a gourmet of sex. He really makes love like a musician makes music or an artist paints a picture. I am more satisfied sexually now than I've ever been in my life before. He doesn't look his age. He doesn't act it either."

Had Harry been—or was he—concerned about AIDS? His quick reply was "Oh, sure I was concerned," and he explained that he had taken all the precautions he knew how: latex condoms, spermicide, even (in one case) double condoms. This was with the women he dated before he met Connie. But what about Connie herself? He had spent several hours talking about it with her before they had "regular sex," as he called it, without a condom. He assured us that he had been monogamous and faithful to his wife for the 42 years of their marriage. Then the women he dated starting about 6 months after his wife's death had all accepted his "condom condition." "At my age, I didn't want to end up with AIDS for being careless and stupid." One woman refused his condition, and he just walked out on her. Connie had also been faithful sexually to her husband of 28 years. She also had been very firm with the men she had dated about safe sex (though now they say there is no safe sex, only safer sex). She had also refused to get sexually involved on a couple of occasions when the man had not taken her seriously and wanted to have sex without protection. Thus Harry felt that Connie and he were safe and he did not have to be concerned about AIDS any more.

Harry introduced us to his friend Sam whom he described with great affection and even admiration.

> *Sam was now a retired dentist, and Harry and Sam had been friends for over 25 years even though Sam was 12 years younger than Harry. Sam had been married for 38 years, had four daughters, all independent and three married by now, and had had a very successful dental practice in an affluent part of town. His wife died of cancer. Four years later, when we interviewed Sam, he told us how much his wife's death had affected him. He had even thought of suicide and had lost almost 30 pounds in less than 7 months. Then a male friend of his, whom he had known for many years when they were both married, helped pull him out of his severe depression and they became inseparable. His friend had been asexual since his wife's death a few years earlier. Then "something happened," and they entered a homosexual relationship, Sam at the age of 61 and his friend at 63. Sam confessed that both were initially embarrassed and even shocked, but that they were unable to deny the happiness and goodness that this relationship was affording them. His friend had no children, but Sam's daughters were never told directly of their father's new committed relationship. "I'm sure they suspect but they haven't asked," Sam said. "I have a good relationship with all of them, and I guess my fear is that this thing might damage our relationship. What the heck, my daughter Bobby is gay and lives with another woman, and her sisters have accepted her gayness without any problem. But I don't have the guts to tell them. Maybe some day in the future, who knows?"*

Both Harry and Sam have accepted their sexuality after the death of their wives, each differently to be sure, but ultimately with a sense of inner resolution and peace. Sam still is affected by the fear of condemnation that is unfortunately quite common in our rather homophobic society. But he is happy and at peace in his relationship with his male lover.

Counseling Strategies

Grief, as painful as it is, heals. Theoreticians (e.g., Bowlby, 1980; Parkes & Weiss, 1983; Sanders, 1989) believe that the process is a developmental one. As such, these authors have described specific stages through which grievers must pass if the process is to change their relationship with the deceased and allow them to emotionally invest in new satisfactions. For the widowed, one potential source of satisfaction may be a sexually intimate relationship.

These developmental theorists have warned their readers that the actual experiences of the bereaved are much more complex than the neat and precise charts that depict the developmental stages might suggest. Counselors ought not be confused, for example, if clients seem to overlap the stages or to regress from time to time.

The previous chapters have described the social, psychological, and sexual issues that are commonly experienced by single parents. Whether they are single through divorce or the death of a spouse, the common factor involved is that they have experienced intimacy dissolution. Specific guidelines and counseling strategies were presented that addressed common issues presented in counseling by these populations. Here some of the main points in the prior sections are summarized and additional guidelines for the counselor presented.

There are sufficient similarities among the grief reactions of these populations to guide, not lead, the counselors' work. Table 1 presents a guide to the process of intimacy dissolution that we have found helpful in clinical practice. It broadly outlines the steps involved in the process and suggests issues likely to be found in each. Counseling techniques are also included. In the clinical use of Table 1, counselors are reminded that it is only an outline, not a roadmap, of the process. As Sanders (1989) emphasized, no two griefs are alike.

The decision to dissolve an intimate relationship is rarely reached quickly or without difficulty and pain, even in unhappy marriages. Counseling during this time frame may help to reconstitute individuals' sense of stability and help them focus on future aspects of their new life style. The general goal of counseling during this time is to help the client optimize personal development as he or she pursues his or her new life style. It is crucial for the counselor to examine his or her own assumptions about this particular life style in order to help the client identify his or her own social role and attitudes toward it. The counselor's attitude should be one that the single life style is a legitimate and viable alternative style of living. Counselors need to help the client explore his or her own personal and interpersonal needs and attitudes, aiding the client to develop and maintain his or her socially constructed identity in a realistic way. In some cases, the counseling process may include educating the client with regard to single life. During the stages of divorce adjustment, it becomes apparent that there are several common problems that clients present. Although these problems may not appear to be initially overtly sexual, the task of the counselor is to be tuned into the possible sexual implications, understand the underlying sexual dynamics, and be comfortable and competent enough to give the client permission to deal with the problems and instill confidence that they can be solved. However, counselors helping clients deal with sexuality or sexual issues after divorce must be keenly aware of the basic emotional process and stages that individuals experience during the divorcing process. It is impossible to separate out the sexual issues a divorcing person experiences from the other strong emotions the person is feeling at this time.

Counselors must recognize the emotional stages of intimacy dissolution—denial, conflict, ambivalence, and acceptance—and the sexual aspects within each stage in order to help their clients with the sexual issues inherent in this time frame. (The stages are also discussed in Chapter 1.)

Denial Stage Issues and Techniques

During Stage I, clients experience denial. At this point in the intimacy dissolution process, clients may not be interested in sex at all, let alone sex with a person other than their spouse. They also may deny the existence of their feelings of sexuality or their fears about sexuality, which may be manifested in a counseling session by a repeated, "I don't have to worry about sex. I'm simply not interested in it. If just isn't important anymore." Or, "I certainly won't have any problems dealing with sex." Most clients still feel married at this point and to encourage them to engage in dating may be detrimental to their healing process. Any sort of denial, repression, fear, and ignorance imperils any type of eventual healthy sexual expression. Clients during this stage usually experience sexual deprivation, although even if the marriage was disintegrating, some individuals still engage in sexual intercourse with their ex-spouse. Counselors dealing with clients in Stage I of the divorcing process should help their clients acknowledge their sexual needs and help them decide how they could comfortably deal with their sexuality.

Also important in Stage I are the client's reactions to loneliness. During this stage, counselors should help the client to explore and deal with feelings of loneliness. Loneliness has many components: One is a feeling of emotional insufficiency. The person may feel empty and sorrowful. This may be a healthy sign, for it may signal that the person is ready to seek out a new emotional partnership. Another component is anxiety. The person may feel as though the world is without comfort, and he or she will never meet anyone satisfactory. This may be accompanied by a sense of impending doom. The person may feel restless, may feel a need to keep busy, may be involved in random activities. The single person must, at times, deal with feelings of loneliness and isolation. Attaining a degree of comfort with solitude and with one's self is essential.

Epstein (1974) has suggested that loneliness appears to be a greater problem for divorced men but autonomy is a greater problem for women. This is especially true for women who have young children still at home. The presence of children may prevent much of the loneliness women can experience in this situation because they provide both organizational structure to every day life and emotional satisfaction. At the same time, however, children impose numerous responsibilities and may further restrict the mother's ability to utilize her new-found freedom. Single parents may find solace in their children's presence, but reliance on children for amusement and company is unhealthy for the parent because it keeps him or her from seeking more appropriate alternatives and, further, may place too much of a burden on the children. Some parents blame the children for their loneliness. "If I didn't have children, I could go out more and meet people."

Loneliness is one of the most painful feelings that accompany divorce and widowhood. The individual often experiences hopelessness at facing the prospect of making new friends as a single person. Clients complain they do not know where and how to meet people. The loneliness can turn to depression after they have tried the singles bars or experienced the Michelletic search to pair up that is common in certain self-help divorce adjustment groups. For some individuals, loneliness may become a chronic condition, a way of life. They feel that loneliness is what they will feel forever. Certain times of day may be more difficult than others. For example, after dinner may be particularly lonely for the individual who prior to the divorce or the death of the spouse socialized until bedtime. For others, the holidays may represent a problem. The counselor, in these cases, must help the person get in touch with his or her own motives and needs, explore the extent to which sexual needs are part of the loneliness, understand the extent to which fantasy of a new ideal partner or of the former spouse dominates their efforts to make new friends, and evaluate options for dealing with the problem in terms of where the person is in the divorce adjustment process.

Counselors need to help their clients openly face feelings about loneliness and understand their own responsibility in its making. Denial of these feelings and the resulting displacement of anger and blame only increases the problem. Often during this time persons feel doubtful about their own capacities to love or to maintain stable relationships. The counselor should help the person understand the feelings of loneliness and aid him or her to gain self-acceptance.

Conflict Stage Issues and Techniques

During Stage II clients experience conflict. At this point in the intimacy dissolution process, individuals may feel curious about dating, interested in dating, or even compelled to date. They may in fact enter the social world, yet still be unsure of themselves in this world. They may push themselves to date and have sex, only to feel ashamed and depressed afterward. Some individuals in this stage may use their sexuality as a weapon to rebel against a sexually restrictive former spouse or a sexually restrictive upbringing. Others may use sexuality as self-punishment in the same way that some individuals allow themselves to be used sexually to prove to themselves that they are indeed worthless. In these cases, sex is used for manipulation, rebellion, and punishment. Areas for exploration in counseling are self-worth and self-esteem. Sexual needs are legitimate; so in these cases, the counselor could help the client understand the basic purposes of sexuality: enjoyment, communication, playfulness, and building deeper relationships. At this time it is not unusual for a man to report impotence or a woman to report orgasmic dysfunction or sexual disinterest. At times individuals may feel quite comfortable dating and engaging in sex only to find themselves guilty and ashamed later on. Their emotions at this point are too unstable to form any long-lasting impressions of themselves or others.

During this stage it is important to help the client clarify values about dating, relationships, and sexuality. When clients clarify their values about sexuality they are becoming aware of the beliefs and behaviors that are important to them and that they are comfortable with. It also helps them to act on their values and beliefs consistently. Counselors need to help clients set up realistic values so that they are not constantly failing to adjust their behavior to their values. After a sexual value has been clarified with the client, planning must be done to optimize the client's chances of carrying the plan into action.

Anxiety about newly achieved sexual freedom and the changes that have taken place in sexual codes and behavior is a problem commonly reported by clients in the counseling situation. Some persons appear to enjoy the freedom to have many sexual partners without commitment; others find the expectation that they must have sex with every new friend or date oppressive. Somewhere between these two extremes, others explore by trial and error their new sexual self-concept. With the individual who feels that sexuality should be free and easy, it may be useful for counselors to help the person fit sexuality into his or her life, to put sexuality into a perspective. Sexuality may be very important to these and other clients, but it is not their whole life.

As clients cope with dating and the sex game, they often find they have to confront additional feelings of anger at having been used sexually, guilt over sexually exploiting others, or depression when intimacy needs are not met. In addition, both male and female clients often express concerns about the new emphasis on female orgasm and other changes in sexual mores. For these kinds of sex-related anxieties, the counselor could help the client recognize specific fears and anxieties; bring to consciousness personal needs, expectations, and values about sexuality; and hasten the reintegration of the sexual self so that the person can deal openly and honestly with potential sexual partners and choose whether and when to engage in sex and on what terms.

Counselors can help clients deal with prioritizing and setting boundaries on their sexuality. Boundaries are basically set at the dividing line between constructive and destructive sexual expression. Thus once values are set up and a plan of action established, people ultimately have to mobilize their will power in order to incorporate the values into their life style. Only with this kind of self-knowledge and comfort with one's needs and values can a person communicate honestly about sex, take responsibility for his or her own sexuality, and gain protection from the hazards of trial-and-error sexual encounters. After clients have accomplished this, they need to evaluate and assess their sexual value system. If they feel comfortable with their actions, then they have affirmed their value system; if they feel uncomfortable, more value clarification work is needed.

Counselors should help the client approach new roles and responsibilities from a positive perspective. The individual may feel a new sense of pride in his or her newly found competencies. For example, the client needs to be helped to find emotional support in friendships and family relations. It is crucial for the single parent to establish a support network outside his or her family system. Only in this way can the person achieve a new level of communication with adults whose uncritical acceptance can greatly aid in reducing the person's feelings of guilt and shame.

Ambivalence Stage Issues and Techniques

During Stage III, clients experience ambivalence. At this point in the intimacy dissolution process, persons may experiment sexually. They may date and have sex with several individuals in an attempt to learn about their new sexual identities. One client reported having sex three times in one weekend with three different partners. Feeling youthful and free, a client may enter into a relationship with a much younger person and engage in youthful activities. Some clients seem to be picking up where they left off as a socially and sexually involved individual before they were married. Usually, these relationships are time limited, and eventually the individual typically begins dating someone closer to his or her own age, emotionally and biologically. During this time a person may feel that "My body is not getting any younger. I'd better have sex with this person now." In situations like these, persons feel as though they are bartering sex for something else. In other words, clients are not engaging in sex for appropriate reasons; rather they are acting out of curiosity, or to affirm their attractiveness to the opposite sex. Individuals who engage in sexual encounters based upon these reasons usually lack self-esteem, commitment, and intimacy, characteristics that most people consider to be important in sexual and social relationships. Counselors should help their clients understand what their values are regarding sexual motivations.

During this stage the client may report specific sexual dysfunctions. Counselors should initially universalize and thereby detoxify these specific sexual dysfunctions. Loss of sexual desire, erectile dysfunction, premature ejaculation, and orgasmic difficulties may be present either alone or in

Table 1

The Psychological Issues and Counseling Techniques Utilized During Specific Stages of the Intimacy Dissolution Process

Stages	Issues	Counseling Techniques
Stage I: Denial	Loneliness Sexual deprivation Lack of sexual interest	Help clients develop outside support 　networks. Aid clients in dealing with 　emotionally associated with 　separation shock.
Stage II: Conflict	Possible sexual acting out Emotional instability	Help clients to clarify values about 　dating relationships and 　sexuality. Help clients "own" their 　ambivalent 　feelings.
Stage III: Ambivalence	Identity problems (social, 　psychological, sexual)	Help clients make the identity 　transition from defining 　themselves 　within a married script to the 　context of a single script.
Stage IV: Acceptance	Stability maintenance	Help cleints internalize their new 　social-psychological identity.

context of the kinds of problems already discussed. The therapeutic assessment of these dysfunctions must encompass the individual's previous sexual functioning, the dynamics of the previous marriage, sexuality with the marriage, the overall impact of the divorce process on the person's sexual self-concept, and the present circumstances in which the sexual dysfunction is manifested. Regarding the extent to which the problem existed in the previous marriage and the possibility that it may have been a factor in the divorce, the counselor has to be content with the client's version of the problem and its causes. The direction that the counseling takes depends on the overall assessment and on the counselor's level of competence for treating sexual dysfunctions.

Acceptance Stage Issues and Techniques

During Stage IV clients experience acceptance. At this point in the intimacy dissolution process individuals are aware of and can accept their own needs and desires and thus can maintain healthy social and sexual relationships. They have attained a balance of self and relationship and should now be able to enter into an intimate relationship.

To reiterate: Counselors working with individuals going through the intimacy dissolution process must also consider the individual's sexual needs, problems, and issues, and it is crucially important for both coun-selors and clients not to separate out the sexual areas of counseling from the psychological or emotional. The wonderful complexity of human be-havior should not be simplified.

Chapter 8
THE IMPACT OF AIDS

Disease and illness can be examined at many different levels. Typically disease is explored from a biological, medical point of view, but illness reflects the social and psychological reaction. This chapter concerns itself with providing counselors with psychoeducational information about acquired immune deficiency syndrome (AIDS) and discusses the social and psychological reactions to the disease. This coverage is brief. Exploring the social construction of the psychological reactions to this disease is impossible, yet counselors must be aware of the socially constructed aspects of the disease so that they are better able to assist their clients. From a social level of analysis, AIDS represents a disease that carries with it the effects of its early association with certain marginal or stigmatized risk groups, its sexual transmission, its contagious nature, and its deadly nature.

AIDS is one of those illnesses that carry with it an aura of stigma, or moral judgment. Like leprosy, cancer, mental disorder, and venereal disease, AIDS reflects moral shame to the persons who were unfortunate enough to contact it. Generally speaking, stigmatized illnesses are usually those illnesses associated with "deviant" behavior in some way. Its initial discovery in the homosexual population gave AIDS this stigmatized socially created image. Shortly thereafter, AIDS also came to be associated with such other risk groups as IV drug users, thus increasing the public's image of the disease as belonging to deviants.

AIDS, with its connection to numerous sexual partners, promiscuous sexual activity, so-called deviant sexual activity (i.e., sodomy), and sexual irresponsibility, revived Puritanical sexual concerns absent in the 1970 pre-AIDS generation. This connection served to increase fears and anxieties about sexual activity, associating sex with death. The contagious nature of the AIDS epidemic, and the fact that AIDS basically kills 100% of its victims, further revived panic reactions toward contagious diseases absent since the polio epidemics of the 1940s and 1950s. Reports that the AIDS virus was found in saliva and tears added to the notion that AIDS could be caught anywhere and transmitted casually. The term *courtesy stigma*, described by Irving Goffman (1963, pp. 30–31) as a taint that has spread from the stigmatized to his or her close associations, is now applicable to the way many feel about AIDS. Taken together, these definitions have socially created an image of AIDS that is socially, psychologically, and medically devastating. In addition, these definitions also make some of those infected obviously visible.

The image of AIDS that counselors (as well as their clients) hold is infiltrated with these social definitions. In order to better assist and educate their clients, counselors must educate themselves about the AIDS virus so that they have accurate information about the disease, can examine prejudices and assumptions in light of the facts, and be aware of the disease process involved in AIDS.

The Facts About AIDS

Because of the impact of AIDS, counseling sexually active adults in the 1990s in very different from counseling sexually active adults in the 1970s and early 1980s before people knew about AIDS. This section contains basic factual information that is useful for counselors when working with individuals who are sexually active on the history of the AIDS explosion as well as on the nature, prevalence, transmission routes, risk factors, nonsexual infections, onset, and symptomotology of AIDS.

The AIDS Explosion

In the late 1970s thousands of homosexual and bisexual men came to San Francisco's public venereal diseases clinic to participate in a government-sponsored study of hepatitis B. In 1981 the hepatitis study produced a major victory: A hepatitis vaccine tested on the San Francisco group and in several other cities worked. But there was little reason to celebrate because health officials found they had to worry about something far more ominous than hepatitis. At a May 1981 meeting in San Francisco, there was talk of a mysterious new illness that had caused homosexual men in New York and California to die of rare forms of pneumonia and cancer. Something was apparently attacking their immune systems. A few weeks later the first five cases were announced in a Centers for Disease Control (CDC) report on morbidity and mortality. Many of the first AIDS cases—11 of the first 24 in 1981—turned out to be participants in the hepatitis project. Many of the hepatitis participants had filled out extensive questionnaires about their lives, from sexual habits to drug use. In 1983, CDC and the San Francisco city health department agreed to contact a sample of the participants and question them again to see if they could isolate special risk factors for AIDS.

When they gave blood for the project, these men had no way of knowing that a time bomb was ticking for a then-unknown disease far more threatening than anyone could have imagined, and that the signs of the future AIDS epidemic lay hidden in the vials they filled.

By the spring of 1984, researchers in Paris and the United States had isolated the cause of AIDS, a new virus that attacked key immune system cells, and the CDC began using an experimental blood test to look for antibodies to the virus. Using the test and samples of the frozen blood, the researchers tracked the footprints of the AIDS epidemic in the San Francisco men. They found that undetected the virus had spread rapidly among this group of sexually active men. With participant consent, CDC tested random stored blood samples and found that 3% of the gay men in the hepatitis study showed antibodies to the then-unknown AIDS virus in 1978, rising to 12% in 1979. By 1983, 61% were positive.

Although the rise has since slowed, preliminary results showed that 69% of those tested in 1986 follow-up studies were positive on the AIDS antibody blood test. A positive antibody blood test generally signals long-term infection. Many people initially hoped that it meant past exposure to the AIDS virus without long-term consequences. But CDC studies using data from the San Francisco project have since found that the virus can in fact be found in the blood of most of those who are positive.

Because many people in the hepatitis vaccine study gave frequent blood samples, conversion from negative to positive can often be pinpointed to within months. For every case of actual AIDS, far more people may be infected with the virus but show no symptoms. The government's often quoted projections that more than 1.5 million Americans may already be infected with the virus are based in part on what has happened to the San Francisco men.

In a selected sample of 66 infected men followed for an average of about 6 years, one fourth have already developed AIDS, and more than one third have already developed symptoms of illness that sometimes precedes AIDS. Only 25 men—38%—remain free of symptoms. There are exceptions. Four people who have been antibody positive for at least 9 years still have not come down with AIDS. Most findings have been disturbing. At first it was believed that the vast majority of people would not get sick. Now there is a very different picture.

By 1987, at least 600 of the 6,700 participants had acquired immune deficiency syndrome. About 400 of them were dead from it, and a sample survey taken showed that 70% of the participants tested positive for AIDS antibodies, indicating that they were carrying the virus and that it probably was a matter of time before they too manifested symptoms of AIDS. For them, and for all of those involved in the hepatitis study, the figures are tragic testimony to the speed and virulence of the epidemic that some experts predict could become the worst in modern history. But their participation in the study brought at least one priceless benefit: The stored frozen blood has offered an unexpected opportunity to track the path of the AIDS virus over time in a large, vulnerable group, teaching researchers more about the progress of the disease than any other single study. It is also an indicator of what can happen when the AIDS virus goes unchecked.

Thus the study, which eventually evolved into one focusing on AIDS, showed that the incubation period for AIDS is much longer than many had earlier suspected and that the chance of becoming sick increases with time among those infected, with the likelihood of getting AIDS greater in the second 5 years after infection than the first.

The Nature of AIDS

A person who has AIDS is in the final stages of a series of health diseases caused by a virus. This virus is called HIV or HTLV-III or LAV. The virus attacks white blood cells (T lymphocytes) in human blood. The AIDS virus attacks a person's immune system and damages his or her ability to fight off other diseases. When a person is left without a functioning immune system to ward off other germs or bacteria, he or she becomes vulnerable to becoming infected by bacteria, protozoa, fungi, and other viruses and malignancies that then may cause life-threatening illnesses, such as pneumonia, meningitis, and cancer.

When the AIDS virus enters the bloodstream, it begins to attack certain white blood cells (T lymphocytes). Substances called antibodies are produced by the body. These antibodies can be detected in the blood by a simple test, usually 2 weeks to 3 months after infection. However, even before the antibody test is positive, the victim can pass the virus to others by methods that are explained in the sections that follow. It is important to note that in some cases it takes even longer for the antibodies to build up so that an infected person can test negative for AIDS and still be able to infect others.

The Prevalence of AIDS

The number of people infected with the AIDS virus in the United States is estimated to be about 1.5 million. In addition, there are over 40,000 new AIDS cases reported nationally every year. All of these individuals are believed to be capable of spreading the virus sexually (heterosexually or homosexually) or by sharing needles and syringes or other implements for intravenous drug use. Of these, an estimated 100,000 to 200,000 will come down with AIDS-related complex (ARC). It is difficult to predict the number who will develop ARC or AIDS because symptoms sometimes take as long as 9 years to appear. Based on present knowledge, scientists predict that those infected with the AIDS virus will develop an illness that fits an accepted definition of AIDS within 5 years. The percentage increases with each passing year.

The incidence of HIV infection is also difficult to estimate because new infections are largely asymptomatic, and reported AIDS cases have a long and variable incubation period. However, there are indications that prevention efforts are succeeding. Because the prevalence of infection among gay men, intravenous drug abusers, and persons with hemophilia is high and infection persists, the prevalence of HIV is likely to remain high even without further transmission. Sexual intercourse with an infected partner, or with a risk-group member whose infection status is now known, is likely to constitute a substantial risk for the future. Simply reducing the number of partners is not enough to avoid infection if infection status is unknown and adequate precautions are not taken.

Transmission of the AIDS Virus

Although the AIDS virus is found in several body fluids, a person acquires the virus during contact with an infected person's blood, semen, vaginal secretions, or breast milk. The virus then enters the blood stream through his or her rectum, vagina, penis, or mouth. Small unseen tears in the surface lining of the vagina or rectum may occur during insertion of the penis, fingers, or other objects, thus opening an avenue for entrance of the virus directly into the blood stream. Therefore, the AIDS virus can be passed from penis to rectum and vagina and vice versa without a visible tear in the tissue or the presence of blood.

Risk Factors

What is clear and what everyone should know is that unprotected intercourse, vaginal or anal, is an efficient way to transmit the disease. Although it has been said often that the virus is more easily passed during anal than vaginal intercourse, evidence to support the statement is lacking. There is no reason to doubt that a woman can acquire the disease from an infectious male partner and that men can contact the virus from their women partners, although probably not as easily. In Africa, the disease is primarily a heterosexual one, with the major route of transmission penile/vaginal and visa versa.

Though the risk groups for AIDS are well understood, little is known about the absolute risk of acquiring infection through sexual contact. This risk depends on two variables: the number of sexual contacts with an infected person and the likelihood of transmission of infection during sexual contact with an infected partner.

The number of sexual contacts with an infected partner depends on the number of partners, the number of sexual contacts with each partner, and the prevalence of infection in those partners. If infection with the AIDS virus is like other sexually transmitted infections, repeated exposure to an infected person is not necessary for infection, but the probability that transmission will occur increases with the frequency of exposure. As the prevalence of infection in the population increases, the likelihood of infection in a random partner also increases. Therefore, in an epidemic an increasing risk of infection can be expected as the prevalence of infection increases.

The risk of transmission during sexual contact with an infected person depends on the type of body fluid the uninfected partner is exposed to, the anatomic area that is exposed (or the possible route of entry of the virus), and the level of infection in the infected person. Although the AIDS virus has been isolated from blood, saliva, semen, and vaginal secretions, little information is available on the relative infectivity of these body fluids. Because the virus preferentially infects lymphocytes, the concentration is probably highest in secretions containing lymphocytes, such as blood, semen, and vaginal secretions. The ease with which the virus enters the body depends on the physical properties of the exposed area. It is highly unlikely that the virus crosses intact skin. The fragility of the lining of the rectum may account for the positive association between AIDS and receptive anal intercourse reported in many studies of AIDS and HIV infection in gay men. However, some infected gay men and nearly all infected heterosexuals, including the majority of infected prostitutes and other women in Africa, have no history of receptive anal intercourse, indicating that AIDS is transmissible through heterosexual penile/vaginal intercourse.

Human immunodeficiency virus seems less likely to be transmitted during a single contact than other sexually transmitted infections. The transmission rate of gonorrhea is estimated at 22 to 25% after a single exposure in a man to an infected woman and at 50% for a women whose male partner is infected. The risk of transmission of other infections after a single exposure is less well understood. Evidence for infection is found in about 30% of the sexual contacts of an individual with primary or secondary syphilis, but this often includes multiple exposures, and some of the contacts may represent source rather than the spread of infection.

Human immunodeficiency virus is transmissible from men to women and from women to men, but the risk of transmission per single sexual exposure is not well defined. Two studies of the wives of hemophiliacs have each found that 2 (.5%) of 21 were seropositive. As part of a study of infected male military personnel, seven of the steady heterosexual partners of these men were tested; five were infected. A fourth study tested heterosexual partners of intravenous drug abusers with AIDS or AIDS-related complex and found that 20 (48%) of 42 were seropositive. None of these studies accurately quantified exposure because the date of infection for the initial case was not known. However, because the people with HIV infection were probably infected for a much longer period of time than the people with acute hepatitis B, HIV is probably less easily sexually transmitted than hepatitis B.

A study of the sexual transmission of hepatitis B among heterosexuals concluded that a significant risk of contracting the virus occurs when someone has had more than five sex partners within 4 months.

Nonsexual Infection

AIDS can be transmitted nonsexually by injecting the virus directly into the blood stream during drug use, by blood transfusions, by a pregnant mother to her child, or through breast milk. In other words, the virus must be passed from the infected person into the immune-system cells in the blood stream of the uninfected person. Therefore contact must be made between the body fluids of one person and the blood of the other in order for infection to occur.

Drug abusers.   AIDS can be nonsexually transmitted to drug users who inject drugs into their veins. These users are at high risk and have high rates of infection by the AIDS virus. Users of intravenous drugs make up about 25% of the cases of AIDS throughout the country. The AIDS virus is carried in contaminated blood left in the needle, syringe, or other drug-related implement, and the virus is injected into the new victim by reusing dirty syringes and needles. Even the smallest amount of infected blood left in the needle or syringe can contain live AIDS virus to be passed on to the next user of those dirty implements.

No one should shoot up drugs because of the risks of addiction, poor health, family disruption, emotional disturbances, and death that follow. However, many drug users are addicted to drugs, and for one reason or another have not changed their behavior. For these people, the only way not to get AIDS is to use a clean, previously unused needle, syringe, or other implement for the injection of the drug solution.

Hemophilia.   Prior to 1985, some persons with hemophilia (a blood clotting disorder that makes them subject to bleeding) were infected with the AIDS virus either through blood transfusions or the use of blood products that helped their blood clot. Now special heat processes have virtually eliminated the risk of infection for the nation's 20,000 hemophiliacs whose lives depend on regular infusions of special blood-clotting products, and studies of these patients have not found a single case of AIDS infection since late 1984 when drug firms first began heating the blood concentrates. Infected hemophiliacs represent a very small percentage of the cases of AIDS throughout the country.

Transfusions. Blood screening tests have made the nation's blood supply much safer, although there is still a slight risk that the AIDS virus can be passed on from transfusions (about 1 in 50,000 units). That translates to about 70 transfusion-related AIDS cases a year nationally for the 3 to 4 million patients who get transfusions each year. Currently all blood donors are initially screened, and blood is not accepted from high-risk individuals. Blood collected for use is tested for the presence of antibodies to the AIDs virus. With such routine testing of blood products, the blood supply for transfusion is now safer than it has ever been with regard to AIDS. However, some people who had blood transfusions prior to March 1985, before it was known how to screen blood for safe transfusion, became infected.

Some experts remain concerned about transfusions. These experts say the source of today's few units tainted with the AIDS virus is a window period that occurs right after infection. There is a lag time of several months before antibodies to the virus appear and tests sensitive to them can be effective. However, the risk of getting AIDS from blood must be put in perspective. Transfusions are a life-sustaining therapy given only under critical circumstances. Blood is probably one of the safest parts of the life-saving effort.

Casual contact. There is no known risk of nonsexual infection in most situations encountered in daily life. Family members living with individuals who have AIDS do not become infected except through sexual contact. There is no evidence of transmission of AIDS virus by everyday contact, even though these family members shared food, towels, cups, razors, even toothbrushes, and kissed each other. A person cannot get AIDS from casual social contact. But casual social contact should not be confused with casual sexual contact, which is the major cause of the spread of AIDS. Casual social contact is kissing, shaking hands, hugging, crying, sneezing, or coughing and will not transmit the AIDS virus. People cannot get AIDS from swimming pools and hot tubs or from eating in restaurants (even if the restaurant waiter has AIDS or carries the AIDS virus). People cannot get AIDS by sharing bed linens, towels, straws, dishes, cups, or any other utensils. Persons cannot get AIDS from door knobs, telephones, doorbells, or household furniture. Nor can people get AIDS from mutual masturbation, body massage, or nonsexual contact.

About 2,500 health care workers who were caring for AIDS patients when they were sickest have been carefully studied and tested for infection with the AIDS virus. These doctors, nurses, and other health care givers had been exposed to the patients' blood, stool, and other body fluids through spills or being accidentally stuck with a needle. Upon testing, only three who had accidentally stuck themselves with a needle had a positive antibody test for exposure to the AIDS virus. Because health care workers had much more contact with patients and their body fluids than can be expected from common everyday contact, it is clear that we can be confident that the AIDS virus is not transmitted by casual contact.

Onset

Once an individual is infected, there are several possibilities. Some people may remain well for a relatively long time, but even so they are able to infect others. They may have no physically apparent symptoms of the illness. The majority of infected antibody-positive individuals who carry the AIDS virus show no disease symptoms and may not come down with the disease for many years. However, if proper precautions are not used with sexual contacts and/or intravenous drug use, these infected individuals can spread the virus to others. Anyone who thinks he or she is infected or involved in high-risk behaviors should not donate his or her blood, organs, tissues, or sperm because they may contain the AIDS virus.

Other people may develop AIDS-related complex, a disease less serious than AIDS but caused by the AIDS virus. These patients test positive for AIDS infection and have a specific set of clinical symptoms, which are often less severe than those with classic AIDS and include loss of appetite, weight loss, fever, night sweats, skin rashes, diarrhea, tiredness, lack of resistance to infection, and swollen lymph nodes. These are also symptoms of many other diseases, and in such cases, a physician should be consulted.

Only a qualified health professional can diagnose AIDS, which is the result of a natural progress of infection by the AIDS virus. The virus destroys the body's immune system and allows otherwise controllable infections (caused by bacteria, protozoa, fungi, and other viruses) and cancers to invade the body. These opportunistic diseases might not otherwise gain a foothold in the body, and they may eventually cause death.

Symptomotology

The earliest symptoms of AIDS are like those of many common infections such as colds or the flu. Some can also be caused by anxiety or depression. These symptoms and signs of AIDS and the opportunistic infections may include unexplained swollen glands (lymph nodes) for more than 3 months, unexplained fever for more than 10 days, drenching night sweats (that make it necessary to change bed sheets), prolonged fatigue that is not explained by physical activity, emotional depression, persistent severe diarrhea, unexplained weight loss (more than 10% of ideal body weight) not due to dieting or exercise, oral thrush (a thick, whitish coating of the mouth or tongue), fever associated with shortness of breath or difficult breathing, recent appearance of purplish blotches or discolored lesions of the skin or mucous membranes that do not go away and gradually increase in size, easy bruising or unexplained bleeding, and a dry cough, cold, or sore throat (in nonsmokers) lasting several weeks.

Any persistent combination of these symptoms is a good reason to see a health provider, even though it rarely signifies that a person has AIDS. Most symptoms are also characteristic of many common minor ailments. The AIDS virus in all infected persons is essentially the same; the reactions of individuals may differ.

The CDC currently lists several criteria for the diagnosis of AIDs:

- **Pneumocystis carinii pneumonia.** One of the most common symptoms is pneumocystis carinii pneumonia. AIDS patients who have pneumocystis carinii generally have no structured treatment regimen to follow that will help them cope with the fear of the progressive effects of the disease. Infections must be treated as they occur. Even though some patients are helped with the drug known as AZT, AIDS patients cannot hope that the cure of this opportunistic infection represents a remission of the underlying disease. Multiple reinfections become progressively more relentless, and the patient is chronically tired and uncomfortable and rarely experiences any signs of improvement.
- **Kaposi's sarcoma.** Another common manifestation of AIDS is Kaposi's sarcoma. Patients with Kaposi's sarcoma develop purplish splotches over their body, leaving them with a constant visual reminder of their disease. The treatment regimen for this manifestation of AIDS is intense and has many side effects. However, although the treatment is stressful, the regular involvement with hospital staff that it requires provides patients with emotional support and encourages the hope of remission. Patients often use their regular contacts with the treatment staff to ventilate their fears, obtain information, and learn new ways of coping with the disease.
- **Neurologic disease.** Evidence shows that the AIDS virus may also attack the nervous system, causing damage to the brain. Many AIDS patients have central nervous system disease, which is often characterized by a slowly progressive dementia that eventually becomes incapacitating. Some patients become confused, disoriented, and have short-term memory deficits. Others experience symptoms such as weakness of the legs and blurred vision or blindness. Patients with these symptoms often need extensive help in the home with eating, bathing, dressing, and other basic activities of daily living as well as assistance in traveling to and from the hospital because they may become confused about directions. These cognitive changes also have a tremendous impact on the patient's relationship with people close to him or her. For example, when one patient grew suspicious and accused his friends of stealing

from him, they became reluctant to enter his apartment to provide the care that he so desperately needed.

- **Chronic lymphadenopathy syndrome.** Some AIDS patients have a chronic lymphadenopathy syndrome, that is, a chronic disease process affecting lymph nodes. Although the relationship between this condition and AIDS is unclear at present, investigators suspect that the syndrome actually may be a prodrome of AIDS. Thus patients with chronic lymphadenopathy ultimately may be found to be at high risk for AIDS. There is presently no known cure for AIDS. There is presently no known vaccine to prevent AIDS.

What should be kept in mind about the CDC's criteria for diagnosis of AIDS is that many individuals with AIDS die of diseases different from the ones listed but never receive a diagnosis of AIDS because they do not meet the CDC's criteria. This is especially evident in the case of women who die from pelvic inflammatory disease and test positive for the AIDS virus but never become part of the national percentage. This also implies that the number of infected persons, persons who have been diagnosed as having AIDS, and persons who die of AIDS are grossly underrepresented.

AIDS Risk Among Heterosexuals

AIDS is not a homosexual disease, although the initial discovery was in the homosexual community. AIDS is not a black or white disease. AIDS is not just a male disease. AIDS is found in heterosexual people. AIDS is found in women, and presently AIDS is increasing at alarming rates among heterosexual women. AIDS is found in children. Eventually, if left unchecked, AIDS will probably spread among people in the same manner as other sexually transmitted diseases (like syphilis and gonorrhea, which are increasing at alarming rates).

What started out as a disease afflicting homosexual men and IV drug users has not only spread to certain heterosexuals—the sex partners of bisexual men, partners of intravenous drug users, babies of IV drug users—but also into the general population. For heterosexuals, fears about the spread of AIDS through casual contact have yielded to concern over catching it in a brief sexual encounter. It is becoming clear that acquired immune deficiency syndrome is a profound killer that is not going to go away soon.

The virus does not distinguish between heterosexuals and homosexuals. AIDS can be transmitted by men and women. According to the CDC, an estimated 500,000 heterosexuals carry the disease. Some studies have indicated that women do not spread AIDS as easily as men. In fact, some studies have suggested that women may be acting as a buffer, slowing the spread of the virus to the general population. Other researchers have referred to women as vectors, providing the connections to many areas of the population. These statistics indicate that heterosexual women thus face greater danger than heterosexual men in casual sex. Many experts have suggested that a key factor in the course of AIDS in this country may be the efficiency of transmission from women to men. But one head of AIDS surveillance at a city health department has indicated that American women may not be efficient transmitters and may instead be temporarily holding back the spread of the virus into the heterosexual population. No one has any idea how many people are infected but asymptomatic, or how much transmission is going on. Men and women outside of monogamous relationships, and many people in them, must ask themselves "Am I at any risk of exposure to the virus?" and more frightening, because 10 years can pass before someone exhibits any visible sign of infection, "Have I ever been exposed?" People perceive themselves as immune and possessed of an intuitive power that enables them to choose safe partners.

Women and AIDS

   Michelle is a 53-year-old administrative assistant to a top executive in an exclusive department store. Prior to her divorce, she had been married to Bob since she was 18. They grew up in the same neighborhood and knew each practically their whole lives. They have two grown children who are both married.

   About 5 years ago, Bob decided he wanted a divorce. Michelle was devastated, especially when she learned he (age 57) was seeing a 23-year-old woman. She could not understand how this could happen to her at this time in her life. She had devoted herself to Bob and the children, and now without these roles to fall back on, she felt lost and alone. Her early abandonment fears were triggered and often, terrified in the middle of the night, she called Bob to come and hold her. She entered therapy, and after about a year began to feel better about the possibilities for the future.

   Although she was an attractive woman, she had no interest in other men and was extremely reluctant to begin dating. Finally, after being "dragged out by her friends," she met Herman and started dating. Herman was 62 and was retired but worked part time. He adored Michelle. After a few months they began sleeping together. Michelle was very surprised because she experienced sexual pleasure with Herman such as she never experienced with Bob. They had an excellent sexual relationship for the next year—loving and free.

   One day Herman became ill and couldn't breathe. She took him to the hospital, and he was diagnosed with AIDS 2 weeks later. He was unable to breathe because he had AIDS-related pneumonia. Apparently, he was given contaminated blood when he had bypass surgery many years before. Michelle was once again devastated; she knew he was going to die. She was also terrified: Did she have it? She was tested for AIDS and spent 3 weeks waiting for the results in a state of chronic terror, crying constantly and feeling rage for Bob, because "it's his fault that I was out there in the first place." Fortunately Michelle tested negative. She has to be tested again in 6 months just to make certain, but the doctor seems to feel that she's probably okay.

Now she has other problems. She is terrified of catching the AIDS virus from Herman. She doesn't want to kiss him; she cringes at the thought of having him sleep in her bed; and sex is out of the question. Herman is depressed, scared for his life, lonely for Michelle's touch, and guilty about the possibility of having given her AIDS. He hardly sees her anymore.

The route of HIV for women in the United States over the past few years has been through male IV drug abusers, but this is changing quickly. If a male is an IV drug abuser, his risk of contacting HIV is very high to begin with, especially if he is homosexual or bisexual. When this male has intercourse with a woman, her risk increases dramatically. Almost 30% of women with HIV contracted the virus through a male IV drug abuser. Heterosexual transmission appears to occur more easily with IV drug abuse than with any other risk factor. When men acquire the virus, they pass it on to women, who are at phenomenal risk of getting the disease today as compared to 5 or 10 years ago. In the United States the transmission of HIV is more likely to occur from male to female. Although there is not much known as to the reason for this, one theory is that men may be the first round of the epidemic because they are the majority of those infected. Men inoculate their partners with a substantial dose of virus during intercourse (in the ejaculatory fluid) while most women do not. Counselors should keep in mind that HIV/AIDS disproportionately affects poor women, women of color, and drug users.

According to a study conducted by the CDC in Atlanta, Georgia, regarding the transmission of HIV (Whipple & Scura, 1989), less than 8% of HIV cases are contracted from women. The CDC studied families of persons who have contracted the disease via blood transfusions. To the family members who did not have sexual relations with the infected person, there was no transmission. This is important to note because it shows that families who share cups, food, razors, and even kiss did not contract the disease from the infected member. Of the sexually active couples, of the 50 men with HIV who did not use condoms during intercourse, 8 passed on the virus. Out of the 20 women infected, only one male contracted HIV when not using condoms. All these people had vaginal intercourse. This shows that rectal intercourse is not the only route of transmission. In almost all cases, HIV was contracted with only one exposure.

AIDS and Adolescents

Although few studies of seroprevalence have included adolescents, rates in military recruits are 1.5 per 1,000 nationwide; the Job Corps, which contains adolescents 16 to 21 years of age, had a seroprevalence of 0.33% (Hein, 1989), roughly double the military. Recent data reported during testimony before the Presidential Commission on the HIV epidemic by James Kennedy from Covenant House revealed that about 7% of the runaway or homeless youth who came to Covenant House were HIV positive in the anonymous seroprevalence study. About 15% were positive among the 19 and 20 years olds (Kennedy, 1989, pp. 190–203). These rates are very high compared to any other group in the nation. According to the Centers for Disease Control (Whipple & Scura, 1989), adolescents now represent 1% of reported cases of AIDS, and people in their 20s account for 21% of all cases. Many of them were infected as adolescents.

Romanowski and Brown (1986) reported that little change in sexual behavior has been noted among heterosexual college students (Hirschorn, 1987; Simpkins & Eberage, 1984; Simpkins & Kushner, 1986; Weinstein, Rosen, & Atwood, 1991). For example, Weinstein, Rosen, and Atwood (1991) found that although college students are informed about safer sex practices and the consequences of contracting AIDS, they inconsistently use safer sex practices. This is substantiated by others (Manning, Barenberg, Gallese, & Rice, 1989), who found that college students (and others) know intellectually that AIDS is a deadly disease, know intellectually how to prevent contracting this deadly disease, but continue to feel that practicing safer sex techniques is "too much trouble."

AIDS and Monogamy

Couples who remain in mutually faithful monogamous relationships are protected from AIDS through sexual transmission. Thus if a person has been faithful for at least 10 years, and his or her partner has also been faithful, neither is likely to be at risk. If neither have been faithful, both are at risk. This is true for both heterosexual and homosexual couples. Unless it is possible to know with absolute certainty that neither person is carrying the AIDS virus, protective behavior must be practiced. Absolute certainty means not only that the partners have maintained a mutually faithful monogamous sexual relationship but also that neither has used intravenous drugs.

AIDS Testing: Who Should Have the Test?

Deluged in recent days by calls from worried patients, many physicians are reluctant to urge tests to detect infection with the AIDS virus among those who are worried about being infected. Although some frightened patients may have their fears allayed by taking the test and getting a negative result, doctors interviewed said that for others taking the test posed real psychological problems.

How can counselors best help worried clients? They can recommend that anyone who is unsure about whether or not to get the test for AIDS should ask him- or herself the following questions:

- Are you a man or woman who has had unprotected sex that involved the exchange of body fluids at any time since 1977? A single contact may have been sufficient for infection to occur.
- Have you shared syringes, rubber bulbs, "works," "cookers," or needles for intravenous drug use (such as shooting heroin or cocaine) at any time since 1977?
- Could any of your sexual partners since 1977 have belonged to any one of the groups just mentioned?
- Did you receive whole blood or blood products, donor sperm, organs, or tissues at any time before March 1985?
- Have your or any of your sexual partners been sexually active in Haiti or central Africa (e.g., Zaire, Rwanda, Zambia, Uganda)? These are countries where prevalence of HIV infection seems to be high among people not included in one of the acknowledged high-risk categories in the United States (that is, gay or bisexual men and IV drug users).

If clients answered "Yes" to any of these questions, it will be wise for them to follow the guidelines described in the Counseling Strategies section that follows and consider getting tested, both to avoid exposing themselves and to avoid exposing their sexual partners. Counselors can be extremely helpful to persons worried about their HIV status. It is never too late for individuals to begin protecting themselves against HIV. Even if they have reason to believe that they have already been infected, it is always to their benefit to avoid further exposure because multiple exposures may help to trigger the illness.

Counseling Strategies for Safer Sex

If the AIDS epidemic is to be stopped, the disease must be understood—its cause, its nature and, its prevention. Counselors can play an important role in helping their clients achieve this understanding.

In the absence of a vaccine or therapy, the major hope for preventing transmission is the adoption of safer sex behavior. Control of certain behaviors and knowing the facts about AIDS can prevent the further spread of the disease. Educating those at risk for infecting themselves or infecting other people is essential. Because certain types of behaviors lead to infection by the AIDS virus, personal measures must be taken for effective protection.

Preventing the transmission of the virus is the best way to fight the virus. Transmission occurs through the exchange of infected blood or semen; it is this exchange that must be prevented. Certain actions and behaviors may help avoid exposure, or further exposure, to HIV infection. Utilizing these risk-reduction actions and behaviors may require a substantial change in sexual behavior for those at increased risk for HIV infection. Everyone should assess his or her level of risk and undertake risk reduction behavior as necessary.

Risk-Reduction Guidelines for People Who Are HIV Positive

People who have an HIV infection should observe routine and reasonable precautions against accidental contact by others with their blood or semen. Hands or skin may be washed with soap and water. Other surfaces where blood or semen have been spilled may be cleaned with soap and water or a mild disinfectant solution such as 10% bleach solution. Caution should be exercised so that toothbrushes, razors, tweezers, and other instruments that may carry blood are not shared. This is good advice not only for avoiding HIV infection but also for avoiding more common diseases. Remember that the lining of the rectum is fragile. Do not engage in activities that might damage the rectum. Unprotected oral-anal contact (rimming) should be avoided; it might spread the virus and certainly can transmit other diseases (such as amebiasis and hepatitis B).

Alcohol and nonmedical drugs impair judgment and lower the efficiency of the immune system. Avoid using nonmedical drugs, and be aware of the side effects of alcohol consumption. Poppers (amyl- or butyl-nitrate) inhalant drugs are immunosuppressive and may be associated with increased risk of contract AIDS. A spermicide called Nonoxynol-9 is found in some diaphragm contraceptive jellies and creams as well as on some lubricated condoms. It has been shown to kill the virus and so may help prevent transmission.

General health is also important. A person with any infection does better if he or she is well-nourished, rested, exercising regularly, not smoking, not drinking to excess, and not stressed out. The same is true with persons with an HIV infection. Note that urine may contain the virus and so should not be allowed to enter the mouth or come in contact with open cuts on the body. In order to protect themselves and their partners, HIV positive persons must evaluate their risk factors in order to determine how to modify their sexual behavior.

Counselors can assist HIV positive persons to follow the risk-reduction behaviors in any future sexual encounter. Simply reducing the number of different sexual partners provides no protection if a person continues to have unsafe sexual relations.

If persons are not sure whether a sexual partner belongs to one of these groups and they feel they cannot talk about sexual and drug use histories with their partner, then they should always follow risk-reduction guidelines. The guidelines divide common sexual behaviors into three categories of risk for transmitting HIV: high risk, no risk, and lower risk.

- **High-risk behaviors.** These involve the contact of blood or semen with mucous membranes and are therefore extremely dangerous. High-risk behaviors should be avoided at all costs if one of the partners may be carrying the HIV.
- **No-risk behaviors.** These do not involve any exchange of bodily fluids and are therefore completely safe; they can be practiced whether or not either of the partners is carrying the virus.
- **Lower risk behaviors.** The situation is less clear cut. Behaviors in this category involve some risk of the exchange of bodily fluids other than blood or semen. These fluids occasionally contain HIV, but at a lower concentration that makes infection less likely. Saliva is almost certainly safe, and preliminary studies suggest that oral sex is unlikely to transmit the virus. Despite this, it is impossible to prove that lower risk behaviors will never transmit the virus. The best that can be said is that these behaviors are much less dangerous than those in the high-risk category.

In cases where one or both sexual partners may be carrying the virus, the partners should carefully discuss which activities and what level of risk are acceptable to both of them.

General Precautions

General precautionary measures that clients—or anyone else—should be urged to take include the following:

1. If a client has been involved in any of the high-risk sexual activities or has injected illicit drugs into his or her body, the client may want to consider taking a blood test to see if he or she has been infected with the AIDS virus.
2. If the test is positive or if the client engages in high-risk activities and chooses not to have a test, the client should be counseled to tell his or her sexual partner(s). If the partners then jointly decide to have sex,

they must protect each other by always using a condom during inter-course.

3. If the client's partner has had a positive blood test showing that he or she has been infected with the AIDS virus and there is a possibility that he or she has been exposed by previous heterosexual or homosexual behavior or intravenous drug use with shared needles and syringes, a condom should always be used during sexual intercourse.

4. If the client is at high risk, mouth contact with the penis, vagina, or rectum should also be avoided.

5. The client should avoid all sexual activities that could cause cuts or tears in the linings of the rectum, mouth, vagina, or penis.

6. Clients should not have sex with prostitutes. Infected male and female prostitutes are frequently also intravenous drug abusers; therefore, they may infect clients via sexual intercourse and other intravenous drug abusers via sharing their intravenous drug equipment.

Thus the most certain way to avoid getting the AIDS virus and to control the AIDS epidemic in the United States is for individuals to avoid promiscuous sexual practices, maintain mutually faithful monogamous sexual relationships, avoid injecting illicit drugs, and use condoms.

Sexual transmission of HIV can be prevented only if precautions are taken. The need for precautions depends on whether either sexual partner is infected. If neither partner is infected then precautions need not be taken. If only one partner is infected, the most certain way to avoid transmission is to avoid having sexual intercourse. This does not preclude massage and mutual masturbation if there is no exposure of the mucous membranes (e.g., rectum, mouth, vagina, or penis) to body fluids of the infected partner.

Another approach that reduces, but does not eliminate, the risk of transmission is the consistent use of condoms or condoms plus spermicides.

Condoms. For individuals who wish to remain sexually active, the best protection against AIDS is condoms. They are recommended for use in oral sex, anal sex, and sexual intercourse. A study reported that in laboratory tests HIV cannot pass through either a synthetic or a natural skin condom, but many experts are skeptical and believe that natural skin condoms are more porous, offer less effective protection, and therefore should be avoided. It is important to note that condoms, which can break, leak, or be used improperly, are associated with an annual 10% failure rate in pregnancy prevention—and a woman is fertile only a few days of each month, whereas a person with the AIDS virus always has it. Improper use of condoms or a tear in the condom could lead to infection.

Counselors often assume that clients know how to use condoms and that specific instruction is not necessary. This assumption is often incorrect.

Women, for example, who have been in a long-term marriage, who have not had experience with partners other than their former spouse, may not have knowledge in this area. Many times men may have knowledge about condom usage but do not know that only specific types of condoms are effective against the AIDS virus. The following list provides a summary description of how to use condoms. It may be a useful handout for counselors to give to their sexually active clients.

How to Use Condoms Effectively:

1. The use of condoms is strongly suggested. If any individual is unsure of his or her partner's complete sexual history, a condom should always be used. Condoms are useful for preventing the transmission of HIV, and they also provide protection against such diseases as gonorrhea, chlamydial infections, syphilis, and herpes. Note that many other methods of birth control, such as using a diaphragm with a spermicide, do not provide adequate protection against the transmission of HIV infection and other venereal diseases.

2. When putting on a condom, leave about one-half inch of room at the tip to avoid semen breaking the condom upon ejaculation. If the penis is uncircumcised, retract the foreskin before putting on the condom. If intercourse is continued to ejaculation, withdraw promptly.

3. During withdrawal, hold the rim of the condom firmly against the penis so that the condom cannot slip off and no semen can escape.

4. Use proper lubrication. Lubrication is important to avoid tearing the condom or abrading body tissue. Always use a water-soluble lubricant, such as K-Y jelly. Never use oil-based lubricants such as Vaseline because these may damage the latex of the condom.

Spermicides. Spermicides containing nonionic surfactants have in vitro activity against syphilis, gonorrhea, and herpes simplex virus. One of these spermicides, Nonoxynol-9, kills HIV in vitro when tested in concentrations similar to those in the commercially available spermicide product. Uncontrolled epidemiologic studies suggest that women who consistently use spermicides have some protection against gonorrhea, but no studies have been done to evaluate whether the use of a lubricant containing Nonoxynol-9 is safer or effective in preventing sexually transmissible diseases during anal intercourse. Spermicides alone should be considered inadequate to protect one from HIV infection.

Other risk-reduction considerations. If both sexual partners are infected with HIV, the risk associated with unprotected sexual intercourse is not clear. It is not known if reinfection with the virus causes the disease to progress or if other sexually transmitted infections act as cofactors for the development of AIDS in people infected with HIV. Because such cofactors or coinfections are theoretically important, infected couples should take the same precautions with each other by avoiding intercourse or by using condoms consistently.

Further, if the infectious status of a sexual partner is not known, or if either partner is at risk (because of a history of a homosexual contact, intravenous drug use, hemophilia, or sexual contact with another person at risk), it is prudent to assume that the partner could be infected. Heterosexual contact with persons who have had multiple sexual contacts (i.e., prostitutes) also pose a risk for heterosexual transmission, particularly in areas where there is a high prevalence of infection among heterosexuals. Prevention efforts should concentrate on counseling people about ways to reduce risk of transmitting HIV infection. Gay men's organizations have been advising all gay men to practice safer sex at all times.

Other efforts could include educating the general public about the risks and the way infection is (and is not) transmitted. People can then make informed decisions whether to have sexual contact and know how to take precautions during sexual encounters with a partner who may be infected. The use of condoms could be increased by education, greater accessibility, and use of modern marketing techniques.

Even condoms are not 100% reliable in preventing transmission of the AIDS virus; using spermicidal jelly along with condoms is safer yet, but still not totally safe. The natural type of condom is unsatisfactory. For the time being stay with the rubber type.

The AIDS virus is contagious, and control of this disease may be facilitated by the willingness of AIDS patients and those at risk to modify their sexual behavior in ways that reduce the risk of transmitting the disease to others. These behavioral modifications also have direct personal health implications for affected individuals because they reduce the risk of acquiring further infections that may exacerbate the disease. At this time, a clear distinction among the healthy, the infectious, and the infected individual is not possible given the possible long incubation period of the disease.

All sexually active individuals are counseled to alter certain aspects of their sexual behavior that may increase the risk of acquiring any of the sexually transmitted diseases. These behavior changes include:

1. Reducing the number or partners
2. Avoiding anonymous sex partners
3. Modifying those sexual practices that may present a significant opportunity for the exchange of bodily fluids (stool, blood, urine, and semen)
4. Reducing use of volatile nitrites, barbiturates, amphetamines, intravenous and various other illicit drugs, and alcohol because they decrease the person's ability to control his or her behavior.

Implications for the Sexually Single

The appearance of this deadly disease has far reaching implications for the sexually single. First of all, a new type of sexual relating must take place: straightforward and open. The conversation must occur in the beginning of the relationship, not when both partners are in bed. The use of condoms must be discussed early on, and the relationship must be based on the results of that talk.

Clients must be educated about the nature of the AIDS virus and its transmission routes. They need to understand the importance of discussing all these factors with their potential sex partner prior to the bedroom scene. They need to role play with their therapist, discussing the specific words they will use and how and when they will inform their partner that they will not have sex without a condom. This is especially useful for women. Unfortunately, all too often women are educated about the AIDS virus, say they will use condoms, go through the role plays, and then, when they are in the situation, fail to tell their partner to use a condom. This is very distressing because they are putting themselves at tremendous risk. The reasons they give are typically something like "Well, he's only dated three people in the last 3 years so he's safe." Or "He's healthy and very athletic and hasn't been sick in the past 5 years." Or "I was too embarrassed to ask him to use a condom." Or worse yet, "I asked him, and he said he hates condoms, so I just went along with it. I'm sure I'm okay. "Sometimes the woman will tell the man to use a condom, and he will; and then 2 months later, she stops asking—somehow feeling that she knows him now and knows he's okay. These quotes, by the way, were not made by adolescents. They were made by professional, educated women, living in a large cosmopolitan city.

Unfortunately, the women may not be okay. The reasons for why women often do not take care of themselves are varied and complicated, many of them having to do with socially constructed notions about female assertive behavior or not wanting to hurt his feelings. However, being sexually single in the 1990s can be deadly if proper precaution is not taken.

AIDS-related fears are rapidly appearing in therapists' offices. Questions the therapist can explore with the sexually single client include the following:

- Given that AIDS exists, what do you feel you *should* change sexually?
- What do you feel you *have* to change?
- What do you think you *will* change?
- What do you miss about sex in the good old days, the Woodstock days, when sex was free, easy, frequent, and varied? What else do you miss? (If the client experienced the sexual liberation of the 1960s and 1970s and enjoyed it, help the client to mourn the losses.)
- What do you like about safer sex?

- What are some new things you can do, different sexual practices, using safer sex procedures?

The therapist should also:

- Help the client think about intimacy that does not involve genital sex.
- Ask the client to describe how to bring on safer sex with someone.
- Help the client understand that he or she has control over his or her life.
- Help women to understand that they have a right to protect themselves.

Of course, there are also the worried well:

> Ann M., a recently separated client, accepted an invitation to dinner. After the dinner, when the man drove her to her car, he passionately kissed her goodnight. This led to about an hour of passionate kissing in the car. Nothing more. The next morning, she raced to the doctor's office, convinced that she now had AIDS. She demanded and was given the AIDS test, which was negative. She then spent the next 6 months in the library reading everything she could about AIDS and had herself retested 6 months later. Ann M. is an example of the worried well.

Most sexually single people will not get AIDS, but many people worry about it. Depending upon their situation, worry is to be expected. Individuals need to learn to assess their risk realistically. If they have a significant risk factor and they are not following the risk-reduction guidelines, or if extreme anxiety is interfering with their normal living, they ought to explore this in counseling. Characteristic problems are depression, periods of celibacy punctuated by episodes of unsafe sex, and obsessive preoccupation with illness or symptoms.

To summarize: It is almost a decade since the AIDS virus first entered the U.S. population, and there is absolutely no evidence that the disease can be spread by casual contact—shaking hands, sharing meals, or just being near someone with the virus.

AIDS infection can be prevented by using safer sex practices, by having sex only with an uninfected partner, by avoiding sex with multiple partners. The use of condoms during sex can greatly decrease the possibility of transmitting the virus. Practices that injure body tissues (such as anal intercourse) should be avoided, as should oral-genital contact. Drug users should not share needles or syringes. Those addicts who continue to share needles are urged to sterilize needles with common household bleach.

AIDS is no longer the concern of any one segment of society; it is the concern of us all. No American's life is in danger if he or she does not engage in high-risk sexual behavior or use shared needles or syringes to inject illicit drugs into the body. People who engage in high-risk sexual behavior or who shoot drugs are risking infection with the AIDS virus and are risking their lives and the lives of others, including their unborn children.

The full impact of AIDS in our society is not yet known. From a clinical point of view there may be new manifestations of AIDS—for example, mental disturbances due to the infection of the brain by the AIDS virus in carriers of the virus. From a social point of view, it may bring an end to a free-wheeling sexual life style that has been called the sexual revolution. Economically, the care of AIDS patients puts a tremendous strain on our already overburdened and costly health care delivery system. Clinically, it is the therapist's responsibility to educate and help clients who are at risk to use safer sex practices.

PART III

SINGLE AGAIN AND DEALING WITH THE LARGER SYSTEMS

Chapter 9

SINGLE PARENTS, SCHOOL PERSONNEL, AND THE PATHOLOGY ASSUMPTION

Perhaps there is no greater challenge to the counselor's diagnostic skills than the formulation of an understanding concerning the school behavior and academic difficulties of a child from a single-parent family. In examining the literature on single-parent families, it was relatively easy to find research that supported a deficit model of the children living in these families. Many articles focused on the pathology and negativistic ramifications of the divorced family setting. Upon closer investigation, however, it became readily apparent that there were many methodological problems with this research (Emery, 1982; Marsh, 1990a).

In Guttman (1988), bias by teachers and school psychologists, participants in many studies, reflects a low reliability. Because these school personnel not only participate in evaluations of children but also read and utilize the studies for educational purposes, society causes and is reinforced by figures and observations that could be seriously questionable. Flawed teacher ratings of child behaviors have "raised doubt about studies concluding that children from two-parent families function better than do children of divorce" (Blechman, 1982, as cited in Guttman, p. 556).

The deficit model, supported or not by research, seems to enjoy wide acceptance. Guttman (1988) and Santrock (1972) discussed moral behaviors in terms of children of divorce and children from two-parent families. They concluded that differences could be found only on teacher ratings. This is interesting to note because other studies not using teacher ratings failed to find differences in school achievement test scores when comparing father-present and father-absent children. It is Guttman's contention that teacher ratings are based on stereotyped variables derived from middle-class expectations. It was observed that teachers rated boys and girls of divorce lower than those children from two-parent families, although girls were rated better than boys in either case.

155

A very important question arises in light of Guttman's discussion. Does teacher bias, in fact, cause lower student functioning for children of divorce? Is lower rating a self-fulfilling prophesy? In 1978, Santrock and Tracy showed a 20-minute video to 30 teachers. The subject was an 8-year-old boy. When teachers were told that the child was from a divorced family background, they rated him lower on happiness, emotional adjustment, and ability to cope with stress. This evolved into Santrock's and Tracy's Implicit Personality Theory and led Guttman (1988) to conduct a further study. Teachers were asked to view a film of a 9-year-old child from Tel Aviv. Student peers were also asked to view the same film. The teachers and students were told that the child was female or male to account for bias in terms of gender. The child was filmed to demonstrate 23 characteristics spanning emotional and other behaviors. Seven of the behaviors were school related. The subjects were asked to rate the child on a scale of 1 (lowest rating) to 5 (highest rating). The researchers concluded that children were judged less favorably if the rater was told that the child was from a divorced family. Teachers seemed to rate lower than did peer members of the rating panel. Female children of divorce, overall, were rated lower in academics than their male counterparts, but boys of divorce were rated as lower in the affective domain (emotions). The main point is that accurate assessment is made more difficult by the assumption often made by single parents, school officials, classroom teachers, and guidance counselors that the child's problems are always caused by the absence of one parent.

Many other questions have been raised by researchers in terms of bias. As Fassell (1991) suggested, we need to question the manner in which research in the area of divorce reflects the bias of society in favor of the two-parent family. She feels that with research carrying the implication that children of divorce are flawed, the implication follows that these children will eventually make flawed choices themselves. This is not necessarily true.

Although, initially, locating citations was not an easy task, there has been research that supports the position that there can be positive outcomes for children of divorce. These studies are presented here not to convince the reader that divorce should be a precondition for academic achievement but rather that all children do not suffer academically from this transition. When the literature, hypotheses, and interpretations focus on pathology and dysfunction in these children, they serve in many cases to create self-fulfilling prophesies. It is time that professionals working with these children examine their own assumptions about these children so that they do no more harm. The results of a number of methodologically sound studies that examined academic scores of children in single-parent families have clearly indicated that there is no one academic reaction to living in a single-parent family: some children have problems, some children show no effect, and some children improve.

Watts and Watts (1991) studied over 4,000 Canadian high school students from two-parent and female-headed single-parent families. They found that ability and educational aspirations of the student have the largest direct effect on student academic achievement, whereas the effect of family configuration (one parent vs. two parent) was negligible. The authors rated academic orientation, self-concept, involvement of significant others, involvement of parents, and even socioeconomic status as better indicators than the marital status of their parents. Other factors, such as whether the children witnessed any physical violence in their home prior to the onset of the single parent family life and the attitude of the mother toward her status as a single parent, were seen to be more important factors in determining the outcomes of divorce for children.

McCombs and Forehand (1989) studied low, medium, and high achieving adolescents and found that the two variables most accounting for the variance between low and high grade achievers were mother's reports of conflict between her and her ex-spouse in front of the child, and the adolescent's report of the intensity of conflict between him- or herself and the mother. These findings indicated that school performance after divorce is far from uniform and possibly caused by more complex factors than the divorce itself.

In a review of studies between 1970 and 1980, Cashion (1982) concluded that children in female-headed single-parent homes are likely to have good emotional adjustment, good self-esteem, and school success, and do as well in school as children from two-parent families when socioeconomic factors are controlled.

Wood and Lewis (1990) compared 32 second and fourth grade boys and girls from divorced-mother-custody families with a control group from two-parent homes. They examined family structure (one parent or two parents), coparental relationship variables (trust, frequency of contact, and quality of coparental relationship), and the children's behavioral adjustment at school. In contrast to earlier studies, they found no significant differences in behavior problems between children of single- and two-parent homes. Structure of family was not found to be a significant predictor variable accounting for variance in children's school behavior. However, two of the three coparental relationship variables were significant predictors: A lower frequency of coparental interaction was related to greater number of incidences of acting-out behavior in school, and low quality/high conflict coparental relationships were significantly related to acting-out behaviors and distractibility. These results imply that children's behavioral problems are impacted more by problems in the family system (as evidenced by difficult coparental relationships) than by divorce and single-parent status. In other words, divorce itself is neither positive or negative, and the outcomes of divorce are at least in part a function of the behavior of the parents. Thus these researchers cautioned teachers to be aware of basing their judgment of a student's behavior or school performance on their assumptions about the home life of the child, in particular on the child's status as a member of a single-parent family.

The term *resiliency* is discussed in an article by Hetherington, Stanley-Hagan, and Anderson (1989) in that some children exhibit remarkable resiliency and in the long term may actually be enhanced by coping with these transitions. However, although the adjustment of children is related to the adaptation and behavior of parents, what may be a positive event for one family member is not necessarily so for another, and some suffer developmental delays or disruptions. It is interesting to note that only about one third of the divorce group subjects fell into the category of vulnerable in the academic domain. In contrast to the monolithic view that children who experience parental divorce are universally maladjusted, the majority of adolescents from divorced families in the sample demonstrated relatively successful academic careers. The fact that these youngsters were evidencing healthy adjustment in the classroom is interesting. They did not resemble the children of divorce as they usually are portrayed in the literature. Instead, the data indicated that sweeping generalizations must not be made about these children, not only in the domain of academic performance but also in other areas.

Among longitudinal studies dealing with performance and children of divorce is a 5-year study (Kaye, 1989) that involved 457 students (50% from two-parent homes). This research revealed that although achievement scores dropped in the months after divorce, the overall grades did not seem to be adversely affected. The study also revealed that a crisis model of divorce is only partially correct and needs to be complemented by a cumulative stress model focusing on the problems that persist or gradually increase following divorce.

Perhaps the most impressive study was done by the National Center for Educational Statistics (Marsh, 1990b). These researchers tracked a large representative sample of high school students. Across all the various comparisons and all the different outcomes, family configuration had remarkably little effect on student growth and changes during the last 2 years of high school. The lack of effect of single-parent and stepparent families was also consistent for boys and girls in single-mother, single-father, mother-stepfather, and father-stepmother families.

Further research regarding effects of divorce on academic performance was cited by Beer (1989a, 1989b). In this study there were no significant effects for the composite score from the Iowa Tests of Basic Skills when compared to marital status of parents.

According to Gately and Schwebel (1991), divorced parents who value and use appropriate support from friends, counselors, and relatives experience a more positive postdivorce adjustment (Woody, Colley,

Schlegelmilch, & Maginn, 1984). The same is true of children. Support given directly to children by peers, relatives, teachers, guidance counselors, and other caretakers can promote social competencies and reduce behavioral problems. A supportive school environment can facilitate a favorable postdivorce adjustment in children. Although having counseling resources available is beneficial, simply having a safe, orderly, and predictable school environment with high expectations and norms for achievement is associated with positive emotional, behavioral, and academic postdivorce outcomes in children (Guidubaldi, 1983).

Children respond to expectations. Mothers, teachers, guidance counselors, and other involved adults should explore their expectations of children from single-parent families. Do adults expect these children to have problems at home and to fail in school? Or do adults expect these children to be happy and independent with good cognitive abilities and good verbal skills? Children respond to adult expectations and benefit from positive expectations. Stigma is associated with low self-esteem in children, and it results in defining the children as problems even when they do not have problems. It additionally undermines their sense of confidence. Academic personnel can counteract possible stigmatizing effects on children in these families if they are not pessimistic about their success.

In the following sections, some of the more subtle factors that impact upon the assessment/intervention process are considered. An appreciation of these factors helps counselors avoid simplistic diagnoses.

Challenging "Reality"

Mrs. K's divorce had been finalized 6 months prior to the phone call she received from her daughter's fifth grade teacher. The girl's work had been slipping, and she tended to avoid socializing with the other children. During her meeting with the teacher, Mrs. K mentioned the divorce. The next week, with no warning or notification, the girl found herself in a group for children from single-parent families that was conducted by one of the school's guidance counselors.

As incredible as the story sounds, it is true. It illustrates a seminal difficulty in the assessment of children from single-parent families: the belief that death or divorce causes behavioral and academic difficulties. Cognitive psychologists (e.g., Meichenbaum, 1977) and constructivist family therapists (e.g., White & Epston, 1990) suggest that people and systems of people selectively attend to and react to only some portions of reality. They use this selective attention process and language (Mince, 1992) to create a reality for themselves and to co-create a shared reality with others. They behave, believe, and feel as if their subjectively held views are factually true.

It appears as if Mrs. K, the teacher, and the guidance counselor have co-created a reality in which divorce begets academic problems.

Hodges (1991) in his encyclopedic work on dealing with children from divorced families offered a significantly different reality:

> When a child from a divorced home has emotional or behavioral problems, the general assumption is that the problems were caused by the divorce. Statements such as "that child is aggressive because he comes from a two-parent family" are unlikely to be made, even though they may be truer than assumptions that behavior problems in a child from a divorced family were caused by the divorce. (p. 19)

Hodges also pointed out that "The literature and clinical experience reviewed in this chapter have not indicated that delinquency, serious academic problems, depression, and suicide are likely long-term outcomes . . ." (p. 47).

Peck and Manocherian (1988) in their discussion of divorce, and Walsh and McGoldrick (1991) in their consideration of the effect of parental death, also attacked the pathology model of single-parent families. These authors have understood death and divorce to superimpose a list of developmental demands around the issues of separation, loss, and establishment of a new family structure upon the more normative developmental demands on the family and its individual members. If the two sets of developmental tasks are in conflict, behavioral and emotional symptom etiology can occur.

Consider the fairly typical situation in which an older sibling takes on a number of functions previously carried out by the parent now missing. If the family is flexible enough to allow this parental child to also be a child, the result can be beneficial to the remaining parent, the siblings, and the child her- or himself. If, however, the system demands that the child's agenda must be abandoned in deference to the needs of the parent, this parental child can become overburdened and distracted (Brown & Samis, 1986/1987). Preto (1988) described the situation:

> This type of control is often seen in families where . . . forces operate to keep members from leaving the system . . . The message is given that separation is dangerous . . . Members of families that are so tightly bound attempt to meet each others' needs, but fail to promote growth. As a result, adolescents may become stuck when they feel the urgency to grow, but stay home to meet the parents' needs. Parents experience a similar dilemma when fears

of loss interfere with their attempts to help the children grow. The dilemma is often solved by adopting symptomatic behavior.

The adoption of a developmental view of single-parent families is one way in which counselors can avoid the pathology assumption; and appreciation of family structure and communication flow is another (Genovese, 1992). Fulmer (1983) suggested that the covert rules governing a family's interaction may result in behavioral problems in the children. He described one family in which, through counseling, the family's covert rules became overt: Mother must not be allowed to cry; the children act up in order to deflect her sadness; when the children act up, mother directs her attention outward to them and away from her own grief; then mother labels them as bad, not sad.

Knowledge of the literature is also of value to counselors in keeping themselves and their clients from making the gravely reductionistic pathology assumption. Hodges' work (1986, 1991) and the extensive literature review done by Lowery and Settle (1984) indicated that although some research supports the idea that children of divorce are at a disadvantage, other studies point out areas in which these children do better than children from two-parent families. It is important for counselors to be aware of the many factors that can cause academic and behavioral problems in children from single-parent families.

That the stress often accompanying the formation of a single-parent family may impact upon the children and manifest as school problems is not questioned. The counselor's role, however, is not to observe the correlation between family restructuring and academic performance. It is rather to do a thorough assessment of the interacting factors that give rise to and maintain symptoms. The counselor's role is to be aware that often it is not the death or the divorce that lies at the heart of the problem. In many cases other causes such as the residual effects of having lived in an anxiety-filled two-parent family prior to the death or divorce, or the impact of greatly reduced family income, of continued postdivorce parental conflict, or of the existence of growth-stunting relationships with extended family members, friends, and social institutions, may all play important roles in the functioning of single-parent families.

Assessing the Child

The observation that most academic problems vary in their intensity across different situations is not lost upon scholars and educational theorists. Graduate schools of education insist that the proper unit of assessment is not the individual child in isolation but rather the child in the context of his or her environmental envelope. Tombari and Davis (1979) wrote that:

> . . . problems may be of a social-emotional or academic nature involving attitudes, self-concepts, assertion, obedience, reading comprehension, penmanship, math computation, or creative writing. . . . Underlying behavioral consultation is the assumption that the root of the child's problems lies in the setting in which it takes place. Thus, any plans to change children's behavior must involve manifestation of immediate environmental events. (p. 288)

There is commonly a gap between theory and professional practice, however. In dealing with academic difficulties, it is incumbent upon the counselor to assess how the school defines the child's problem. Through consultations with teachers and other school officials, and direct observation of the child in school, the counselor can identify the assumptions (both administrator and classroom teacher) concerning the cause and maintenance of problematic behaviors. The work of the cognitive psychologists and constructionist family therapists provide the counselor with entry into one level of problem analysis: the school's assumptions may be powerful influences on the child's behavior in that they can set up self-fulfilling prophesies.

Psychoeducational Models

Ysseldyke's (1979) work can be help the counselor in ascertaining how the school defines problems. He described five different theoretical positions concerning the nature of academic difficulties. The *medical model* is a deficit model assuming that abnormality is the result of biological factors. Environmental or sociocultural factors play no role in assessment and diagnosis within this model. In the *social-system (deviance) model*, the assumption is that there are many definitions of normal behaviors, and that these definitions are determined by social role expectations. This is a deficit/asset model. For example, the aggressive behavior that a boy shows at school may be abnormal from a student-role perspective but may be highly adaptive when assessed from an abused-child-role view. School interventions involve teaching the child requisite socially expected behaviors when he or she is in the student role.

The *psychoeducational process model* assumes that a child's academic performance is caused by an idiosyncratic pattern of strengths and weaknesses among a number of universal underlying cognitive processes. In this model, the school assessment/intervention process is deficit focused. The deficits are viewed as existing solely within the individual child. In the *pluralistic model*, academic problems are assumed as resulting from the demand that children from all sociocultural backgrounds behave like white middle-class children.

In the *task-analysis model*, academic difficulties of all sorts are seen as predicated on the nonattainment of subskills that are necessary for the performance of more complex behaviors. Skills are assumed to be hierarchical, and the acquisition of complex skills is understood as dependent upon the development of adequate lower level behaviors. Assessment involves finding the student's current position in the skill hierarchy. Intervention consists of teaching the component subskills required for advancement through the hierarchy. In this model of assessment, the child's performance is not compared to that of a norming group but rather to his or her previous performance. Such an approach obviates the problems of validity, reliability, and inappropriate norms that plague assessments carried out by standardized tests.

Hill (1978) demonstrated the value and power of understanding skills as hierarchy. In her study of antisocial adolescent boys with long histories of academic failure, poor relationships with peers and teachers, aggressiveness, negativism, general depression, and hyperactivity, task analysis was employed to study the preconditions required for success in school. These preconditions focused on the personal interaction between the student and the tutor, and the student's acceptance of the tutor. Included were coming to and staying at the sessions, trying a game or craft, accepting primary and social reinforcements from the tutor, and accepting limits with regard to acting-out behavior. Increases in measures of academic achievement after the attainment of the preconditions were reported.

A theoretical position taken by school personnel that combines an appreciation of both skill hierarchies and the importance of environmental factors in the maintenance of problems is prognostic of progress. A position that assumes a deficit, found solely within the confines of the individual student's skin, is contraindicative of good outcome. As consultant to the school and to the single-parent family, the counselor should strive to coconstruct with all involved the most efficacious reality concerning the nature of the child's academic difficulties.

Self-Fulfilling Prophesies

At another level of analysis, diagnosis is informed by the works of Dusek (1975), Brophy and Everston (1978), Dusek and Joseph (1983), and many others who have studied the highly complex interactions between teacher expectations and children's performance. Although it is a vast oversimplification to imply that a self-fulfilling prophecy on the teacher's part is the only potent variable in academic problems, it is safe to assume that the efforts of the school, the student, the family, and the counselor are enhanced by rejecting the reductionistic assumption that single parenthood per se is the pathologic agent. Some school officials are aware that school personnel are vulnerable in this regard. Writing in *Principal*, Ourth and Zakariya (1982) pointed out the desperate need for in-service training for classroom teachers, guidance counselors, and school administrators to address the questions:

> Do we, in our own minds, attach a stigma to separation and divorce? Do we automatically expect the worst when we learn that a child's parents have separated? Are we sensitive to the signs, many of them subtle, that signal real confusion and stress in a child? Do we recognize, and openly acknowledge, the strength and independence many children develop when they learn to cope with that confusion and stress? (p. 31)

In the same issue of *Principal*, Zakariya (1982) discussed the analysis of a study that reported significantly higher achievement scores for children from two-parent families. In-depth analysis, however, indicated that the family's income and the gender of the student had greater effects on achievement scores than did the number of parents in the home. Children from single-parent homes were greatly overrepresented in the low-income group. Only 17.5% of the students studied came from single-parent homes, but they comprised 41% of the lower income group: "This relationship indicates that many factors negatively influencing achievement may be more readily formed in the one-parent home. It does not necessarily say that single parentness is the problem" (p. 36).

Henderson (1981) acknowledged the need to provide in-service training for school personnel in order to challenge certain pervasive myths: the structure of the family has more effect on the child than does the emotional climate of the home; having divorced parents means that the child has only one parent; the single parent's life style is detrimental to the development of a child's mortality; children from a broken home can always be identified; to grow up properly, a child must have both male and female role models present in the home. Henderson cited evidence for the value of group counseling for single parents and for their children that is carried out within the school district. In both the children's and the parents' groups, members were asked to share information on tasks and roles in the new family structure. The focus was on validating the new aspects of the self that each individual developed. The reality that single parenthood, for all its difficulties, represents an opportunity to grow was co-created by the counselors, the parents, and the children.

In assessing the quality of school-based group interventions with children of divorce, the guidelines provided by Hodges (1991) are most helpful. To be effective groups should have the full support of the school's administration, require parental permission before a student is placed, take place during regular school hours, ensure that information shared in group is kept confidential from both teachers and parents, and include pre- and posttreatment meetings for parents. Counselors should remain aware that not all interventions work equally well with all children.

Failure Analysis

A central task in any sophisticated problem analysis is the understanding of why previously attempted solutions have failed. Failure analysis often leads to the formulation of more accurate hypotheses concerning the child's behavior problem.

Consider the following hypothetical situation:

> *Twelve-year-old Bill has been acting up in school since the beginning of the semester. In consultation with the boy's teacher and the school psychologist, Bill's mother institutes a behavior modification program. Both at school and at home, Bill's target behaviors are closely monitored. Frequency records are kept. Charts depicting the occurrence of target behaviors are displayed. Increases in the frequency of adaptive responses and decreases in problematic behaviors are positively reinforced by the teacher at school and by the mother at home. One month after the program is in effect, Bill's behavior is worse than ever. School officials and the mother are convinced that Bill's problems stem from his parents' recent divorce. The officials and the mother agree that a counselor should be consulted to help Bill in dealing with separation issues.*

If our fictitious counselor is one who does a thorough analysis, he or she may discover that Bill's problems are not caused by the historical effects of the separation and divorce but rather by current interactional patterns. The counselor may determine that since the divorce, Bill's mother has related to the boy as her primary attachment figure (Bowlby, 1980). Her involvement with him has been extreme, as have been her subtle demands that he adopt behavior and attitudes more appropriate for an adult than for a preteenager. As a result, the boy acts in anxious and symptomatic ways.

Failure analysis indicates that the behavior modification solution to the problem was sure to fail. By intensifying both the school's and the mother's focus on Bill, the solution appears to magnify the interactional processes that originally gave rise to the problem.

The counselor who was consulted concerning Bill's behavior problems was called in after the family and the school had made a formal and intentional decision to attempt to solve the problem. This is not always the case.

Schools tend to respond to behavior problems differently than to academic problems. Children who are mentally retarded, learning disabled, or hearing or vision impaired often act inappropriately; but all children at some time act inappropriately. Usually, the essential difference between the behaviors of normal children and behavior-disordered children is in the intensity and duration of their behaviors, not in the behaviors themselves (Kirk & Gallagher, 1989).

In those cases in which the duration and intensity of a child's academic and behavior disorders have not reached severe problematic levels, the counselor is positioned to be most helpful to the child. Within the unique context of consultant to both family and school, the counselor is able to help coordinate the efforts of both systems, aid in the clear flow of communication between the systems, encourage the use of those school and family factors that positively impact on the child's behavior, and intervene with regard to factors that are growth stunting. To do so well, the counselor's assessment of the family must be as sophisticated as that of the school environment.

Assessing the Family

Counselors who adopt a systemic view of families share a basic philosophical orientation with interactionist educational theorists: behavior is best understood in the context within which it occurs (Nichols, 1984). A systemic epistemology allows a counselor to understand that symptomatic children from single-parent families are reacting to separation issues, and that this factor may not be the primary maintainer of the problematic behavior in all cases. The systemic approach allows for the possibility that the child who is doing poorly is the symptom bearer who most overtly expresses the dysfunction of the entire family (Goldenberg & Goldenberg, 1991). Analysis of this possibility results in a sophisticated approach to the assessment/diagnosis process.

Some theorists understand symptomatic behavior in children from single-parent homes as the result of an incongruity between the developmental tasks appropriate to the child's age and those of reorganizing a family's basic structure following the departure of one parent (Pack & Manocherian, 1988; Walsh & McGoldrick, 1991). An example is the parental child mentioned earlier: the centripetal forces at play as a family restructures may bind a teenager so tightly to the family that his or her own individuation is stunted. Peck and Manocherian (1988) and Hodges (1991) both provided excellent outlines of the developmental needs of children at various stages of development, and described how the process of transforming from a two- to one-parent system may impact on those needs.

In assessing families from a systemic perspective, counselors move beyond the individual—the monad—to dyadic and triadic analysis. To do so effectively, an appreciation of the Bowenian concept of triangles is required (Kerr & Bowen, 1988). Bowen believed that when a dyad becomes stressed it behaves in predictable, although subtle ways. This concept helps conceptualize these automatic systemic phenomena and suggests that when families become stressed, the tension between a pair of persons is diluted by bringing in a third party. This unconscious solution is short-lived. As the anxiety gets transferred from person to person to person within the triangle, more anxiety is generated than originally existed. Counselors should become familiar with Bowen's theory and with techniques designed to "detriangulate."

In describing the function of the triangle, Papero (1990) made several important clinical observations. It is not uncommon in any stressed pair for one of the two to feel the interpersonal anxiety more than the other. When the felt anxiety surpasses a tolerant level, the stressed partner automatically forms a relationship with a third person. The formation of this relationship tends to lower the experience of anxiety in the originally stressed partner. If, however, the relationship with the third partner is highly intense, the process can generate more anxiety than it absorbs. Papero (1990) gave the example of the affair: an affair of low-to-moderate intensity can, at least for a time, relieve the tension in a marital dyad; but a high-intensity affair can lead to the creation of a huge degree of stress upon the marriage. Children are often the third leg of a triangle, and as such are at risk.

Guerin and Katz (1984) have used their understanding of triangles in dealing with children's school problems. Families of these children usually are involved with one or more of five factors: (1) the symptomatic child is emotionally vulnerable within the family, and this vulnerability is played out among peers or in school; (2) explicit conflict exists between the child and a school authority figure, usually the teacher; (3) covert conflict between the child and one or both of the parent is displaced into a conflict between the child and the teacher; (4) the child has a special relationship with the teacher that makes the child a target of unfavored, but powerful, classmates; and (5) the child is caught up in a triangle based on a conflict, overt or covert, between the parent and the teacher (p. 29). Any of these situations can lead to antisocial behavior or underachievement in school.

Guerin and Katz (1984) described several common triangles that may, among other things, cause academic difficulties. At any moment in time, two of the three individuals are strongly connected, in either a calm or an agitated way. The third person occupies a more distant position from the other two. Trangulating emotional patterns are understood to be most damaging when the positions become relatively fixed.

Most typically, in the Primary-Parent Triangle, the emotional make-up of the family involves an overclose relationship between the mother and child, with the father in the outside position. The mother and child are overly sensitive to each other's level of emotional arousal. Increases in the mother's level of anxiety from an unrelated source, such as continued stress with a former spouse, can be transmitted to the child. Problem behaviors appear as the child's anxiety increases. The child may also become the target of the parent who occupies the outsider position.

In the Parent-Sibling Triangle, the symptomatic child usually occupies an inside position with the parent, and a sibling is on the outside. A variation of this structure is very common in single-parent families. The leadership vacuum created when the single parent leaves for work each day is filled by one of the siblings, most usually the eldest daughter. Not only is this child burdened with much responsibility and with the lack of real power to carry it out, she must vacate the position when the parent returns home. When conflict between the parent and daughter arises, often the daughter overtly displaces it onto a younger sibling. The relationship with the parent becomes distant and passive-aggressive in nature. The younger child is the one most likely to express anxiety in the form of school-related problems.

In the Parent-Child-Teacher Triangle, parent-child conflict is displaced onto the relationship between the child and the teacher. Variations of this triangle include the child's acting out of the parents' anger at the teacher. This pattern is common in families when the parent is a teacher or other professional who feels that his or her expertise is not sufficiently appreciated by the teacher. In another variation, something about the symptomatic child triggers an emotional reaction from the teacher. The source of the teacher's anxiety is to be found in some relationship other than that with the child. When the patient joins with the teacher to "fix" the problem, the teacher's focus on the child intensifies, as do the problem behaviors.

Herz Brown (1988) also suggested the analysis of triangles when working with single-parent families. Central to Herz Brown's thinking is the experience of a power gap in these family systems. Feeling incapable of doing all the disciplining and nurturing required for the healthy development of her children, the single parent often triangulates with the school and extended family members to fill in the perceived power vacuum.

Herz Brown (1988) described how the economic deprivation that often accompanies the formation of a single-parent family can create troublesome triangles with the single parent's own parents. If (as suggested in Nancy's case in chapter 3) in moving in or in accepting financial help, the single parent and her parent(s) recreate an earlier family structure in which the parent is subordinate to her own parents, then the power gap between the single parent and her children also increases.

Should the single parent surrender her right to discipline her children to the school, the same loss of parental power ensues. Isaacs (1987) believed that many symptomatic children in single-parent families have chosen to ignore their own well-being in the service of protecting and helping an overtly stressed single parent. Such a family structure creates a completely reversed power hierarchy in the family: the child becomes nurturer to the parent.

Many authors agree that often it is the continuing conflict between former spouses that leads to problems with the children (Herz Brown, 1988). Meyer's (1992) outline of various types of relationships between parents serves as a guide to assessment. In situations with one cooperative and one uncooperative former spouse, conflict is often caused and maintained by the person who feels that he or she was abandoned by the other. When both spouses are uncooperative, the level of anger is often such that they avoid direct contact. "During these recuperative periods, they work on each other indirectly through the children. Unfortunately, the children suffer from these indirect attacks, even if they themselves are not victims" (p. 163). Meyer appears here to have identified another triadic relationship. In yet another scenario, oppositional former spouses create a love-hate relationship characterized by alternating hostile outbursts and honeymoons. Should one of the honeymoons result in a temporary reconciliation followed by another separation, the impact on children can be devastating (Hodges, 1991).

Guerin, Fay, Burden, and Kaulto (1987) have identified the child-as-refuge triangle, the target-child triangle, and the tug-of-war triangle. In each, a child may become symptomatic as a result of being drawn into parental conflict. In the child-as-refuge triangle, the parent who more acutely feels the anxiety caused by an unsatisfactory marital relationship forms a special relationship with one of the children. The move, as in all triangulations, calms the marital dyad temporarily. The target child is found in an overly close relationship with one of his or her parents. The outside parent directs anger, actually meant for the spouse, at the target child. Although relieving dyadic tension momentarily, this deflection of hostility often causes problems for the child. The tug-of-war triangle is common in single-parent family systems. In this situation, each parent showers the child with affection, attention, and gifts in order to become the child's favorite and to exclude the other parent. (Keep in mind that these triangles can also occur in the two-parent family system.)

Assessing School and Family Interaction

An assessment of a single-parent family is a sophisticated undertaking, as is the analysis of school factors discussed. The counselor's work is made more difficult in that an analysis of the interaction between the two systems is also called for.

Okun (1984) observed that the counselor:

> . . . must consider the reciprocal influences of the family and school systems and the possible impacts of these influences on the child in order to understand fully the possible impacts of these influences on the child . . . [and] the child's behavior in terms of transactions and relationships within subsystems and the larger system. Without assessing the degree of congruence between the operating rules of the family and those of the school system, without evaluating information provided by both parents and teachers regarding the child, and without actually observing the child in both the family and classroom settings, the therapist will overlook important data. (pp. 7–8)

The counselor must also be aware of any form of miscommunication between the family and the school even in those cases when both systems agree on certain rules.

Consider the reciprocal effects of family and school interactions:

> *Mrs. Y is overwhelmed by the responsibilities of single parenthood and expects the school to control her 17-year-old son's behavior effectively at school. The school believes that the boy's behavior problems are related to his mother's permissiveness. The teachers and the school disciplinarian are vigilant for any infraction, and punishment is swift. In actuality, the boy is being punished for offenses committed by many others and which go unpunished by the school. When Mrs. Y is informed of yet another problem at school, she becomes furious: the boy will be grounded for a full month, including weekends. As a result of the miscomminication between the school and the family, the boy is caught in an ever-escalating punishment paradigm.*

Both the mother and the school wish to positively impact upon the boy's behavior. Each perceives an inability on the part of the other to be effective; however, the coconstructed reality is that each believes that they must work alone, and that the best strategy is to employ preventive measures. An analysis of the interaction between the two systems suggests to the counselor more potent intervention strategies than does the assessment of either system in isolation.

Jones (1987) provided another example of uncoordinated family-school interaction in the maintenance of problems. Many schools have a strong interest in promoting parental involvement in academic and behavior problems. If a single parent, either through guilt or a sense of being totally responsible for the welfare of her child, finds it impossible to say "No" to the large number of meetings, exercises, and evaluations suggested by the school, she may find herself living a life centered around the child.

As a result, the needs of the parent and of other children in the family may be neglected.

The Role of the Professional Counselor

The role of the counselor is to coordinate the efforts of the school and family in the resolution of the problem. This is no mean task. Not only must the counselor be knowledgeable about both education and counseling literatures, he or she must also be able to form relationships with family members and school personnel that allow for effectively joining with the two systems. Specifically, the counselor must:

- Strive to avoid the serious error of treating the single-parent family generically (Jones, 1987)
- Strive to avoid the reductionistic pathology model of the single-parent family
- Predicate treatment based upon a thorough analysis of school factors, family factors, and the interaction between the two systems
- Join both the family and the school system in an active fashion but not become part of a particular alliance or coalition
- Be informed of the ways in which school systems operate and conversant with educational jargon
- Be informed of the ways in which family systems operate and able to understand family interactions, roles, rules, as they relate to academic and behavior problems in the school
- Be vigilant with regard to confidentiality issues in acting as consultant to two systems.

The counselor must also be aware that single parents are faced with many reality problems and take the position that the parent actively seeks assistance with these problems. To this end, the counselor makes available to the single parent information on such vital referral sources as the family court support collection unit; personal health division for women, infants, and children; community health centers; social service referral department; county child support services; day care services; county employment programs; food stamp information services; public assistance information; local women's services; and local job service agencies.

Further, the counselor must encourage the family to avoid viewing single parenthood as a temporary family structure (Herz Brown, 1988). Thus the counselor must explore the possibilities for growth and happiness as well as deal with difficulties and dispute any coconstructed reality that suggests the family can wait until some ill-defined white knight appears and solves its problems.

The counselor needs to be aware of the many theories of development found in the professional literature, including Freud's (1952) theory of psychosexual development, Erickson's (1963) of psychosocial development, and Kohlberg's (1969) of moral development. For dealing with children, Piaget's (1952) work on cognitive development suggests which techniques are most appropriate with a particular youngster.

Entire family systems, as well as individuals, can be understood from a developmental point of view (Carter & McGoldrick, 1980, 1988). Walsh and McGoldrick (1991), Parkes and Weiss (1983), and Bowlby (1980) have discussed the developmental course of the mourning process. Herz Brown (1988) as well as Peck and Manocherian (1988) considered the stages of development that entire family systems must negotiate following divorce, while Wallerstein and Kelly (1980c) and Hetherington, Cox, and Cox (1985) traced the same journey more from the perspective of the individual.

The number of different theoretical approaches to development is large, but all share certain common elements. As individuals and family systems grow and develop, demands are placed upon them to respond in increasingly complex and more articulated ways. Some of these demands are primarily internal, such as when the toddler first acquires language or the ability to crawl. The development of the child, of course, engenders a demand that the family adapt appropriately. Other demands are initiated by the family of societal institutions: Children are expected to attend the lessons at school; families expect that children exhibit greater degrees of self-control as they mature. Some external demands are normative. For example, families in Western societies expect to deal with the question of bladder and bowel control. Such demands are nonnormative in the sense that society has provided neither individuals nor family systems with adequate models for the successful negotiation of a particular set of developmental tasks. In this sense, the change from a two-parent to a single-parent family system is an example of a nonnormative developmental process.

Developmental theorists and counselors who adopt a developmental stance regard symptoms not as indicators of psychopathology but as problems in negotiating phase-specific demands. The problem—the symptom—may result from an attempt to use strategies that were adaptive in earlier stages but that no longer are appropriate for the advanced development of the entire family system and of the individuals who comprise the system. For example, the effective discipline of toddlers calls for an essentially one-way, authoritative flow of communication from parents to children in a context of love, care, and concern for the well-being of the young ones. Parents of young children do not need the input of the children to know that running into the street is an unacceptable behavior on the part of a 3 year old. Parents who attempt democratic solutions to such problems by attempting to negotiate rules with children place the children at risk. Toddler are not ready to make this sort of decision.

Regardless of how successful the rule "Parents know best and make decisions for the children" may be through toddlerhood, the family that tries to extend its use with adolescent children is also putting the children at risk. The mutual weaning of parents and children is the primary developmental task of adolescence. The weaning is prerequisite if the children are to become independent adults capable of forming their own relationships, and if the parents' ability is to continue to grow.

The professional counselor is aware of the specific developmental tasks clients are attempting to negotiate and is able to frame problems in developmental terms.

Counseling Strategies

Assessment, unbiased by the pathology assumption, begins even before the counselor meets the family. The initial phone call provides only the merest outline of the difficulty: a child or children from a single-parent family is experiencing academic difficulties. How does a counselor ascribe meaning to the family's story? Is the counselor's thinking directed by deficit models of the family, or does the counselor assume an unbiased position? Hodges (1991) said it best: "It is presumptuous to assume that every problem is due to unresolved childhood conflict" (p. 286). It is also presumptuous to assume that every problem within a single-parent family is due to unresolved loss reactions.

The Education Model

The child's problem in school may simply reflect a lack of skills or knowledge on the part of either the child or the parent with regard to the sorts of behaviors that lead to success in school. As defined by Hodges (1991), skill implies knowing how to do what needs to be done, and knowledge implies knowing what needs doing. Counselors are well positioned to help families in both areas.

Consider, for example, the possible impact of being a parental child, as described earlier. It is common, and may be growth promoting, that children in single-parent families take on additional tasks and more responsibilities than children with two parents. There are simply fewer hands to do what needs to be done in order for the system to run smoothly. It is not growth promoting, however, when being a parental child expands into areas beyond the child's capacity. Putting the child in charge of all of his or her own academic decisions is also not healthy or growth promoting.

Structural Moves

Herz Brown (1988) described how many overburdened single parents tend to divest themselves of parental authority in the daily interactions with their children. Awareness of the potential impact of being a parental child with regard to study behaviors allows the counselor to provide parents with the knowledge that children need their leadership and guidance in this area. The generational boundary-making techniques of Minuchin and Fishman (1981) are of value in this process. For example, the counselor and parent discuss the problem together, with the children at a peripheral position in the room; the children brainstorm solutions to the problem that are subsequently evaluated by the parent.

Sherman and Fredman (1986) suggested a number of structural moves designed to reinforce generational boundaries and to support the parental position in the family's power hierarchy. Among these are seating the parent apart from the children during sessions; allotting different household tasks to the children and the parent; meeting alone in executive session with the parent to deal with parenting issues; asking parental permission to interact with the children; reinforcing the need for privacy by instituting a closed-door policy for the parent's and children's rooms; scheduling alone time for both parent and children; allying with the parent in matters of discipline; encouraging the parent to conference with other adults and school personnel, and not with the children, concerning the problem; encouraging mature, controlled parental behavior and discouraging frustration-propelled, regressive parental behavior; encouraging age-appropriate behavior on the part of both parent and children; and helping the parent and children contract responsibilities, duties, and consequences of behavior.

The counselor can help provide requisite skills through the use of basic behavioral principles. Stimulus control procedures can be employed to set up both a particular time and a particular place when and where only studying occurs. The counselor can help with time-management procedures by having the family construct daily calendars for the children that include time for school, chores, play, and study. The concept of contingency management can be employed by having reinforcement depend upon following the negotiated schedule.

Herz Brown (1988) provided the counselor with a valuable warning. She suggested that overly burdened single parents may look to others—extended family members, school personnel, friends, and counselors—to take over parenting responsibilities. Such a move may temporarily relieve the parent of some stress, but it also decreases the parent's power in the family. What results is a short-term gain for long-term pain. In consulting with parents, the counselor provides insights, skills, and intervention, but does not assume responsibility for the children's academic success.

Supporting Hierarchy

Madanes (1981) has made the systemic observation that often parent and children interact in ways that lead to inversions and incongruities in the power hierarchy. Counselors must respond appropriately when one hierarchy places the children in a dependent place with regard to shelter, food, and finances while another places them in a power position concerning decisions such as whether or not to study. This situation is not uncommon within single-parent families with adolescents.

The existence of incongruent hierarchies manifests in several ways. The first is via communications suggesting that the parent is unable to participate actively in counseling due to an inability to occupy an executive position within the hierarchy. Such a belief is indicated when the parent takes the position that the solution to the problem is to be found by some external expert—a psychiatrist or counselor. Madanes suggested a therapeutic response that relabels the problem as one which is in the arena of parental expertise. The child's problem is not labeled as an emotional upset or as the result of psychological conflict, but rather as laziness or choosing to fail.

Parents further disqualify themselves by pleading ignorance as to what is appropriate behavior on the part of their child, by using meaningless phrases such as "I just want him do to well," or by turning to the child for advice or asking the child what is best. The therapeutic response is to frame the problem as one born of the child's confusion, and to demand that the parent provide simple, concrete guidelines and definitive limitations on behaviors.

Madanes (1981) suggested that families also may undermine therapy by disqualifying the counselor. At times, this takes the form of a direct attack on the counselor's competence. In this instance, a nondefensive and brief description of the counselor's qualification is called for.

At other times the attack is veiled, as when the parent cites contradictory expert opinion or previous failures in counseling. Replies that suggest that the counselor is aware of other theoretical positions but does not agree with them all, and that underscore the differences between this and previous counseling experiences, are called for. Labeling interventions as behavioral experiments whose outcome can be evaluated after a limited time is also helpful.

Content or Process

The counselor must remain aware that academic difficulty as the presenting problem may be a manifestation of less than adequate systemic functioning. The problem may be the metaphoric expression of some more fundamental family difficulty, an attempt to deflect tension onto the child by some other dyad, the result of some cross-generational coalition, the replication of issues from previous generations. It is our experience, however, that traditional approaches to family therapy are more effective if the anxiety around the presenting problem can be reduced. The counseling techniques just described are helpful in this regard.

Several writers have suggested techniques for dealing with academic and school behavior problems at the systemic level. Titler and Cook (1981) proposed that counselors aid in the communication between family and school by adopting the Bowenian position of insisting that all intersystem messages be clear, mutually respectful, and nonemotional. Bagarozzi (1980) stated that a counselor who is prepared to assess and intervene around academic problems from the systemic, psychoanalytic, and behavioral perspectives is more effective than one who adheres to only one therapeutic ideology.

Guerin and Katz (1984), in discussing the impact of triangular relationships, suggested that these interactions be broken down into their dyadic components. If analysis indicates that difficulty between student and teacher results from a covert alliance between single parent and child, the counselor is advised to coach the parent to build a more explicit relationship with the child.

If the symptoms-maintaining triangle involves a former spouse, the counselor must be very careful in intervening. Only if it is apparent that the ex-spouses can put their dyadic issues aside and agree to work on parenting issues should conjoint sessions be considered. To allow former spouses to rehash old angers and hurts is to put the child in jeopardy. Latent nonadaptive family structures may be reactivated. Rather than allow this possibility, the counselor who is unsure of the former couple's capacity to put the needs of their children ahead of their own is wise to coach the custodial parent around the issue of putting children "in the middle" of parental battles.

Both Weltner (1982) and Herz Brown (1988) called for counseling strategies aimed at supporting the executive functions of the single parent and at strengthening intergenerational boundaries. Weltner suggested fostering an understanding in the parent that the collective tasks facing her may be too much to deal with alone; that a parental child may be of great value if the child is well supported and not exploited; that several children may be employed to parcel out certain of the parent's executive functions. The boundary defining techniques described in chapter 5 are applicable. The in-session and between-session interventions outlined by Minuchin and Fishman (1981), Sherman and Fredman (1986), and Sherman, Oresky, and Raintree (1992) are also useful. Herz Brown (1988) cautioned that the power vacuum created at the executive level may foster the formulation of triangles that serve to keep the single parent impotent. Identification of such triangles is the first important counseling strategy. The single parent is then coached on how to employ children, friends, and extended family members in ways that do not disempower her or him. In the later stages of counseling, interventions are aimed at solidifying extrafamilial activities. Herz Brown (1988) has been convinced of the importance of work (outside the home) to the single parent. (This is a topic of the next chapter.)

Consultation With the School

In assessing both the family and school systems and any recursive interactions between the two, the ecomap is a helpful tool. Holman (1983) described the ecomap as a dynamic diagram of the connections between a family and the people and institutions that together comprise the family's life space.

The construction of the ecomap begins with the family creating a family map (see chapter 5) depicting the relationships among the individual family members. Next, in the form of large circles, important forces outside the family's boundary are identified. These include the extended family, the school, the church, work, health care agencies. The nature of the relationship between the family and each of these other systems can be indicated by the use of different sorts of lines to connect the various systems to the family graphically: ——————————— can indicate a strong relationship; - - - - - - that the relationship is weak; -/-/-/-/-/ a stressful relationship. By adding arrows to these connections, the direction of flow of energy, resources, or communication can also be mapped.

Holman (1983) wrote that:

> The ecomap provides a visual overview of the complex ecological system of the family and shows its organizational patterns and relationships. It maps the major systems that are part of the family's environment and provides a picture of the balance between the demands and resources of the family system. In highlighting the nature of the connections between the family and its ecological system, the ecomap demonstrates the flow of resources from the environment to the family as well as deprivations and unmet needs. (p. 63)

The ecomap thus serves to direct the counselor to the optimum point of intervention—the troubled student, or his or her family, or his or her school environment, or the relationship among these factors.

To consult effectively with school personnel, the counselor must join with this system as well as with the family system. An attitude that reflects the school's position as expert in educational issues, one that fully appreciates the school's conceptualization of the problem, and one that encourages cooperation and coordination of the effort of both systems should provide the desired outcome.

In observing the child in class, the counselor frames the interaction between the teacher and child, and those among the child and other students, in terms of his or her knowledge of behavioral psychology and systems theory. With input from the teacher, guidance personnel, and the parent, interventions both for at home and at school are negotiated. The school is better positioned than the family to provide extra help and instruction in study skills such as active listening, active reading, and note taking. The school is also more able to monitor and modify classroom behaviors and peer interactions. The parent has greater control over scheduling time for home study and the other such variables. Differential task division should reflect these variations.

Chapter 10

SINGLE PARENTS, WORK, AND WELFARE

Single-parent families headed by divorced or never-married mothers are much more likely than two-parent families to be not only poor but also dependent upon public assistance programs. In the aggregate, the data that describe what has been referred to as the *feminization of poverty* are shocking. For example, in reviewing the statistical picture of the economic deprivation of these families, McLanahan, Garkinkel, and Ooms (1987) and Holder and Anderson (1989) reported that:

- The average standard of living for men, postdivorce, increases by 40% while that of women declines by 73%.
- In 1977, 67% of poor persons older than 16 years were women.
- By 1985, 55% of all poor families were headed by women.
- Although 75% of all employed women work full-time, in 1985 their average income was only $14,404.
- In female-headed single-parent families, the mother's income accounts for 60 to 70% of the family's total.
- From 1960 to 1981, the number of poor female-headed households increased by 40%. During that same time period, there was a 45% decrease in all other categories of poor families.
- In 1988, 50% of children living in female-headed households were poor.
- Even among the more prosperous of divorced mothers, income was only 60% of the predivorce level measured 1 year after the divorce.
- It is estimated that of children born in the late 1970s, 45% of white and 84% of black children will live, for some time at least, in a female-headed single-parent family.
- In 1983, approximately 58% of single mothers were awarded child support payments from the courts. Of these, 50% received the full award, 26% some portion of the award, and 24% received none.
- The organization of programs for Aid to Dependent Children can serve to keep single mothers unempowered. Poor mothers are often

left with choosing between a kind of full-time work that provides only a marginal economic position or becoming dependent upon welfare.

The ultimate solutions to problems such as the feminization of poverty are to be discovered at the level of profound changes in social policies, social institutions, and attitudes. We cannot stress this enough. If we are to assist children of divorce, then we must assist their mothers. Feminists have described the problems and have called for fundamental societal changes to address questions such as those of the low earnings of single mothers, the inadequacies in child support, and the unfairness in work requirements for public assistance (McLanahan et al., 1987).

That sweeping cultural change does not occur quickly leaves the professional counselor and his or her clients in a dilemma. While supporting the sort of political and cultural evolution that serves to alleviate the problems associated with economic (and therefore power) inequities, the counselor and client must negotiate within the context of the current societal milieu.

The first step in one possible solution to this dilemma is to study the feminist critique of the salient societal beliefs about single parenthood. These beliefs can lead clients to form and maintain non-growth-promoting and abusive relationships with former spouses, governmental agencies, and others. The second step is to assess the degree to which the client may have incorporated these belief into her own reality constructions. The third step involves exploring with the client ways in which a difficult situation may be made better.

It must be emphasized that in assessing and intervening at this level, the counselor must in no way blame the victim for her predicament. To ascertain the degree to which a client may have internalized societal myths, such as framing the single-parent family in pathological terms, or assuming that single mothers cannot be effective workers, is most certainly not to imply that the client is the author or the maintainer of the myth. The purposes of the analysis, rather, are to make overt any covert agreement on the client's part with the various cultural biases that put her in a one-down and unempowered position, and to aid the client in disputing the validity of these constructions.

As suggested in chapter 5, the counselor should help the client dispute any belief system that suggests she should wait, passively, until some white knight comes to her rescue. The approach is similar here. When a client assumes that she is unable to make adaptive changes in her life until great and sweeping alterations in the cultural climate are initiated by others, she will remain passive and powerless.

Poverty and Psychological Distress

Hicks and Anderson (1989) pointed out that the drop in income that many single mothers incur impacts not only the pocketbook. The degree of correlation between financial security and self-esteem implies that persons with money feel better about themselves than those without. Impoverished people are often perceived to be of less value by outside observers as well. If the single mother's predivorce status was based upon her husband's salary and position, the counselor may find a client whose negative self-images are reinforced by "friends, relatives, acquaintances, and shopkeepers who regard her as less important" (p. 319).

As income declines, so also does the range of possible interactions with the environment. Braver et al. (1989) listed common changes for divorced families. These include relocation to a less desirable abode, problems with child care, the loss of a familiar neighborhood, and the disruption of friendship networks. Even in those instances in which the custodial mothers remain in the family home, the number of pleasant experiences available to her and her children are generally greatly reduced. The loss of discretionary income not only means fewer trips to restaurants and theaters, but for some it also implies worry concerning the availability of basic needs such as food, clothing, and transportation. Given the bleak situation these mothers face, the attendant loss of self-esteem, and the likelihood that these parents hold little hope for improvement in the future (Braver et al., 1989; Weitzman, 1985), the stage is set for clinical depression. Using a cognitive epistomology, Beck et al. (1979) described the depressive triad: a belief in one's inability to cope with the world's demands, a belief that these demands are unfair and impossibly difficult, and a belief that the incongruity between the perceived enormity of the demands and one's ability to meet them will not diminish in the future. Single mothers, as described by Hicks and Anderson (1989) and Braver et al. (1989), seem to be extremely at risk for adopting a depressive stance.

An experimental study designed by Braver et al. (1989) examined the relationship between economic hardship and postdivorce psychological distress of custodial mothers. In comparing 77 custodial mothers to a control group, several statistically significant results were reported. Perhaps of greatest import to the professional counselor was the finding that drop in income was related to measured psychological distress but actual income level was not. The sociological term of *relative deprivation* appears to be a strong factor here:

> The finding that drop in income related to poorer psychological adjustment at all levels of current income suggests that the impact of psychological factors such as loss of status and self-definitions involving the former standard of living should not be underesti-

mated. It may be that although wealthy women who are reduced to middle-class status do not experience great economic hardship, they nonetheless do experience disruption in social networks, life style, and self-esteem, which may cause considerable psychological distress. (pp. 30–31)

Given the small numbers involved in this particular study, counselors are warned against overgeneralizing its findings. There may, however, be considerable clinical value in thinking in terms of drop in income, selfesteem, and status as well as in terms of absolute family income.

The Therapeutic Value of Support Networks

Although Braver and his coauthors (1989) call for significant societal changes to address the problem of postdivorce drop in income, some custodial mothers have been able to design their own solutions in the here and now. Their successes can be most informative as counselors work with single-parent families. For example, in the case history described in this section, Flo's artful use of various support networks was of enormous value to her as she transformed her family from an upper-middle-class, two-parent system to a single-parent family comprised of five children, a mother who had never worked outside the home, and a woefully inadequate child support award.

> Dave and Flo met during the summer between their freshman and sophomore years of college. He was a lifeguard at the swim club to which Flo's family belonged. She was immediately attracted to his aggressive and assured demeanor. He seemed to be a "can do" sort of fellow. He was attracted to her classic beauty and refinement. The sparks flew, and for the next 3 years they carried on an impassioned, long-distance relationship. Perhaps the fact that Dave's college was in Boston and Flo's in New York served to keep their need for one another intense.
>
> During their senior year in college, Flo and Dave were married in a civil ceremony. This "first" marriage was one of convenience: it served to keep Dave out of the Vietnam war. They were married in a religious ceremony during the summer of 1965. Both were 21 years of age.
>
> Dave had been a prelaw student at college, Flo a French major Immediately after graduation, Dave's drive to succeed manifested itself. He simultaneously enrolled in law school at night and opened an insurance practice. He was successful in both endeavors. Although Flo was eligible for certification as a French teacher at the secondary school level, she did not follow through on the necessary paperwork.
>
> Within a year, the first son, Rick, was born. A second son, Tommy,

followed in 1967. By the time Paul was born in 1972, Flo was the mother of three sons under the age of 8. She was the wife of a successful young attorney, and she was not yet 29 years of age.

Despite the social upheaval characteristic of the 1960s and early 1970s, and despite the early stirrings of the feminist movement, the young couple seemed happy, in an anachronistic way, during the early years. They seemed to be following a script, one described by McGoldrick (1988):

> Women have always played a central role in families, but the idea that they have a life cycle apart from their roles as wife and mother is a relatively recent one, and still is not widely accepted in our culture. The expectation for women has been that they would take care of the needs of others, first men, then children, then the elderly. . . . They went from being daughter, to wife, to mother, with their status defined by the male in the relationship and their role by their position in the family's life cycle. (p. 29)

The script is all about gender roles. Holder and Anderson (1989) succinctly restated the different stories ascribed to men and women. Women operate within the world of relationships, the most important of which is the family. Men deal with the world of work. It is as if the front door of the home divided the world into the spheres of influence as neatly as do "His" and "Hers" towels: "Women managed the home and children and were socialized to perform more nurturing activities. Men were schooled to actively compete in the larger community, to influence policy and norms, and to earn money" (p. 360).

The difficulty with this view of a marriage partnership is, of course, that it is not a partnership at all. Although both husband and wife are mutually dependent upon each other's functioning for as long as the marriage continues, the disparity in economic power permits the husband to purchase what the wife provides should their union dissolve. The woman has no such option.

As Dave became increasingly more successful as a matrimonial attorney, the family's life style and social status grew proportionately. Dave replaced his cars and boats more frequently, it seemed, than his brothers-in-law replaced neckties. The homes of Flo's three sisters were filled with furnishings discarded by their well-to-do sister. But although Flo and Dave were financially "flush" during this period, their relationship was on the way to bankruptcy.

Over time, each began to resent the other's noninvolvement. Dave devoted essentially all of his energies to his practice, the social networking required to have the practice grow, and recreation. Flo felt often as if she had to play the role of the single parent. She viewed Dave as nonfunctional with regard to his parental role and unsatisfactory in his role as husband. From Dave's perspective, Flo had opted to put all her resources into the home and children. He considered Flo to be unable or unwilling to "play." As Flo turned to her sisters for support, Dave turned to his female office manager for companionship.

It is not uncommon for angry, distancing couples to forge temporary reconcilations. The decision to divorce, after all, is almost never an easy one. Questioning one's own ability to survive without a partner often takes on an obsessive quality. Wondering about the possible deleterious effects on the children, reminiscences of better times, and considering ways of making things better all add to the inertia.

Religious beliefs, antidivorce family legacies, and a simple refusal to admit failure especially daunted Flo. She felt unequal in the struggle. Dave had the money, the power; and he was a divorce attorney. For his part, Dave believed that his marriage was no different from the other areas in his life, and that if he worked on the problem with sufficient diligence, success would be assured.

It is also not uncommon for children to be born during these trying, vacillating times.

Laura was born in 1976, Kevin in 1978. When the divorce was formalized in 1980, Flo was 36 years old. She was the custodial parent of five children ranging in age from 15 to 2. She received 50% from the sale of the matrimonial home, $100 per week in alimony, and $75 per week per child in child support. With the proceeds from the sale of the house she had shared with Dave, Flo bought a comfortable, but somewhat rundown, home for herself and her children. Her primary problem was how to maintain the household. If Dave was prompt with alimony and child support payments, she received $475 per week. Dave was not prompt, although the payments were ultimately made. Flo felt that she needed to go to work if her family was to survive economically. But how does a 37-year-old French major with five children, one who has never worked outside of the home, choreograph this most difficult dance?
　The divorce was a particularly bitter one, and Flo could not rely on Dave to provide any help, financial or otherwise, that was not court mandated. There was nothing that the courts or other societal institutions could do for her. She turned to her family and friends to provide the various sorts of support she needed.

It is important to remember that Flo went through this time without benefit of counseling. She seemed somehow to sense what her needs were and was able to develop several support systems that, as a whole, provided her with what she required. In a sense, Flo's moves provide a road map for counselors who work with single-parent families.

In moving to a town in which two of her sisters and her father resided, Flo took the first step in meeting her needs for nurturance. In their family of origin, Flo and her sisters assumed the typical sorts of roles: There was a responsible one; the popular, well-liked one; the physically and emotionally weak one; the studious one (McGoldrick, 1989). Flo was popular, and the sisters to whom she turned during the transition to single parenthood were the studious and responsible ones. A fourth sister, the weak one, was significantly less available to Flo during the time of crisis as a result of both physical and emotional distance.

The relationship among Flo and her two nearby sisters was remarkably growth promoting. In a very real sense, these women became Flo's primary attachment objects. They provided her with the sort of emotional assuredness and calmness that is prerequisite for making good life choices. Flo knew that she belonged, that she was loved, and that she was not alone. Some of her most basic needs were met: She was therefore able to focus on personal growth and other issues found higher up the need hierarchy.

McGoldrick (1989) referred to the unique relationship that may exist among sisters:

Often it is not until midlife that sisters reconnect with each other, through the shared experiences of caring for a failing or dying parent, a divorce in the family, or perhaps a personal health problem. Such events inspire them to clarify their priorities and to redefine the relationships in life that really matter to them. (p. 255)

Flo created another web of relationships among her neighbors. She became very close with a number of women who did not work outside the home. What all of these women shared with Flo was the responsibility to care for their children. Several of them became acutely aware of Flo's particular predicament. How was she to be freed of the responsibility of caring for her daughter and sons while simultaneously making the sorts of decisions that would assure her economic emancipation?

This friend network support Flo magnificently when she decided to train to become a computer programmer. With great humor and with much effort, an incredibly complex juxtaposition of time scheduling on the part of Flo and her friends allowed her to take the required courses. Within a year, Flo was a working mother with an adequate personal income. The relationship networks among Flo and her sisters and Flo and her friends maintained, albeit changed in some degree, even after her return to work. These relationships were and are mutually rewarding for all involved. Flo gives as well as takes, but in no way has she assumed a one-down, dependent, or infantilized role in her interactions with family and friends. Flo and her relationship networks ingeniously empowered her when she was needy. Now she can use her strength in the service of her friends and family. Each of Flo's support networks helped in a far more subtle, but equally important, way in addition to meeting her needs for nurturance, substitute parenting, and mutuality. They allowed Flow to become free of the sociological constraint, the construct, that suggests to women that to work is to be less of a mother.

Ferree (1984) described the conflict between mothers and work:

> In the classic sociological model, the relationship of family and job for women is portrayed as one of conflict and competing demands. Family demands are assumed to have the higher priority, while work performance and satisfaction are influenced by family circumstances, with work commitment and actual labor force participation viewed as contingent upon "prior" home responsibilities. (p. 58)

Flo's case history provides an alternate construct, that is, that a woman can be successful and happy in both her professional and family roles simultaneously.

Carter and McGoldrick (1988) pointed out that as a result of gender-specific socialization patterns, most women are oriented toward relationship. Hicks and Anderson (1989) underscored the need for single mothers to establish support networks:

> The development of a support network is imperative for women who live outside the boundaries of marriage. . . . A strong support network is crucial in beginning the healing process and continuing it once it has begun. . . . However it happens, if a women can become active in her community, join women's groups, develop relationships with those who have similar interests, the new single state can provide a sense of freedom, independence, or autonomy that can be very satisfying and enjoyable.

Professional counselors must be aware, however, that a woman's ability to form relationships does not always result in the sort of personal growth experienced by Flo. Some relationships can be growth retarding.

McLanahan, Wedemeyer, and Adelberg (1981) provided an outline of some of the various types of relationship networks common among single-parent families. The family-of-origin network, the extended network, and two variations of conjugal networks are described.

One response to single parenthood is for the mother to reunite with her original family. The reunion may be a physical one, as in those instances when a single-parent family moves back into the grandparental home. The reunion is essentially a psychological one in those cases in which kin become the single mother's primary attachment objects even if there is no physical move back home. Often either a female or male best friend is included in a peripheral way within this support network.

Because membership in this sort of network is limited by kinship, these relationship configurations tend to be small. Usually they include only those family-of-origin members who live near to the single mother. The degree of interaction among the members, referred to as the density of the relationship, is, however, very high. The content of the relationship is multiplex in nature in that it is based on multiple ties within the relationship. Support tends to be divided along the traditional gender division of labor assumptions, with fathers and brothers helping out financially while mothers and sisters assist with child care and with personal problems. Often there is the implicit assumption of future intergenerational reciprocity. These single mothers often provide the same sort of support that they themselves received to the children of the next generation.

Flo's family-of-origin network was very much as described by McLanahan et al. (1981). In addition to adding the necessary extra hand required for family functioning, the network provided a sense of security, of belongingness, that the authors have reported as typical in this form of network. Another sort of emotional support readily available from family-of-origin networks is a feeling of personal worth, of self-efficacy, of a "can-do" orientation. Single mothers who use their kinship network well often do not feel the need for a husband.

For all their value, family-of-origin networks can have a down side for single mothers. The authors identified the issues of intimacy and social integration as potentially problematic areas. At the beginning, relationships among the single mother and other members of her family tend to be asymmetrical in that she, clearly, is the needy one. Emotional asymmetry tends to limit mutual confiding and other behaviors associated with intimacy. Further, although the family network protects the single mother from becoming dependent upon outside relationships, it may also serve to isolate her from social supports and new social interactions. These mothers may be swallowed up by their intensely loyal families.

Another response to single parenthood is the creation of an extended support network based essentially upon new friendship ties. The structure of these friendship networks, as well as the kind of support they provide to single mothers, vary considerably from those of the family-of-origin networks. McLanahan et al. (1981) saw these networks' heavy concentra-

tion of postdivorce women friends as their most distinguishing characteristic. In addition to sustaining individual friendships, these networks
often connect single mothers to organizations such as women's support
groups and community action and social groups. Compared to family-of-origin arrangements, extended networks are quite large. Single mothers often
interact intensely within many of the components of the network, but
interaction among the groups is quite low: The members in the car pool, for
example, are unlikely to be involved with the Parents Without Partners
people.

There is differentiation among the kinds of support single mothers
derive from the various network components, and this tends not to break
down along stereotypical gender lines. The family of origin and the ex-
spouse often provide financial support. Baby-sitting cooperatives, car pools,
and food cooperatives help in the performance of the tasks required for
family functioning. Emotional support and intimacy needs are met by
others in the network who share a strong identification with the role of
single parent and the commitment to autonomy and success. Those inti-
mates often also share lofty professional and career aspirations.

As relationships within extended networks are predicated upon the ad
hoc needs of members, and as the members enjoy great mobility in entering
and leaving, relationships tend to be, on the whole, less permanent than in
the family-of-origin paradigm. Commonly, however, a few of the networks'
relationships are stable, enduring, and reliable.

The McLanahan et al. (1981) study found several interesting results.
For example, although most of the women who had been involved in
extended networks were quite satisfied and functioning well, a few in this
group were in considerable distress. Common to the women was a nostalgic
longing for the past and a belief that occupational success does not undo
marital failure. To the professional counselor's ear, such affect, cognition,
and behaviors are strongly indicative of the need to explore the question of
mourning and relationship restructuring discussed in earlier chapters. In
Flo's case, mourning work was apparently done in the safe and secure
bosom of her family-of-origin network. What emerged was a woman eager
to grow and possessed of the attitudes, emotions, thinking patterns, and
behavioral repertoire to forge the kind of extended network that allowed
for and nurtured the growth.

McLanahan et al. (1981) described how women may incorporate a key
male or spouse substitute into either the family-of-origin network or the
extended network without altering the essential nature of either type of
support. Perhaps the most interesting finding of the study was the interaction effect between the kind of support group formed and the mother's role
orientation on perceived psychological distress. Women reported stress
when their support network contradicted their personal orientation.
Change-oriented women trapped in a close-knit family-of-origin network

are not happy, nor are stability-oriented women operating within a loose-knit and somewhat unreliable extended network.

Of singular diagnostic importance to professional counselors who work with distressed single mothers is ascertaining the most appropriate level at which to intervene. In some cases what is called for is an alteration in the existing support network; in others, it is changes in the single mothers' self-definitions and role orientations. A thorny counseling problem arises when the single mother's role orientation and support group are syntonic but nonadaptive. These women are often aware that something is not right in their lives, but they are unable to connect their discomfort with the fact that, although comfortable, their support networks are growth inhibiting.

> *Twenty-five-year-old Lynne had successfully put together a family-of-origin network with Jack functioning as a much older key male spouse substitute. With his financial support, Lynne was able to live in her own apartment and raise her two children, the youngest of whom was Jack's daughter. Lynne was accepted into Jack's close-knit extended family, and she also enjoyed a close relationship with her older sister. In addition to Jack's financial support, Lynne was receiving public assistance. Although bright and highly articulate, she had no desire to work outside the home. Her relationship with Jack had to be kept from the authorities or she would lose her benefits. Lynne, most certainly, is not the only single mother to be dissatisfied with her relationship with welfare-type agencies.*

Tillmon (1976) stated starkly that Aid to Families With Dependent Children is:

> . . . a supersexist marriage. You trade in a "a" man for "the" man. But you can't divorce him if he treats you bad. He can divorce you of course, cut you off any time he wants. But in that case "he" keeps the kids, not you. "The" man runs everything. In ordinary marriage, sex is supposed to be for you and your husband. On AFDC you're not supposed to have any sex at all. You give up control over your body. It's a condition of aid . . . . "The" man, the welfare system, controls your money. He tells you what to buy and what not to buy, where to buy it, and how much things cost. If things—rent, for instance—really costs more than he says they do, it's too bad for you. (In Imber-Black, 1989, p. 159)

A central tenet of this book is that single parents need not passively accept negative societal constructs of who and what they are. They need not behave in ways confirming the stereotypes that are used to define them.

Lynne's financial insecurity derived not only from her dependence on welfare but also from her dependence on Jack. Here, too, she was in constant danger of being cut off. Any movement in the direction of her own autonomy was punished by Jack's threats of economic and personal abandonment. Lynne was depressed, but she did not recognize the source of her distress. Having lost her father at age 5, she had been constantly in search of relief from her fear of being emotionally and physically alone. The price she paid for the security derived from welfare and Jack was enormous.

Counseling was in the service of restructuring her support network to foster autonomy while helping her in the work of mourning her many previous losses. Insight into the problem is insufficient. Action also is required. The professional counselor must be aware that when clients say they want change in their lives they are often talking about an end point and not the difficult process of change. In Lynne's case, she wanted to be more independent financially and emotionally. However, much of the counseling was in the direction of understanding and overcoming her resistance to making the sorts of changes in her life necessary for the attainment of her goals.

The work within the counseling sessions had several foci. Lynne needed to examine her relationship with her father, see him in a more realistic light, and mourn his loss. Two conjoint sessions with the older sister aided in the process and also enabled Lynne to examine the nature of her family-of-origin network. Conjoint sessions with Jack enabled the couple to understand the complementary roles each played within their relationship.

Helping Lynne to establish an extended network—the action side of her counseling—was difficult. Her first venture out was to join a group of adult survivors. Although she recreated her preferred dependence orientation in relationships with the members of the group at first, she soon found herself involved in more mutual interactions with the other members. Jack showed his support for Lynne's growth by baby-sitting during the meetings. At some level, he seemed to be relieved to have Lynne less dependent upon him.

This first step back into community opened some important doors for Lynne. One member of her survivors' group introduced her to a community theater organization. Now more open to begin the construction of extended networks, Lynne became fully involved and enjoyed her small role in the company's musical presentation. It was during this period that she decided to go to school to earn a high school equivalence diploma: As her world expanded, her dependence shrunk.

Another case further illustrates the point. Daniella's needs were different from Lynne's when she entered counseling following a divorce. She had endured an emotionally and physically abusive relationship until her ex-husband began to beat her two sons.

As a secondary school teacher, Daniella was not in jeopardy of becoming dependent upon the welfare system. She had, however, incorporated the societal construction that without a partner she could not be both a successful worker and a good mother to her boys. Her depression was fueled by irrational feelings of inadequacy.

Daniella was an aerobics instructor as well as a teacher, so a latent extended network structure was available to her. At the time when she began counseling, she was making no use of this structure, however. She had no family of her own other than her sons, and so it was in counseling that certain of the functions of the family-of-origin network were carried out. Within the context of an open, honest, and caring relationship with her counselor, Daniella was able to dispute her belief around the question of inadequacy, work, and mothering. Over time, in a process similar to the one that Flo and her sisters created, Daniella came to see her strengths and weaknesses realistically and to feel accepted and respected. The reduction in anxiety made it rather easy for this highly talented woman to make use of her extended network in ways that brought about much satisfaction for herself, her sons, and her friends.

Although Flo, Lynne, and Daniella have become happy and successful in their single parenthood, their lives are far from ideal. Each would prefer to be involved more intimately with one special man, but none defines her life as a failure because of this particular aspect. To a greater rather than lesser degree, each feels in control of her life and less at risk of becoming involved in abusive relationships with either other persons or social institutions. To a greater rather than lesser degree, each feels that she has more control over who and what she and her family are rather than any societal stereotypes.

The Role of the Professional Counselor

The counselor serves as a reality check for the single mother by asking her to assess the degree to which she has accepted the social system's deficit model of her and her family.

The interaction of many single-parent families with larger social systems such as social services, schools, and/or human service agencies is influenced by the expectations that these families place on larger systems and in return, by the expectations and constructs that the systems maintain about single-parent families. The agencies, as well as the families themselves, often seem to perceive the single-parent family as deficient or somewhat lacking in one or more necessary components. The families may look to the agencies to augment or fill in the gaps initially created by the exiting of a parent. Single mothers may attribute difficulties with their children to the absence of the father—traditionally the disciplinarian. For example, mothers with preteen or teenage sons often look to outside agents as potential surrogate disciplinarians. They may request a male counselor or worker with the hopes that this worker can function as a role model for their sons. Frequently, however, they are more likely to be seeking parenting assistance than role modeling from the male counselor. Too often both the single mother and the male adolescent maintain the erroneous assumption that the difficulties the family is having with his adolescence result from an inadequacy in the family's structure rather than considering that this assumption may be a significant component of the problem.

Single parents, experiencing a sense of overload from what seems like too many roles and responsibilities, may look toward larger systems to pick up some of the slack. Mothers, eager to compensate for self-assessed deficiencies, are apt to become overly reliant on mental health and school professionals, organizations such as Big Brothers and Big Sisters, or the local Little League coach to supplement their family system. This can be particularly taxing to a mother who is transporting two or three children to myriad support groups and activities while attempting to hold down a full-time job.

And, although any of these representatives of the larger systems may adequately fulfill the requirements of their designated roles, they are unlikely to be equipped to meet the emotional functions of the roles the family may be assigning them. In many cases, this results in a continuous loop of social systems disappointing the single-parent family, which places on these agencies excessive expectations that, inevitably, they fail to fulfill. This is more likely to occur in social service systems such as Public Assistance or welfare, which are primarily constructed to supply emergency financial assistance and are neither designed for nor capable of fulfilling a co-parenting function. These systems can quickly become a source of frustration rather than empowerment for the single parent. Social and eligibility workers with large caseloads are not likely to address the emotional needs of their clientele, and at times these systems seem designed to deter access to the types of assistance they were created to provide. It is not surprising, therefore, to find single mothers, particularly younger single mothers, diminished by their inability to negotiate the system. Frequently, social services function as a persistent source of stress to the family, and as the family may seem to be absorbed by social services, so may social services be absorbed into the operation of the family system. Rather than attributing these difficulties to social service systems, the family is apt to perceive these dilemmas as intrinsic to a single-parent family.

Unfortunately, the larger systems are likely to do the same. Despite the ever-increasing awareness of the preponderance of single-parent families, larger social systems continue to approach the single-parent family as inadequate and incomplete, thereby conceivably reinforcing the family's negative self-constructions. Families that look toward social services or other larger systems to replace a missing parent may be operating from the pretense that single parenthood is a temporary status that eventually can be remedied. In doing so, they may be relinquishing the opportunity of experiencing their family system as capable and, essentially, complete.

The professional counselor ensures that no pathologizing of single-parent families goes unchallenged.

Counseling Strategies

In working with single mothers, McGoldrick (1988) provides the preferred counseling milieu: "Urging women to accept and move toward 'male' values is not the solution to female powerlessness. It is important to validate women's focus on relationships at the same time that you empower them in the areas of work and money" (p. 65).

Thus counselors can:

- Arrange to have each new single-parent client put into contact with a network of other single parents. This aids in the formation of extended support networks that empower single mothers with regard to their careers and their economic well-being.
- Give clients permission to mourn their losses, and help with the work of mourning.
- Help clients identify and dispute negative societal stereotypes concerning single mothers and their families.
- Help clients assess how their own cognitions, affects, and behaviors and those of their support networks either promote or retard personal and financial autonomy.
- Encourage clients to use support networks in novel ways to have their needs met. From car pooling to joint living arrangements with other single-parent systems, any and all potential solutions may be entertained.
- Help clients with specific issues such as self-esteem and assertiveness.
- Help clients find training in specific skills.
- Help with regard to financial matters. As pointed out by Hicks and Anderson (1989), "Whether it be the stress of adjusting to a lower standard of living, the need to develop very specific skills for managing finances, or the need to overcome a socially ingrained fear of money, women must be helped to get control of financial matters. Without

their control they will never fully experience their own power, selfesteem, pride, and autonomy" (p. 331).

- Adopt a construction of reality that suggests single parenthood need not be understood as a problem-saturated role. Rather, the formation of a single-parent family can present a large number of options that, in sum, can lead to a most satisfying family experience. Counselors can help clients to co-create this reality for themselves.

PART IV

SOCIAL CONSTRUCTION THERAPY WITH THE SINGLE-PARENT FAMILY

Chapter 11
THE SINGLE-PARENT FAMILY AND SOCIAL CONSTRUCTIONS

The preceding chapters have presented counselors with research findings and traditional family therapy theory and therapy techniques applicable to the single parent. This chapter presents the underlying assumptions and theoretical concepts of social constructionism and a six-stage model that describes how social construction theory can be applied as a therapy in working with a single-parent family. This application is illustrated through a case history. The approach to therapy presented here is based on the belief that we create our own reality. Persons, couples, families make sense of their ongoing experience, and it is this process of making sense that is the object of this therapy. The therapy takes as its focus client meaning systems, viewed from the past, present, and future, both negative and positive. The initial focus of the past is affective, on understanding how the meanings developed and how clients believe these meanings affected them in the past. Once the past is put in perspective, the second focus of the approach is cognitive, on client scripts for behavior in the present and the maintenance of the meaning system, on helping the person, couple, family to be aware of the processes and facilitating learning about and amplifying exceptions to the process in order to provide possibilities for new solutions. Future focus enables clients to image how different meanings and the resultant scripts could effect their lives in a positive way. Re-visioning their lives, or their relationship, or their family is the last stage of this therapy, and emphasizes future visions of their life without the problem.

Some believe social construction theory is a paradigmatic shift in the field of family therapy and represents leading edge theoretical formulations in the field. Social construction theory has profound implications for how we do therapy and how we view our clients. It also provides a framework whereby we can examine our own biases and assumptions about the divorce experience (intimacy dissolution) and being a single parent.

Social Construction Therapy

Social construction therapy flows from the work of Kelly (1969), Berger and Luckman (1966), and Gergen (1985). Social constructionism places emphasis on social interpretation and the intersubjective influences of language, family, and culture. As Gergen (1985) stated, "From the constructional position the process of understanding is not automatically driven by the forces of nature, but is the result of an active, cooperative enterprise of persons in relationship" (p. 267). Thus social construction theory proposes that there is an evolving set of meanings that continually emerge from social interactions. These meanings are part of a general flow of constantly changing narratives.

Berger and Luckman (1966) have indicated that the socially constructed meanings that we have inherited are "opaque" (p. 55). That is, the ways in which our meanings are constructed are as invisible to us as the elements that compose them. The social world we are born into is experienced by the child as the sole reality. The rules of the world we are born into are nonproblematic, they require no explanation, and they are neither challenged nor doubted. Through socialization, the socially constructed meanings are internalized; they are filtered and understood through meaningful symbols. From these socially constructed meanings flow psychological meanings and scripts for behavior. A person attempts to match his or her own experience with the available meanings and scripts. The person learns the language, the appropriate behavior for his or her gender, age, and culture. In this way, a person develops an individual identity, an individual script, and individual meanings—all of which are created by and embedded in the dominant culture. This process of the development of an individual's world view is illustrated in figure 5.

Social construction therapy thus explores the family meanings that incidents, behaviors, and encounters with single-parent families have for individuals and how these meanings are determined by the sociocultural environment. The sociocultural environment equips individuals and families with methods and ways of understanding and making judgments about aspects of the single-parent family, ranging from how they felt and feel about the divorce or the death to their religious values. These ways of making sense of experiences are embedded in a meaning system that is accepted as reality by the social group and in the scripts (ways of behaving) that are a part of the individual's meaning system. The dialectical relationship between individual realities and the socially constructed meanings around the single-parent family is the focus of this chapter.

Before discussing the actual social construction therapy model for counseling the single-parent family, a comparison of deficit- and solution-focused therapies is useful. (See table 2.) One of the first theorists respon-

Figure 4.   Social Construction World View

MODEL OF SOCIAL CONSTRUCTION THERAPY

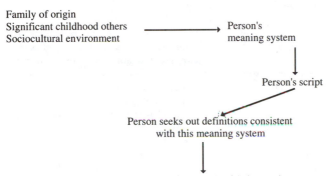

```
┌─────────────────────────────────────┐
│  DEVELOPMENT OF THE WORLD VIEW       │
└─────────────────────────────────────┘
```

Family of origin
Significant childhood others ─────────────▶   Person's
Sociocultural environment   meaning system

                                                      │
                                                      ▼
                                              Person's script

Person seeks out definitions consistent
        with this meaning system

                    │
                    ▼

The single-parent family that sees a problem as part of their meaning system seeks out information consistent with this view. Behaviors, interactions, and affect (the person's script) reflect this view. A cycle is set up whereby the person/family experiences the problem as flowing from the past, reinforced by interactions in the present, and not having a solution in the future.

sible for solution-focused therapy was de Shazer (1985). His work led him away from a focus on the problem in therapy to a focus on solution that the clients defined as more helpful. He stated that often the solutions that clients constructed had very little to do with the problems they presented but that their solutions "fit" with the clients' definition of the problem. Consequently, the therapy moved in a direction away from the therapist trying to understand the client's problem, and therefore trying to design a solution to it, to a focus on questioning the client about his or her own goals and exploring his or her self for potential resources for problem solving. While doing this, Molnar and de Shazer (1987) noticed that there were exceptions to the client's story—times when the problem was not happening. These therapists then focused on what that experience was like (when the problem was not happening) and developed the solution-focused therapy model. White (1986a, 1989) proposed a similar model of alternate descriptions, building on Bateson's (1972) notions of restraints (the beliefs and values that people hold and make them less likely to notice other aspects of their problem-saturated lives). In so doing, he developed a narrative therapy through which people explore their ongoing stories. Therapy thus involves assisting individuals to reauthor their lives.

Some of the assumptions that arise from a social construction approach are as follows:

Table 2. Comparison of Problem/Deficit Models of Therapy With Solution-Focused Models

Traditional Approaches	Solution-Focused Therapy
• Therapist is an expert—has special knowledge regarding the problem to which the client needs to submit (colonization/missionary model).	• Client and therapist both have particular areas of expertise (collaborative model).
• Client is viewed as damaged by the abuse (deficit model).	• Client is viewed as influenced but not determined by the abuse history, having strengths and abilities (resource model).
• Remembering abuse and the expression of repressed affect (catharsis) are treatment.	• Goals are individualized for each client, but do not necessarily involve catharsis or remembering.
• Interpretation.	• Acknowledging, valuing, and opening possibilities.
• Past oriented.	• Present/future oriented.
• Problem/pathology oriented.	• Solution oriented.
• Must be long-term treatment.	• Variable/individualized length of treatment.
• Invites conversations for insight and working through.	• Invites conversations for accountability and action and declines invitations to blame and invalidation.

Note: From W. O'Hanlon, in S. MacNamee & K. Gergen, 1993, New York: Sage. Copyright 1993 by Sage Publications, Inc. Reprinted by permission.

1. Every human has a biological drive to unfolded and to grow—to be the fullest he or she can be: ". . . you can let the organism take over without interfering, without interrupting we can rely on the wisdom of the organism" (Perls, 1969, p. 17).
2. There are no absolute truths and no absolute realities.
3. We coconstruct reality through language with one another in a continual interaction with the sociocultural environment. Thus what is real is that which is coconstructed through language and interaction by persons in continual interplay with the surrounding sociocultural environment.
4. Our inner world is a construct, colored by the past, and our past is a construction.
5. People tend to re-create an image of their world by noticing behavior in others that confirms their self-definitions and definitions of situations and by selectively ignoring disconfirmatory behavior.
6. How we see problems, roles, and relationships does not simply reflect or elaborate on biological givens but is largely a product of sociocultural processes.
7. People who come for therapy are experiencing problems in living. They have tried many solutions—many of which have been unsuccessful. The problems they report are not seen as being functional in

maintaining the system or as a manifestation of underlying pathology. They are seen as problems—problems that have negative effects for the person, couple, or family. The way that people use language about problems is the way they can use language to coconstruct a new story.

8. Repetitive knowledge of behavior that is discrepant with the perceptual view of the person results in a change in the person's perceptual view. This is accomplished by focusing on and amplifying exceptions in the person's description of his or her world.

9. Social construction therapy focuses on challenging the person's view of the problem. It accomplishes this by breaking up the meaning that the problem holds and questioning his or her behavioral script. This is achieved through the use of techniques like metaphors and reframes that amplify the person's process and by finding exceptions (deconstruction or de-scripting) and providing seeds (construction or rescripting) for transformation.

Theoretical Concepts

Among social construction theoretical concepts important for therapists are ideas about constructed perceptions, social construction of meanings and scripts, constructive time lines, collapsing time, and therapeutic change.

Constructed Perceptions

Gergen and Gergen (1983, 1988) used the term *self-narratives* to describe the social psychological processes whereby people tell stories about themselves to themselves and others. These theorists characterize selfnarratives as the way individuals establish coherent connections among life events. They believe that individuals have a set of schema by which they attempt to understand life events as meaningful and systematically related. In this way, events are rendered understandable and intelligible because they are located in a sequence or are part of an unfolding process. It is this process that enables individuals to make sense out of nonsense and to interpret events in a coherent, consistent manner. This chapter looks at single-parent family problems as sociocultural symbolic constructs, and inquiry into the sources, processes, and consequences of their construction and organization is the therapy that flows from this view.

The Social Construction of Meanings

These narratives or *meaning systems* are originally created and maintained by interactions with significant others. The process begins at birth and continues until death. If a person holds a particular meaning system, he or she then seeks out events and persons that are consistent with that meaning system. These meaning systems in turn lead to *states*, the emotional reaction to the meaning system, and *behaviors* that are consistent with the meaning system.

These meaning systems are socially constructed and embedded in the larger sociocultural environment. Berger and Luckman (1966) described social constructions as the consensual recognition of the realness and rightness of a constructed reality, plus the socialization process by which people acquire this reality. A social construction includes not only the routines and the mechanisms for socializing the children of the system but also the means for maintaining the definition of reality on which the system is based. Language is one way that a community reaffirms the dominant reality and discredits competing social constructions. Meanings, which are social constructions, refer to the complex and unique definitions in each individual that can influence behavior. These meanings were constructed in childhood and are maintained by ongoing sociocultural perturbations. These meanings are created, embedded in, and recognized by the larger social group and thus operate at social, interpersonal, and intrapersonal levels.

The Social Construction of Scripts

Individuals' meaning systems determine the content of their scripts. The notion of scripts was initially introduced by transactional analysts and later by social psychologists Simon and Gagnon in 1973 when they applied this notion to the area of sexuality. For these researchers, people are like actors with parts in plays, and these parts, or scripts, exist in all areas of life, including the sexual. The scripts are the organizers for our behaviors and are involved in learning the meaning of internal states, organizing the sequences of specific acts, decoding novel situations, setting the limits on responses, and linking meanings from different aspects of life to specific experiences (Gagnon, 1990, p. 6). People develop scripts out of their meaning systems. A script is a "devise for guiding action and for understanding it" (p. 6). Scripts are plans that people have about what they are doing and what they are going to do. Scripts justify actions that are in agreement with them and challenge those that are not. Scripts are the "blueprints for behavior" that specify who, what, when, and why an individual does a particular behavior, and they ". . . constitute the available repertoire of socially recognized acts and statuses, and roles and the rules governing them" (Laws & Schwartz, 1977, p. 217). Scripts operate at social, personal, and intrapsychic levels. They are embedded in social institutions and as such are internalized by individuals. The overriding, dominant scripts receive most attention because of their primacy and potency among people's options. It is against the dominant social scripts that people attempt to match or reject their own personal social scripts. "It is clear that the . . . scripts that individuals bring to treatment exist at the intrapsychic and the interpersonal levels and most, though not all, interventions involve changes in both" (Gagnon, 1990, p. 33).

Constructing Time Lines

The concept of time is an important part of this model (Atwood, 1991; Penn, 1985; White, 1989). For example, by asking questions such as "How long has this problem been around?" and "When did you first start becoming depressed about this problem?" the therapist introduces a historical context with a beginning, a middle, and, hopefully, an end. These types of questions give persons, couples, and families information about the origins and persistence of problems and how the trends developed over time. This also helps to dispel beliefs that people are born that way, or are just like one of their parents, or any other genetic causality. The problem becomes located in time rather than in the person, and its characteristics are then examinable and observable.

Collapsing Time

Clients are asked, "If I were to take a rubber band and stretch it back to when the problem was not there, what was your life like?" Then, by asking "How long has this problem been around?" and "When did you first start having this problem?" the person's experience of the problem can be placed within a developing trend. Stretching the rubber band into the past and asking about what life was like before the problem implies that there was a time when the problem was not there. (As will be discussed later, the rubber band can also be used, if requested by the client, to stretch farther back in time to explore the person's story when he or she was a child in the family of origin.)

Stretching the rubber band into the future enables the person to envision a future without the problem: "If I were to take the rubber band and stretch it forward, say 3 months from now, and the problem was gone, what would your life be like?" Questioning about development over time is an effort that not only draws attention to the fact that the intensity of the problem varies over time but also identifies that there are times when the problem is absent and presents the possibility that the problem might not be there in the future. This lays the groundwork for ideas that the person has some control over the problem and by implication that at some point the problem will no longer be there. The progressive use of directional description of the time metaphor allows clients to understand their participation in the problem's persistence at different points in time (White, 1986b).

Change

Watzlawick, Weakland, and Fisch (1974) described two types of change: first- and second-order change. Simply, first-order change is a change that occurs *within* a system; and second-order change is a change of the system itself, a *change of change*. First-order change maintains homeostasis, whereas second-order change is a change of the premises governing the system as a whole. First-order changes are incremental modifications that make sense within an established frame (Watzlawick, 1978, 1984). Second-order change changes the frame itself. In order to accomplish second-order change, the therapist phases in particular material and phases out other material. First-order change is exemplified by traditional psychotherapy. Second-order change is represented by the approaches of Haley (1967), Minuchin (1974), Watzlawick (1978, 1984), Watzlawick, Weakland, and Fisch (1974), and White (1985, 1986a, 1986b, 1989).

Because the focus of intervention is on meaning systems and scripts, the change model described here is a second-order change model. It is similar to Epston and White's (1990) recent work whereby the therapist initially assists clients in learning processes that help them amplify (be aware of) their processes, provides techniques that they can use to generate new possibilities, and is someone who creates a safe environment for them to explore their processes, generate new possibilities, consider the implications of the possibilities, and negotiate frames around the chosen change. These ways of learning can be used by each person outside therapy. Over time, as the person learns to rely on his or her own self-healing processes, he or she becomes more confident in the processes and in his or her own abilities to generate growth and change. In this case, the result is new structures that are of a higher order—ones that are more connected and integrated than the prior ones. They are more complex, more flexible, and more susceptible to further change and development.

Counseling Strategies

Changes in the narratives that families hold about their meaning systems can lead to opportunities for change. Social construction therapy focuses on helping clients to reconstruct what is important to them, in order to provide them with more options for action (Viney, Benjamin, & Preston, 1988), and on the meanings clients place on the events they experience. It also provides clients with alternative perspectives of those events in order to enable them to change their behavior if they choose to do so. The aim of the social construction therapist is to see his or her clients' world through the clients' eyes not in order to change their view but to help them develop a variety of alternative perspectives (Viney et al., 1988).

Social construction therapy assists single-parent families by exploring the role of narrative (the family's story about the problem) in maintaining the family meaning system with the problem, and by presenting ways of challenging this meaning system. A six-stage model of therapy is described and illustrated here: (1) joining the family meaning system, (2) proposing the notion of a family meaning system, (3) learning the family's meaning system, (4) challenging the family's meaning system, (5) amplifying the new family meaning system, and (6) stabilizing the new meaning system. (See figure 6.)

Stage 1: Joining the Family Meaning System

Underlying the beginning of any therapy is the importance for the therapist of joining the family meaning system or constructing a workable reality. The dynamic interplay of joining and constructing a workable reality initiates the process of change. The *construction of a workable reality* can be defined as the process in which the view of the problem is transformed from a paradigm of individual causality to a paradigm of family interaction. It is a process analogous to socializing by which an empathic rapport is developed with the clients. The therapist's reflections serve to create an environment conducive to change. In this environment, the therapist listens to the family's language, learns it, and uses it to create a comfortable environment. The basic assumption is that the client is the expert in knowing what is best for him or her. The role of the therapist is that of curious observer—interested in learning about the family's story. The therapist interacts with the family orthogonally so as not to become part of the system.

Exploring the past.   If the family feels there are unresolved past issues contributing to the problems, the therapist can use the rubber band method described earlier to help the client move back in time. "If I were to take a rubber band and stretch it back to when you were a little girl or boy, could you tell mom or dad what it was like for you? Could you tell mom or dad what you wanted from them and didn't get? Could you tell mom and dad what you learned about yourself from the way you were treated by them? What meanings did you give these experiences? Could you also tell mom and dad what you appreciated about her or him? Could you tell mom and dad what they taught you that was helpful for you as a very young person growing up? And mom or dad, could you reflect that back?" Similar questions could be asked of the parent: "Could you tell your son or daughter what wishes, desires, hopes you had for him or her when he or she was born? And son or daughter, could you reflect that back?" This phase of therapy is used not to blame the child or parent but only if the family feels there are old unresolved issues that need to be settled. Further, the focus of this phase of therapy is not to ascertain the truthfulness of the memories but rather to put the perceptions in perspective, along with recognizing that multiple perceptions of the same event exist.

Put the past in perspective. After both parent and child(ren) have explored the story of the past, the past can be put in perspective. This can be facilitated by a ritual. The family members can write down all the important childhood events that relate to the explored issues, both negative and positive, and place the paper in a shoe box and bury it (i.e., symbolically burying the past). Family members may wish to write letters to each other, forgiving them for their mistakes and thanking them for the gifts they gave them. These letters can either be mailed or buried. The family members can have a ritualistic ceremony whereby they symbolically let go of their pain, and the effects of the pain, by setting a balloon or kite free at the beach. They can symbolically show appreciation for early gifts from each other by doing something special for them.

Stage 2: Proposing the Notion of a Family Meaning System

For single-parent families, therapy around the theoretical concepts of social constructionism can be divided into three different stories: the family's story about their families of origin (whether there are old skeletons or not), their story about their present relationships (how the problems they are experiencing are maintained), and their story about what they see for their future (how their family meanings and resultant scripts can change). Knowledge of each of these three stories helps the therapist understand the family's frame of the problem and helps the family learn about their frame of the problem. Hoffman (1990) stated that "Problems are stories people have agreed to tell themselves . . . . we have to persuade them to tell themselves a different, more empowering story, have conversations with them, through the awareness that the findings of their conversations have no other reality than that bestowed by mutual consent" (pp. 3, 4).

Thus family members are asked about what the problems associated with being a single-parent family member mean to them in their given sociocultural contexts. The notion of single-parent family is treated as a symbol invested with meaning by society. The approach to the family problem becomes a matter of symbolic analysis and interpretation, and the family problem is seen as emanating from various forms of action or practice within the family's life.

Stage 3: Learning the Present Family Meaning System

Berger and Kellner (1979) defined family as a definitional process. At this point in therapy, the family members tell their present story, and the therapist attempts to obtain as complete an understanding as possible of the family's story about the problem. By paying careful attention to linguistic symbolizations such as family myths, legends, rites, and metaphors, the therapist begins to uncover the family meaning system.

An individual's reality is maintained by developing a personal sense of self that is congruent with the social constructions. As noted earlier in this chapter, based on early interactions and ongoing socialization, individuals construct a reality around meanings that includes a preferred way of relating to others. This then becomes the basis for how they view others and how they expect others to view them. In many ways, these perceptual sets determine predictable ways of interacting with others. Here relevant questions might be "How do you think of the problem? Do you see any other options? What solutions have you attempted?"

When uncovering the family's story about the present, both the therapist and the family members learn what information the family selects out of their environment and how family members fit that information into an already existing meaning system so as to reinforce that system. For example, in a family with an adolescent with a problem, differentiating the fine line between being an adolescent with a problem and being an emotionally disturbed adolescent becomes particularly important. It makes a great difference for the family's general expectations and perceptions of the capabilities of the teenager. The therapist and the family learn how the family's patterned conversations and attempted solutions reflect this meaning system. When families learn about their meaning systems and connect them to the way they see their problems, they gather information about how they have inadvertently participated in the perpetuation of the problem. For many families, telling their stories invokes the image of a revolving door with no exits: They begin to see themselves as going around and around, unable to break out of the pattern. It is here that family members begin to reflect on the implications of their meaning system. This reflection eventually leads to the reconstructing that is crucial in social construction therapy and facilitates the relinquishment of old family sensitivities and promotes healing (see also Levine, 1987; Siegel, 1986).

Once it is accepted that a family's meaning system is socially constructed, it then becomes possible to deconstruct it. The family's meaning system can be uncovered and then challenged in order to make room for new experiences. Techniques to amplify the family's process can be used, helping the family see where they are stuck. At this point the family can choose whether to keep the uncovered meaning system or to change it, and choice has been introduced.

To amplify the family's process, tracking, circular questioning, and reflexive questioning may be used. Tracking is when the therapist focuses on the symbols, metaphors, themes, and language in order to help family members better understand their transactional process. Circular questioning is when the therapist invites one family member to comment on the relationship of other family members. Through circular questioning, a view of the meaning the problem holds for the family emerges that allows both the therapist and the family to appreciate its interconnectedness and circular nature. Reflexive questions are questions that enable the family's own healing processes to emerge. "If you make no changes, what do you think the consequences will be? What has to happen in order for your to realize that the problem is getting a little better?"

In this phase, practical issues are also explored. The therapist helps the family get unstuck by reinforcing old coping skills, reaching new skills, and providing education—about the social and community services available to them. Education is provided to the family in order to enhance its effectiveness. Educating families about family conferences (i.e., support groups for teenagers and parents) is another method that therapists can use at this time to assist these families. The conferences give the families ways to discuss sharing responsibilities; they can also give family members an opportunity to express their feelings and concerns. Support groups for adolescents can be recommended: These can normalize the experiences of the family members by helping them feel that they are not alone. The therapist also helps family members prioritize any overwhelming issues they may face. Here the therapist learns about the current situation, the family's definition of the crisis, and which decisions the family feels must be made. Family rules and roles that hinder family coping skills are explored, along with family communication styles clouding the family's definitional process. The division of labor within the family is also explored, and anger expression techniques taught and utilized.

Stage 4: Challenging the Family's Meaning System

Once the notion of a family meaning system is accepted by the family, and the individual family meaning system is uncovered, a competing meaning system can be introduced. It is not apparent to most individuals that there are alternative ways of behaving at each stage of the life cycle. Our meaning systems make areas outside the dominant ones appear invisible. This invisibility serves to maintain and foster adherence to the dominant definitions. In fact, the function of socialization and of the sanctions against moving outside the dominant script is to keep individuals within it. To find, name, focus on, and help the family experience alternative meanings and scripts is the intention of this stage.

Change is normal, and people have a choice in change. Knowledge about how to behave is learned by social definitions of appropriate and inappropriate ways of behaving; however, individuals can choose to develop their own personal attitudes and concepts that differ from the traditional ones. Numerous scripts are available for examination. Here the role of the therapist is to notice competing constructions or exceptions in the family's meaning system. Change requires a two-sided perspective, and a therapist may seek to construct a relational definition by developing two (or complementary) descriptions of the problem (White, 1986b). Complementary questions are derived and introduced to challenge or help deconstruct the dominant explanation and assist families in achieving a relational or double description of the problem. This double description then provides the source of new responses (Atwood & Levine, 1991; White, 1986b). The family's explanation, or frame, begins to overlap the frame offered by the therapist (like two overlapping Venn diagrams), and it is in this overlap that there is the possibility for change.

Bateson's (1979) original concept of restraints has been expanded by de Shazer (1991) and White (1989), who use the concepts of *exceptions* and *unique outcomes* to refer to those ideas, events, experiences less likely to be noticed by people because they are dissonant with individuals' description of the problem. Exceptions are noticing the flip side of the coin. White believed that as a family's view of reality is challenged through questioning about these exceptions, family members ultimately recognize other aspects of their reality that do not involve the problem. In so doing they create another story (narrative), a second story, about their lives that does not include the problem.

For de Shazer (1991), exceptions refer to times in the client's life when the problem was not happening. The therapist "seeks to find the element in the system studied (their conversation about the client's complaint, goals, etc.) which is alogical, the thread . . . which will unravel it all, or the loose stone which will pull down the whole building" (de Shazer, 1991, p. 158).

The therapist reinforces alternatives to the dominant description of the problem—helping to make visible areas outside the dominant meaning system. In so doing, he or she begins to undermine what previously had been specifying and justifying the family's reality (Amundson, 1990). Anderson and Goolishian (1988) stated that:

> . . . to deconstruct means to take apart the interpretive assumption of the system of meaning that you are examining, to challenge the interpretive system in such a manner that you reveal the assumptions on which the model is based. At the same time as these are revealed, you open the space for alternative understanding. (p. 11)

Now the therapist begins to plant new seeds, and the old frame begins to break up. The old frame breaking up is the basis of a different level of order. "Are there ever times when the problem is not there?" The receipt of news of differences is essential for the revelation of new ideas and a triggering of new responses for the discovery of new solutions. An exception is found. Now it must be amplified. A piece has been found that does not fit the overall puzzle. This piece has the possibility to grow, beginning the deconstruction of the old frame (meaning system) and amplification and activation of the new construction—the new frame.

Here the family is encouraged to focus on the positive elements of their interactions. They are encouraged to observe what they are doing right and to increase those behaviors. The therapist highlights and emphasizes the smallest positive difference through obtaining thorough descriptions of exceptions, changes, or possible solutions.

Stage 5: Amplifying the New Meaning System

The amplification of the exception is essential for the triggering of the new construction that holds the possibility of new solutions (Bateson, 1972). The therapist now amplifies the competing constructions in the family's meaning system. "When the problem is not there, how is your relationship? If you were to enjoy your relationship more frequently, how might you notice? What might be different? What else might be different? How might that be for you?" By helping the family deepen the experience of the relationship without the problem, the therapist is facilitating a new construction, a more positive relationship. This new construction holds new meanings for the family. Thus the therapist creates an environment that amplifies the family's strengths, resources, and solutions (Lipchick, 1988).

Stage 6: Stabilizing the New Meaning System

At this point, alternative meaning systems are available to the family, and what once was invisible now holds potential for new solutions. The original meaning system that held the problem has been deconstructed and replaced by a new description. The family can now being to focus on the future. Future focus enables them to visualize their relationship without the problem. Ask questions like "If you could stretch the rubber band 3 years into the future and the problem was gone, what might that look like? How might your relationship be different? How else might it be different?"

By asking questions around future trends and choices, the therapist is making that future more real and more stable. As Penn (1985) suggested, when faced with questions about the future—even if that future really only has the status of the hypothetical—"the system is free to create a new map" (p. 300). Questions such as "How will your future without the problem be different from the future with the problem?'' require speculation about difference and help consolidate the emerging new meaning system for the family. Often rehearsal precedes performance. A version of de Shazer's (1991) miracle question can be used: ''If a miracle were to happen tonight while you were asleep and tomorrow morning you awoke to find that this problem were no longer a part of your life, what would be different? How would you know that this miracle had taken place? How could your mom or dad be able to tell without your telling them?''

Another way of stabilizing the new meaning system was put forth by Epston and White (1990) when they discussed how they invite family members to a special meeting where, through questioning, they discuss the persons' story of their therapy adventure. The family members are asked to recount how they became aware of their problem and what steps they took to solve it. They then recount how and which resources they mobilized as they generated solutions to their problems. That is, they can recount their transition from a problematic status to a resolved one. In addition, the therapist also can provide his or her story of the person's therapy adventure, and they can then discuss their collaborative efforts, thereby helping to reinforce the notion of a new meaning system.

Using the Six-Stage Model

The successful functioning of single-parent families clearly requires a flexibility in structure and roles and the development of responses to new developmental needs and challenges. Patterns that may have been functional in earlier stages may no longer fit and new options must be explored. The following case history and discussion illustrate how the six-stage social construction therapy model assists family members through this life cycle transition.

> Carol is a 35-year-old single parent. She has been divorced from her husband Edward for 4 years. She is the custodial parent of their two children, Danielle, age 14, and Michael, age 15. They came for therapy because Michael was called down to the school principal's office when he cursed at his soccer coach. Carol reported to the counselor that Michael had failed three subjects the past quarter, and although he never was a straight A student, he usually managed to receive Cs or better. In addition, fighting with his sister had increased over the past few months.
>
> Because Carol was having a difficult time living on the money Edward gave her for child support, she had taken a job as a bank teller at a local bank. The job helped, but the family had to tighten its belts. This was difficult because before the divorce they had a very comfortable life style. Michael was no longer able to go skiing with his friends over winter break,

and he had to wait until Carol saved the money before he could get new soccer equipment. Danielle had to stop her dance lessons and was only able to buy one new outfit in September when school started. The children were often resentful, complained bitterly about their financial straits, and blamed Carol for the divorce.

Their bitterness peaked when they had to sell the house in which they had lived all their lives and move into an apartment. Although Carol tried to make it into a nice home, she felt that no matter what she said, they would never be happy. The children hated the fact that their dog Snuffy had to be given away because there was a no-pet rule in the new apartment. They hated that they had to go to a new school where they had no friends. They hated that all their friends lived on the other side of town. They hated that they only saw their Dad every other weekend. They hated that they had to help their Mom with the household chores. They hated each other, and they hated their Mom. They hated the idea that their parents were divorced and were ashamed to tell anyone about their family situation. So they didn't invite any of their friends over after school for fear that someone would learn of their single-parent status. They felt that the only sane person was their Dad who, when he picked them up for the weekend, bought them presents and let them stay up very late watching television.

Figure 5.   Summary of Social Construction Therapy

SOCIAL CONSTRUCTIONIST THERAPY FLOWING FROM THIS VIEW

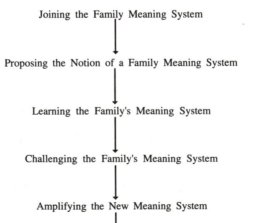

Joining the Family Meaning System

Proposing the Notion of a Family Meaning System

Learning the Family's Meaning System

Challenging the Family's Meaning System

Amplifying the New Meaning System

Stablizing the New Meaning System

After the divorce, but before Carol began working, Carol had to apply for food stamps, much to the embarrassment of her children. They felt as if they were now lower class, and it was all Carol's fault. Carol was exhausted. She was tired from trying to keep the family together only to listen to the children argue incessantly during dinner. When she began working, she was tired of working all day and then having to cook dinner. She caught a glimpse of herself in the mirror one day and saw an old woman. At first she almost didn't recognize herself. Her sister encouraged her to date, or to at least occasionally go to the movies, but Carol was simply too tired. She could not see any solution to these problems and was very resentful of Edward, who was an attorney and who could well afford to give the family extra money. Instead, Edward paid only what the court stated, which was not enough money for even one person to live on, let alone three. At times, she almost felt as if she had made a wrong decision to divorce Edward, but then she remembered the humiliation of his countless affairs and knew better. Carol felt as if she had no life. She didn't see any hope for the future. As far as dating or going out with her friends, she had no energy left at the end of a long day and felt that even if she did, no one would be interested in a "tired old hag."

When Carol came in for therapy, she expressed great concern over "the tension and hostility that existed within the home." She also reported that she was experiencing depression because of having "no life." In the first stage of therapy, the therapist *joined with the family's meaning system*. As a curious observer, the therapist listened and learned the family's language and story about the problem and then used this language to join and create a comfortable environment.

The second stage of therapy involved *proposing the notion of a family meaning system*. To do this the therapist needed to understand the family's frame of the problem. Each member was asked to tell his or her stories about the problems, about the present family relationships, and about what he or she sees for the future. The therapist learned through Carol's story that she had been a housewife for her entire life, just like her own mother. Carol's story contained the belief that "children need their mother at home." Her story was filled with feelings of guilt and incompetence as well as anger at Edward for causing this situation. She felt the need to defend herself and her role in the family to Michael and Danielle. Another belief present in Carol's story was "a good mother is judged by the amount of time she spends with her children." When Carol told her story about her family or origin, she shared with her children the controversy that existed and still does between her and her mother. She was never "close to her mother, feels like a disobeying child even now when she is around her, and fears that this will happen with her own children." Michael's story repeated the theme that "My mother is never around any more, and even when she is, she's so miserable, no one wants to be around her." He, like Danielle, wished that Karen stayed home with them even though rationally they both knew that financially she could not afford to.

The children believed that Carol "overreacted" to their father's affairs, although they did admit that he "sometimes" went too far. When asked to tell their story about "Carol's depression," they all agreed that it stemmed from the loss of the marriage. They could not predict when it might hit Carol, but when it did, it bothered everyone. Carol hardly spoke to anyone and she remained in bed sometimes for days."

The third stage of therapy involved *learning about the family's meaning system* in the present. The goal was to identify what information the family was selecting from the environment to fit into each of their meaning systems and how it was reinforcing the present system. It is at this time that the family learned about how each one of them inadvertently participated in the perpetuation of the family's problem.

When Michael was asked, "How do you think of the problem?" his story was that his mother was going through a hard time without dad and that she should reconsider her position about divorce. If she went back to Dad for a little while, "things would be better for her and us. Mom has always been involved with her family and in doing for others, and this is what makes her happy. It's no wonder she gets tired from working and depressed with all the fighting and tension in the house. Everyone is always fighting. It never used to be this way when we lived with Dad."

Danielle was asked to answer the same question. She said, "The problem is not that I don't appreciate Mom's help. It's just that she isn't there enough. We're always alone!!" Danielle believed the fighting started when Carol came home from work and asked the children to either help with dinner or to clean up their mess. Carol's rule was that they were to do their homework when they returned home from school before they went outside to play or watched television. What often happened instead was that they called their father to ask his permission to go out, and he said, "Sure, go out and play and have fun. You're only young once. You can do your homework later." Then Carol came home, saw their homework not done, started yelling, and then called Edward to yell at him also. By the time they all sat down to dinner, the tension level was high. And their homework was still not done. After dinner, she was too tired to yell at them to study, so she went to her room and fell asleep. The principal said that Michael hands in about one out of every five homework assignments and that this was the main reason for his failures. Carol said that at this point they fight almost everyday over similar incidents and that she feels completely alone because Edward never supports her with the children.

Edward was resentful about the divorce and felt also that Carol overreacted to his indiscretions. "After all," he said, "he still was a good father and husband." The only times when he at all supported her was when

Michael cursed at his soccer coach and when he failed three subjects on his report card. Then he came over, and the two of them had a long talk with him. But Carol felt that instead of things getting better after the talk, they seemed to have gotten worse. And now every time Michael got into trouble at school, he shouted, "Go ahead, Mom, why don't you call Dad? Can't you handle things?" The counselor believed that at least some of Michael's problem behavior was serving to keep Edward involved in the family.

For the future, Danielle wished that Carol could just "be a mother." When asked to define *just a mother*, Danielle said "someone to spend time with us, not work and be there after school." Carol believed that the problem is Edward's. She has done everything she could think of and that now it's Edward's turn. If he gave them more money, or supported her decisions, the problems would cease. She should not have to come home from work and into a house filled with yelling. Carol stated that she did feel that "Edward should be more adamant with Michael about staying home after school and doing his homework." Carol told stories about her own role as a caretaker. She was very proud of the job she did caring for her family. Now Carol no longer thought of herself as being a "good mother" and caretaker. When asked to define a *good mother*, Carol said "A good mother is there for her kids emotionally and physically until the are older and more independent, and even then she is still there if they need her." Carol believed that if she were a better mother and not working so much, then she could spend more time "mothering the children." The family agreed that the construct *mothering* had different meanings for each of them, and that because of their different views, each was perpetuating the problem in the family.

Challenging the family's meaning system was the fourth stage of therapy. Michael was grateful for all his mother did when he was little. He also stated that "mothers need to be appreciated and respected for all the work they do." Michael was questioned and confronted on this belief because Carol did not feel appreciated or respected by him. Michael's reply was "I guess I never thought about it that way because her mothering now is different than it used to be." Carol's belief was that she is not a good mother because she is not spending time with her children. She was then asked who was taking that quality time from her. She replied "No one." The counselor asked "When the children do not have their homework done before dinner, who helps them?" She replied, "Most of the time it winds up being me after dinner." "So then is that considered quality time?" Carol replied "Yes." "So, in essence, Carol, the children not doing their homework when they return home from school is actually supplying you with the opportunity for more quality time when you come home so you can be a good mother?" After a long pause Carol answered "If you look at it that way then, yes." Carol then added "Most of the fighting happens during the week. We seem to get along better on the weekends." Carol was asked "Is this because you spend more quality time over the weekend?" "Yes." "I'm sorry Carol, I'm confused, which is more important to you: the quality of time or the quantity?" Carol said "The quality of time."

Carol's beliefs about mothering and caretaking were also challenged. Carol stated that she has been a mother practically her whole adult life and considered herself an expert at it. She defined an expert mother as someone who can provide for her children's needs—both physically and emotionally. The belief that she had reached expert mother status was then challenged because Carol, "although a very good and accomplished mother (i.e., caretaker) had forgotten recently to take care of one person—herself." Carol agreed that she would like to be a little selfish and care for herself sometimes. She was told to go slowly with this idea because once she started to take care herself, this could be scary. Carol disagreed. "I can take care of myself first and still use any extra time to spend with the children." The family was then asked to talk about times when they were not fighting and what were they doing instead that made the problem disappear.

The fifth stage of therapy focused on *amplifying the new meaning system.* The therapist amplified the exceptions found in the family's original story. The goal was to deepen the family's experience of their relationships without the problem. The family and therapist conversed about times when the family was problemless. Each member described how it would be for them in the future and how it was for them now when the problem was not there. By doing this the family co-created a new, more positive, construction of their family.

The last stage of therapy was *stabilizing the family's new meaning system.* The family now was focusing on the future. When the rubber-band method was used with the family, and they each were asked to stretch it 2 years into the future, Carol saw herself participating in "single activities" at the church and taking up offers from friends to go out. She also saw herself managing her job and family. She felt she could be secure and confident and maybe have a polite relationship with Edward. Michael saw himself spending more time with his father. He felt that the quality time his mother and he spent together could strengthen their relationship. Michael and Danielle were both happy and proud of Carol that she was now "doing for herself," and they both appreciated what she adds to their life.

By speaking of the future, the family formed a new and more positive family map. Their future without the problem was becoming more stable and realistic and was within their control and reach. The family had co-created through language a new family meaning system and had come to realize that they are in control of their own future.

Chapter 12

CONCLUSIONS

Whether or not the single-parent household, or any other kind of family arrangement for that matter, becomes a personal or social disaster depends upon the availability of sufficient material resources, supportive social networks, and the quality of culturally shared beliefs around it. No single family form produces an optimal milieu for a growing child. No family type is more natural to the human species than any other. Children need to have their emotional and physical needs met, but this can be accomplished by a wide variety of social arrangements. It is not necessary that this be done exclusively by biological parents in a nuclear family structure.

Re-examining the Pathology Assumption

Children of divorce are often viewed in the social science literature as pathological creatures, victims of an inherently deviant event, destined to suffer a lifetime of failure. The same view holds true for their divorcing parents. These deficit models of divorce present a pathological picture, citing prominent studies in which divorce is deviant and its effects deleterious. The literature does, however, present research that alludes to healthy reactions to and because of divorce. For example, a growing body of research suggests that the consequences of divorce are far from uniform, and that many adults and children appear to be able to cope well with the stressful events generally associated with divorce. Even some early studies demonstrated that a sizable portion of the population appears to be able to emerge from the periods of transition resulting from the divorce psychologically healthy, and even possibly stronger for having successfully mastered the challenge caused by the break-up of the home. More and better studies methodologically are sure to follow, and the message is an important one to get out to parents through the schools and public agencies as well as through an informed population of counselors and therapists.

The positive evidence beginning to accumulate in clinical, empirical, and theoretical studies suggests that children of divorce often experience

217

outcomes less or no more difficult than children from two-parent family structures. There is a growing recognition that the effects of family configurations that differ from the model two-parent nuclear family need not be negative and that the stigmatization associated with this phenomenon appears to (or should) be lessening. In light of this body of research, it is becoming more apparent that a rethinking of the social value system that fuels the thought that divorce is bad and shameful should be addressed.

In American society, romantic love is not only an expectation for a potential marriage partner but a demand. Combined with socially transmitted, unrealistically based sets of expectations around the institution of marriage and the marital roles, it is not surprising that the divorce rate is approaching 60% of all first marriages. The natural outcome of this combination is profound disappointment when individuals fall in love with the man or woman of their dreams and find they are not living happily ever after. The reality is that the "Father Knows Best" traditional two-parent family, where dad works and mom stays home with the kids, represents a clear minority (less than 10%) of all American households. If we continue to accept the concept that those who do not achieve the ideal are failures, then we are a society of failures. It is these same socially constructed definitions that create the ideas of broken homes and broken dreams—in response to social definitions that no longer reflect the world—and so help to create self-fulfilling prophesies in millions of people in the United States.

It is hoped that in writing this book we have shown (or at least presented) the possibility that the effect of divorce can be a positive, even healthy move toward growth and maturity. Divorce may represent a transition from an unhealthy or untenable situation, for not only are adults and their children not necessarily negatively impacted by the ensuing single parent status, but also a sizeable number of our broken-home population appear to be happy.

As we have shown, a body of research is beginning to emerge that demonstrates that the outcomes of divorce for children and their parents can be positive and growth enhancing. As professional counselors, we can help single parents recognize that the difficulties associated with the one-parent family are part of the life experience of a single head of a family, not part of a deviant family structure. We can assist them in handling these difficulties—whether they be struggling with social definitions or the associated psychological reactions—and in so doing play a crucial role in helping these families adjust to this transition. However, we need also to be certain that we are sending a clear message to these families that one-parent families can be healthy, vital, nurturing family systems. We can encourage the understanding that different kinds of family structures are okay and that transitions can create stronger, better families.

We have stressed the theme that counselors must be alert to the probability that the single-parent families themselves, the professionals who work with them, and the institutions they encounter have defined these families in some way as deficient. The crucial issue from a counseling perspective is simply stated: If the response to a single-parent family through death or divorce is pathologically defined, then family members are relieved by these professionals of the responsibility of making any adaptive changes. If the locus of power to make change is assumed to be always outside the family system, that is, society's definitions about what it means to be a single parent or a child living in a one-parent household, then family members will address their situation with a passive perspective. They will learn to be helpless much like Seligman's famous dogs (1975). They will think, feel, and behave as if they have no personal power or authority to control their own lives. It is the responsibility of counselors to be aware of the effects of these negative assumptions about the single-parent system, and to understand the negative impact that these assumptions might have on the family. It is also the responsibility of the counselor vigorously to investigate and dispute any constructions adopted by themselves and by the family that suggest powerlessness.

The Myths of Pathology

The most common myths of pathology cluster around such central issues as the raising of children, the redefining of relationships, the maintaining of a sexual self, the interacting with larger systems, the creating of constructs of reality. Should the actions, beliefs, or affects of family members appear to be shaped by one or more of them, the counselor is urged to refute them through the use of the research presented in this book within the context of a systemic behavioral approach to counseling (Atwood, 1992).

These nonadaptive cognitive structures encountered every day by single parents include the following:

- **Children in single-parent families always have deficits.** This myth is pervasive in our society and is based on the assumptions that the physical and/or psychological loss of one parent insures long-term negative effects and that the loss is irretrievable and cannot be dealt with. It is also predicated on the assumption that the new one-parent situation is not as good as the old.
- **Single parents cannot be both parents (nurturers) and breadwinners. One role suffers.** This myth is based on the assumption that single parents may either be the providers of nurturance and guidance to their children, or they may be the providers of material goods by being workers. They cannot be both.

- **Single parents themselves must be psychologically traumatized.** This myth is based on the assumption that the psychological trauma associated with the divorce or death of the spouse leads to a diminution in the ability to parent, to work effectively outside of the home, and to interact with friends, family, and social institutions. Further, the effects of this trauma last forever.
- **The single-parent family is only a temporary situation until the woman finds a new man to marry.** Again this myth is based on the assumption that the two-parent model is better and that all single parents will opt for marriage if it is available to them.
- **Single parents have forfeited their right to be sexual beings.** Because individuals are only permitted to practice sex within a marital situation, if single parents act out their sexual needs, they are not only considered promiscuous but also selfish. Further, single-parent sexual activity traumatizes children.
- **Children in single-parent families are expected to do poorly in school and to suffer emotionally and behaviorally.** This myth is based on the assumption that the one-parent family structure denies these children both proper role models and sufficient discipline to allow them to accommodate to the demands of their academic schoolwork. It also assumes that children are affected psychologically and therefore suffer psychological problems as a result of the loss of one parent.
- **Economic deprivation, absolute or relative, has very little to do with the problems encountered by single parents.** This myth is based on the notion that it is only the psychological poverty of the single-parent families that causes the difficulties.
- **Being a single parent means that life is horrible.** This myth is based on the assumption that being in a two-parent family is the best possible family system for adults and children. It is also based on the assumption that single parents have little or no control over their environment, that single-parent systems that thrive are the rarity or are lucky, and that nothing can be done to improve the lot of the single parent.

Interpersonal and Systemic Circularity

The counseling approaches described in earlier chapters are systemic and behavioral. We think in terms of family systems and the interrelationship among their components. We believe that clients must do (behave) if they are to change, and that insight alone is not enough. We have not, however, in the adoption of this position lost sight of the individual as he or she interacts with family, friends, and society, as demonstrated by the focus of the chapter on social constructionism. We understand the quality of a person's well-being to be the result of a complex and mutual reciprocity among interacting variables (Bandura, 1978).

In a pure pathology model, behavior is seen as the external manifestation of internal characteristics, traits, conflicts. Just as the delusions of a paranoid schizophrenic are deemed to result from the projection of his or her own unacceptable sexual and aggressive drives, the pathology model suggests that the behavior of single parents results from a poor psychological adjustment to the loss of the previous partner. The inability to neutralize the effects of loss is considered to be the dominant personal characteristic that causes nonadaptive behavior in a linear fashion:

Personal characteristic ——————→ Behavior

The pathology model has been criticized by behaviorists as simplistic because it ignores the impact of environmental factors on behavior. Radical behaviorists take the position that internal constructs are unobservable and not subject to direct therapeutic intervention. A functional analysis of those environmental stimuli that maintain problematic behaviors is the key to behavioral interventions. Behavioral therapy aimed at two underachieving students, for example, will probably not be influenced by the fact that one was from a single-parent family and the other from a two-parent system. The internal reaction to loss will not be dealt with as the radical behavioral model posits behavior to be caused, linearly, by environmental factors such as the nature and rate of reinforcement contingent upon particular behaviors:

Environment ——————→ Behavior

Cognitive-behaviorists take a more interactive stance. From this position, environmental factors are filtered by a person's belief systems, which attach subjective meaning to the events. For example, if an underachieving student believes him- or herself to be less than peers with two parents, failure on a single examination may be interpreted as evidence that failure on all future tests is inevitable. Such a combination of an event and the personal belief about the event can cause the kinds of behavior that result in failure:

Personal characteristic ←——————
                                    ——————→ Behavior
Environment ←——————

Our position suggests that behavior may influence both environment and traits as well as being caused by them:

Personal characteristic ←——————
        ↕   ——————→ Behavior
Environment ←——————

For example, if the counselor can assist the single parent in shifting her personal belief system from passive to active, it is likely that her behavior will change. Changes in her behavior will impact on the environment response to the single-parent family. If a single mother comes to believe that her child's difficulty in school is the result of the interplay among the student, the teacher, the guidance counselor, the administration of the school, and the family, and not because she is a child from a broken home, then she will take a more active role in addressing the problem. Armed with the attitude of an informed consumer, she will insist that the family and the school work together to assess and intervene at the most appropriate level to best serve the child's needs. In the face of a parent who demonstrates this sort of strong personal conviction and who demonstrates such goal-directed behavior, it is more likely that the social institution, the school, will respond in an appropriate way. As these sorts of interactions grow, so do the feelings of self-worth and can-do attitudes with the family. And can-do beats waiting for the white knight hands down.

Part of the experience of the divorcing process is structured by the expectations of the professionals encountered. In counseling divorcing adults or one-parent families, it is important to help clients be realistic about the negatives that can result from divorce. Equally important is the other side of the story and assisting clients to understand that one-parent families can help children grow emotionally as well as provide needed support for parents. Counselors and educators can help by informing their colleagues and their clients that divorce does not necessarily result in negative outcomes for children or adults. They can caution them about making unfair and inappropriate assumptions about children from one-parent homes.

In summary, then, we need to examine our own assumptions about the one-parent family system. It is only in this way that we can help single parents learn to draw on their strengths, assist them in not seeing themselves as having failed, and help them greet their future with hope and new confidence.

In contrast to our cherished fantasies about romantic love and marriage, the norm in society is now (or is fast becoming) the single and/or single-parent family home: Over 21% of all American households represent adults living alone, another 3% cohabitations with another adult partner, 13% single-parent homes. Add to that the number of two-parent homes that are remarriages, and it becomes apparent that the definition of what is normal could use some updating.

It is important that we continue to assist children of this and future generations as different family situations arise. Until a time when equilibrium is achieved, we must search out and support families experiencing difficulty. Through a reeducation of society, the currently widespread negative views and connotations could be addressed.

On a macro sociological level, we need to rethink the function of marriage in the 1990s and look beyond into the new society of tommorrow. Changes in economic, religious, educational, and moral values and an extended life span will contribute to transforming our relationships and family structures. This can be seen as influencing children in many positive ways.

With more than 57% of all first marriages ending in divorce, we need to rethink the notion that marriage is a failure when it ends in divorce. Rather we need to look at the social institutions of marriage and the family and the associated socially constructed norms, values, and definitions as part of our analysis. As divorce occurs, we need to look at the problems caused by the writing of new scripts and in turn construct new stories offering healthy solutions. Divorce as a concept must become a psychological shift away from deviance to, if not normative behavior, then one possible normative life cycle transition.

REFERENCES

Adams, B. N. (1968). *Kinship in an urban setting.* Chicago: Markham.

Ahrons, C. (1980). Redefining the divorced family: A conceptual framework. *Social Work, 25,* 437–441.

Ahrons, C. R., & Rodgers, R. H. (1987). *Divorced families: A multidisciplinary developmental view.* New York: W.W. Norton.

Alan Guttmacher Institute (1976). *Eleven million teenagers: What can be done about the epidemic of adolescent pregnancies in the U.S.?* New York: Alan Guttmacher Institute.

Albert, R. S. (1971). Cognitive development and parental loss among the gifted, the exceptionally gifted, and the creative. *Psychological Reports, 29*(1), 19–26.

Amundson, J. (1990). In defense of minimalism: Making the least out of depression. *Family Therapy Case Studies, 5*(1), 15–19.

Anderson, H., & Goolishian, H. (1988). Human systems as linguistic systems: Preliminary and evolving ideas about the implication for clinical theory. *Family Process, 27,* 371–393.

Araoz, D. (1982). *Hypnosis and sex therapy.* New York: Brunner and Mazel.

Arditti, J. A. (1992). Differences between fathers with joint custody and noncustodial fathers. *American Journal of Orthopsychiatry, 62*(2), 186–195.

Atchley, R. C. (1975). *Social forces in later life.* Belmont, CA: Wadsworth.

Atwood, J. D. (1987). Sexually single again. In E. Weinstein & E. Rosen (Eds.), *Sexuality counseling.* Pacific Grove, CA: Brooks/Cole.

Atwood, J. D. (1991). Killing two slumpos with one stone: Therapy with a man with depression. *Family Therapy Case Studies, 5,* 43–50.

Atwood, J. (1992). A systemic-behavioral approach to counseling the single-parent family. In J. Atwood (Ed.), *Family therapy: A systemic-behavioral approach.* Chicago: Nelson-Hall.

Atwood, J. D., & Donnelly, J. W. (in press). Adolescent pregnancy: Combating the problem from a multisystemic health perspective. *Journal of Health Education.*

Atwood, J., & Gagnon, J. H. (1987). Masturbation in college youth. *Journal of Sex Education and Therapy, 13*(2), 35–42.

Atwood, J. D., & Kasindorf, S. (1992). A multisystemic approach to adolescent pregnancy. *The American Journal of Family Therapy, 20*(4), 65–84.

Atwood, J. D., & Levine, L. (1991). Ax murderers, dragons, spiders, and webs: Therapeutic metapors in couple therapy. *Contemporary Family Therapy, 13*(3), 201–217.

Bagarozzi, D. A. (1980). Wholistic family therapy and clinical supervision: Systems, behavioral and psychoanalytic perspective. *Family Therapy, 7,* 153–165.

Balsweick, J. O., & Peek, C. W. (1971). The inexpressive male: A tragedy of American society. *The Family Coordinator, 20,* 363–368.

Bandura, A. (1978). The self-system in reciprocal determinism. *American Psychologist, 32*(4), 344–358.

Barrett, C. J. (1977). Women in widowhood. *Signs, 2*(4), 856–868.

Barrett, C. J. (1978). Effectiveness of widows groups in facilitating change. *Journal of Consulting and Clinical Psychology, 46*(1), 20–31.

Barrett, C. J. (1981). Intimacy in widowhood. *Psychology of Women Quarterly, 5*(3), 473–487.

Barry, A. (1979). A research project on successful single-parent families. *American Journal of Family Therapy, 7*(3), 65–74.

Bateson, G. (1972). *Steps to an ecology of mind.* New York: Ballantine Books.

Bateson, G. (1979). *Mind and nature: A necessary unity.* New York: Dutton.

Baydar, N. (1988). Effects of parental separation and reentry into union on the emotional well-being of children. *Journal of Marriage and the Family, 18*(3), 149–159.

Beal, E. (1980). Separation, divorce, and single-parent families. In E. Carter & M. McGoldrick (Eds.), *The family life cycle: A framework for family therapy* (pp. 241–264). New York: Gardner Press.

Beck, A. (1970). Cognitive therapy: Nature and relation to behavior therapy. *Behavior Therapy, 1,* 184–200.

Beck, A. T., Rush, A. J., Shaw, B., & Emery, G. (1979). *Cognitive therapy of depression.* New York: Guilford Press.

Becker, G. S. (1974). A theory of marriage. In T. W. Schultz (Ed.), *Economies of the family* (pp. 87–110). Chicago: University of Chicago Press.

Beer, J. (1989a). Relation of divorce to self-concepts and grade point averages of fifth grade school children. *Psychological Reports, 65,* 104–106.

Beer, J. (1989b). Relationship of divorce to self-concept, self-esteem, and grade point average of fifth and sixth grade school children. *Psychological Reports, 65,* 1379–1383.

Berger, P., & Kellner, K. (1979). Marriage and the social construction of reality. In H. Bobboy, S. Greenblatt, & C. Clark (Eds.), *Social interaction: Introductory readings in sociology* (pp. 78–99). New York: St. Martin's Press.

Berger, P., & Luckmann, T. (1966). *The Social Construction of Reality.* New York: Irvington.

Berman, W., & Turk, D. (1981). Adaption to divorce. Problems and coping strategies. *Journal of Marriage and the Family, 43,* 179–189.

Besdine, M. (1968). The Jocasta complex, mothering, and genius: I. *Psychoanalytic Review, 55*(2), 259–277.

Blades, J., Gosse, R., McKay, M., & Rogers, P. D. (1984). *The divorce book.* Oakland: New Harbinger Books.

Blauner, R. (1968). Death and social structure. In B. L. Neugarten (Ed.), *Middle age and aging* (pp. 531–540). Chicago: University of Chicago Press.

Bloom, B. L., White, S. W., & Asher, S. J. (1979). Marital disruption as a stressful life event. In G. Levinger & O. C. Moles (Eds.), *Divorce and separation: Context, causes, and consequences* (pp. 55–72). New York: Basic Books.

Bolton, F. (1980). *The pregnant adolescent.* Beverly Hills, CA: Sage.

Boss, P. (1991). Ambiguous loss. In F. Walsh & M. McGoldrick (Eds.), *Living beyond loss: Death in the family* (pp. 20–38). New York: W. W. Norton.

Bowen, M. (1978). *Family therapy in clinical practice.* New York: Jason Aronson.

Bowlby, J. (1969). *Attachment and loss* (Vol. 3). New York: Basic Books.

Braver, S., Gonzalez, N., Wolchik, S., & Sandler, I. (1989). Economic hardship and psychological distress in custodial mothers. *Journal of Divorce, 12*(4), 19–34.

Brofenbrenner, U. (1979). Contexts of childrearing: Problems and prospects. *American Psychologist, 34*(10), 844–850.

Brophy, J., & Everston, C. (1978). Context variables in tracking. *Educational Psychologist, 12,* 310–316.

Brown, C. A., Feldberg, R., Fox, E. M., & Kohen, J. (1976). Divorce: Chance of a new lifetime. *Journal of Social Issues, 32,* 119–133.

Brown, J. H., Eichenberger, S. A., Portes, P. R., & Christensen, D. N. (1991). Family functioning factors associated with the adjustment of children of divorce. *Journal of Divorce and Remarriage, 15*(1/2), 81–95.

Brown, N. D., & Samis, M. D. C. (1986/1987). The application of structural family therapy in developing the binuclear family. *Mediation Quarterly, 14/15,* 51–69.

Bureau of the Census (1989). Studies in marriage and the family. (Series p-23, No. 162). Washington, DC: Government Printing Office.

Cargan, L. (1981). Singles: An experimentation of two stereotypes. *Family Relations, 30,* 377–385.

Cargan, L., & Melko, M. (1982). *Singles, myths, and Realities.* Beverly Hills, CA: Russell Sage.

Carter, B., & McGoldrick, M. (Eds.). (1980). *The changing family life cycle: A framework for family therapy.* New York: Gardner Press.

Carter, B., & McGoldrick, M. (Eds.). (1988). *The changing family life cycle: A framework for family therapy* (2nd ed.). New York: Gardner Press.

Cashion, B. G. (1982). Female-headed families: Effects on children and clinical implications. *Journal of Marital and Family Therapy, 8,* 77–85.

Clapp, G. (1992). *Divorce and new beginnings.* New York: John Wiley & Sons.

Clayton, P. J., & Bornstein, P. E. (1976). Widows and widowers. *Medical Aspects of Human Sexuality, 10*(9), 26–27.

Clayton, P. J., Halikes, J. A., & Maurice, W. L. (1971). The bereavement of the widowed. *Diseases of the Nervous System, 32,* 597–604.

Cleveland, W. P., & Gianturco, D. T. (1976). Remarriage probability after widowhood: A retrospective method. *Journal of Gerontology, 31*(1), 99–103.

Commerce Department survey. (1987, April 17). *Wall Street Journal,* p. 42.

Cornelius, G. M., & Yawkey, T. D. (1985). Imaginativeness in preschoolers and single-parent families. *Journal of Creative Behavior, 19*(1), 56–66.

Demo, D., & Acock, A. (1988). The impact of divorce on children. *Journal of Marriage and the Family, 50,* 619–648.

de Shazer, S. (1985). *Keys to solution in brief therapy.* New York: W.W. Norton.

de Schazer, S. (1991). Putting difference to work. New York: W.W. Norton.

Ditzion, S. (1978). *Marriage, morals, and sex in America: A history of ideas.* New York: W.W. Norton.

Durkheim, E. (1951). *Suicide: A study in sociology.* New York: The Free Press.

Dusek, J. (1975). Do teachers bias children's learning? *Review of Educational Research,* *45,* 661–684.

Dusek, J., & Joseph, S. (1983). The bases of teachers expectancies: A meta-analysis. *Journal of Educational Psychology, 75,* 327–346.

Ellis, A. (1962). *Reason and emotion in psychotherapy.* New York: Lyle Stuart.

Emery, R. (1982). Interactional conflict and the children of discord and divorce. *Psychological Bulletin, 92*(2), 310–330.

Emery, R. E., Hetherington, E. M., & DiLalla, L. F. (1984). Divorce, children, and social policy. *Child Development Research and Social Policy, 1,* 189–266.

Epstein, J. (1974). *Divorce in America.* New York: E. P. Dutton.

Epston, D., & White, M. (1990). Consulting your consultants: The documentation of alternative knowledges. *Dulwich Centre Newsletter,* p. 4.

Erikson, E. H., (1963). *Childhood and society.* New York: W.W. Norton.

Ferree, M. M. (1984). The view from below: Women's employment and gender equality in working class families. In B. B. Hess & M. B. Sussman (Eds.), *Women and the family: Two decades of change* (pp. 39–57). New York: Hawthorn Press.

Everett, C. A. (Ed.). (1989). *Children of divorce: Developmental and clinical issues.* New York: Haworth Press.

Fassell, D. (1991). *Growing up divorced: A road to healing for adult children of divorce.* New York: Pocket Books.

Framo, J. L. (1992). *Family of origin therapy: An intergenerational approach.* New York: Brunner and Mazel.

Frantz, T. T. (1984). Helping parents whose child has died. In T. Frantz (Ed.), *Death and grief in the family.* Rockville, MD: Aspen.

Freud, S. (1952). *A general introduction to psychoanalysis.* (J. Riviere, Trans.). New York: Washington Square Press. (Original work published 1917)

Fulmer, R. H. (1983). A structural approach to unresolved mourning in single-parent family systems. *Journal of Marital and Family Therapy, 9*(3), 259–269.

Furstenburg, F., Brooks-Gunn, J., & Morgan, S. P. (1987). Adolescent mothers and their children in later life. *Family Planning Perspectives, 19,* 142–151.

Gagnon, J. H. (1990). Scripting in sex research. *Annual Review of Sex Research, 1,* 1–39.

Gander, A. M. (1991). After the divorce: Familial factors that predict well-being for older and younger persons. *Journal of Divorce and Remarriage, 15*(1), 175–192.

Ganong, L. H., & Coleman, M. (1984). The effects of remarriage on children: A review of empirical literature. *Family Relations, 33,* 389–407.

Garber, R. J. (1991). Long-term effects of divorce on the self-esteem of young adults. *Journal of Divorce and Remarriage, 15*(1/2), 131–137.

Garfield, R. (1982). Mourning and its resolution for spouses in marital separation. In L. Messinger (Ed.), *Therapy with remarriage families.* Rockville, MD: Aspen.

Gately, D. W., & Schwebel, A. I. (1991). The challenge model of children's adjustment to parental divorce: Explaining favorable postdivorce outcomes in children. *Journal of Family Psychology, 5*(1), 60–81.

Gebhard, P. H. (1968). Human sex behavior research. In M. Diamond (Ed.), *Perspectives in reproduction and sexual behavior* (pp. 391–410). Bloomington: Indiana University Press.

Gebhard, P. H. (1970). Postmarital coitus among widows and divorcees. In P. Bohannon (Ed.), *Divorce and after* (pp. 81–96). Garden City, NY: Doubleday.

Genovese, F. (1992). Family therapy and bereavement counseling. In J. Atwood (Ed.), *Family therapy: A systemic-behavioral approach.* Chicago: Nelson-Hall.

Gergen, K. (1985). The social constructionist movement in modern psychology. *American Psychologist, 40,* 266–275.

Gergen, K. L., & Gergen, M. M. (1988). Narrative and the self as relationship. In L. Berkowitz (Ed.), *Advances in experimental social psychology* (pp. 17–56). New York: Academic Press.

George, V. E., & Wilding, P. (1972). *Motherless families.* London: Routledge and Kegan Paul.

Gibb, J. C. (1979). Kohlberg's moral stage theory: A Piagetian revision. *Human Development, 22*(2), 89–112.

Gilchrist, L., & Schinke, S. (1983). Coping with contraception: Cognitive and behavioral methods with adolescents. *Cognitive Therapy and Research, 7*(5), 379–388.

Glick, P. C. (1988). The role of divorce in the changing family structure: Trends and variations. In S. A. Wolchik & P. Karoly (Eds.), *Children of divorce: Empirical perspectives on divorce* (pp. 3–34). New York: Gardner.

Glick, P., & Norton, A. (1971). Frequency, duration, and probability of marriage and divorce. *Journal of Marriage and the Family, 33,* 307–313.

Glick, P., & Norton, A. (1979). *Update: Marrying, divorcing, and living together in the United States today.* Washington DC: Population Reference Bureau.

Glick, I. O., Weiss, R. S., & Parkes, C. M. (1974). *The first year of bereavement.* New York: Wiley-Interscience.

Goffman, E. (1963). *Stigma.* Englewood Cliffs, NJ: Prentice-Hall.

Goldenberg, I., & Goldenberg, H. (1991). *Family therapy: An overview* (3rd ed.). Pacific Grove, CA: Brooks, Cole.

Gorer, G. (1967). *Death, grief, and mourning.* Garden City, NY: Anchor Books.

Greenberg, J. B. (1979). Single parenting and intimacy: A comparison of mothers and fathers. *Alternative Lifestyles, 2*(3), 308–331.

Guerin, P. J., Fay, L. F., Burden, S. L., & Kautto, J. G. (1987). *The evaluation and treatment of mental conflict: A four-stage approach.* New York: Basic Books.

Guerin, P., & Katz, A. (1984). The theory in therapy of families with school-related problems: Triangles and a hypothesis testing model. In B. F. Okun (Ed.), *Family therapy with school-related problems* (pp. 150–182). Rockville, MD: Aspen.

Guidubaldi, J. (1983). Divorce research clarifies issues: A report on NASP's nation-wide study. *Communique, 10,* 1–3.

Guidubaldi, J., Cleminshaw, H. K., Perry, J. D., & Mcloughlin, C. S. (1983). The impact of parental divorce on children: Report of the nationwide NASP study. *School Psychology Review, 12*(3), 300–323.

Guidubaldi, J., & Perry, J. D. (1984). Divorce, socioeconomic status, and children's cognitive-social competence at school entry. *American Journal of Orthopsychiatry, 54*(3), 459–468.

Haley, J. (1967). Toward a theory of pathological systems. In G. H. Zuk & I. Boszormenyi-Nagy (Eds.), *Family therapy and disturbed families* (pp. 78–102). Palo Alto, CA: Science and Behavior Books.

Haley, J. (1977). *Problem solving therapy.* San Francisco: Jossey-Bass.

Hammarskjold, D. (1966). *Markings.* London: Faber & Faber.

Hanson, S. H. M., & Sporakowski, M. J. (1986). Single-parent families. *Family Relations, 35*, 3–8.

Hayes, C. (Ed.). (1987). *Risking the future: Adolescent sexuality, pregnancy, and childbearing.* Washington, DC: National Academy Press.

Hein, K. (1989). AIDS in adolescence: Exploring the challenge. *Journal of Adolescent Health Care, 10*(3), 10–35.

Henderson, A. J. (1981). Designing school guidance programs for single-parent families. *The School Counselor, 29*(2), 124–131.

Herz Brown, F. (1988). The impact of death and serious illness on the family life cycle. In B. Carter & M. McGoldrick (Eds.), *The changing family life cycle: A framework for family therapy* (2nd ed., pp. 63–93). New York: Gardner Press.

Hetherington, E. M. (1989). Coping with family transitions: Winners, losers, and survivors. *Child Development, 60*, 1–14.

Hetherington, E. M., Cox, M., Cox, R. (1985). Long-term effects of divorce and remarriage on the adjustment of children. *Journal of the American Academy of Child Psychiatry, 24*, 518–530.

Hetherington, M., Cox, M., & Cox, R. (1976). Divorced fathers. *The Family Coordinator, 25*, 417–428.

Hicks, S., & Anderson, C. M. (1989). Women on their own. In M. McGoldrick, C. M. Anderson, & F. Walsh (Eds.), *Women in families: A framework for family therapy* (pp. 308–334). New York: W.W. Norton.

Hill, E. L. (1978). Goal analysis for problem learners. *Academic Therapy, 13*(3), 289–299.

Hiltz, R. S. (1975). Helping widows: Group discussions as a therapeutic technique. *Family Coordinator, 24*(3), 331–336.

Hirschorn, M. (1987). AIDS is not seen as a major threat by many heterosexuals on campuses. *Chronicle of Higher Education*, pp. 1, 32–33.

Hodges, W. F. (1986). *Interventions for children of divorce: Custody, access, and psychotherapy.* New York: John Wiley and Sons.

Hodges, W. F. (1991). *Interventions for children of divorce: Custody, access, and psychotherapy* (2nd ed.). New York: John Wiley and Sons.

Hoffman, L. (1981). *Foundations of family therapy: A conceptual framework for change.* New York: Basic Books.

Hoffman, L. (1990). Constructing realities: An art of lenses. *Family Process, 29*(1), 1–12.

Holder, D. P., & Anderson, C. P. (1989). Women, work, and the family. In M. McGoldrick, C. M. Anderson, & F. Walsh (Eds.), *Women in families: A framework for family therapy* (pp. 98–115). New York: W.W. Norton.

Holman, A. M. (1983). *Family assessment: Tools for understanding and intervention.* Newbury Park: Sage.

Holmes, T. H., & Rahe, R. H. (1967). The social readjustment rating scale. *Journal of Psychosomatic Research, 11*, 213–218.

Hoult, T., Henz, L., & Hudson, J. (1978). *Courtship and marriage in America.* Boston: Little, Brown.

Hunt, M. (1974). *Sexual behavior in the 1970s.* Chicago: Playboy Press.

Hunt, M., & Hunt, B. (1977). *The divorce experience.* New York: Signet.

Hutchinson, R. L., Valutis, W. E., Brown, D. T., & White, S. J. (1989). The effects of family structure on intitutionalized children's self-concepts. *Adolescence, 24*(94), 303–310.

Imber-Black, E. (1989). Women's relationships with larger systems. In M. McGoldrick, C. M. Anderson, & F. Walsh (Eds.), *Women in families: A framework for family therapy* (pp. 335–353). New York: W.W. Norton.

Isaacs, M. B. (1987). Dysfunctional arrangements in divorcing families. In M. Lindblad-Goldberg (Ed.), *Clinical issues in single-parent households* (pp. 111–130). Rockville, MD: Aspen.

Isaacs, M. B., Montalvo, B., & Adelson, D. (1986). *The difficult divorce: Therapy for children and families.* New York: Basic Books.

Jacobson, D. (1978). The impact of marital separation on children: Parent-child separation and child adjustment. *Journal of Divorce, 1*(4), 341–360.

Jacobson, G. F. (1983). *The multiple crises of marital separation and divorce.* New York: Grune & Stratton.

Jacobson, D., & Margolin, G. (1979). *Marital therapy: Strategies based on social learning and behavioral exchange principles.* New York: Basic Books.

Jacobson, D., & Margolin, G. (1981). Assessment of marital dysfunction. In M. Herson & A. S. Bellack (Eds.), *Behavioral assessment: A practical handbook.* Elmsford, NY: Pergamon.

Jenkins, J. E., Hedlund, D. E., & Ripple, R. E. (1988). Parental separation effects on children's divergent thinking abilities and creativity potential. *Child Study Journal, 18*(3), 149–159.

Jones, C. W. (1987). Coping with the young handicapped child in the single-parent family: An ecosystem perspective. In M. Lindblad-Goldberg (Ed.), *Clinical issues in single-parent households* (pp. 210–231). Rockville, MD: Aspen.

Jones, A., & Placek, P. (1985). Teenage women in the United States: Sex, contraception, pregnancy, fertility, and maternal and infant health. In T. Ooms (Ed.), *Teenage pregnancy in a family context* (pp. 49–72). Philadelphia: Temple University Press.

Kalter, N., Alpern, LD., Spence, R., & Plunkett, J. W. (1984). Locus of control in children of divorce. *Journal of Personality Assessment, 48*, 410–413.

Kaslow, F. W. (1981). Divorce and divorce therapy. In A. Gurman & D. Kniskern (Eds.), *Handbook of family therapy* (pp. 87–109). New York: Brunner and Mazel.

Kaslow, F., & Hyatt, R. (1981). Divorce: A potential growth experience for the extended family. *Journal of Divorce, 5*, 115–126.

Kavanaugh, R. E. (1974). *Facing death.* Baltimore: Penguin Books.

Kaye, S. (1989). The impact of divorce on children's academic performance. *Journal of Divorce, 12*, 283–289.

Kelly, G. (1969). Man's construction of his alternatives. In R. Maher (Ed.), *Clinical psychology and personality: The second papers of George Kelly* (pp. 180–205). New York: Wiley.

Kelly, J. (1988). Longer term adjustment in children of divorce: Converging findings and implications for practice. *Journal of Family Psychology, 2*, 119–140.

Kennedy, E. (1989). *Sexual counseling: A practical guide for those who help others.* New York: Continuum.

Kerr, M. E., & Bowen, M. (1988). *Family evaluation.* New York: W.W. Norton.

Kinsey, A., Pomeroy, W., & Martin, C. (1948). *Sexual behavior in the human male.* Philadelphia: Saunders.

Kinsey, A., Pomeroy, W., Martin, C., & Gebhard, G. (1953). *Sexual behavior in the human female.* Philadelphia: Saunders.

Kirk, S. A., & Gallagher, J. J. (1989). *Educating exceptional children* (6th ed.). Boston: Houghton Mifflin.

Kohen, J. A. (1981). From wife to family head: Transitions in self-identity. *Psychiatry, 44,* 230–240.

Kohlberg, L. (1969). Stage end sequence: The cognitive developmental approach to socialization. In D. A. Goslin (Ed.), *Handbook of socialization theory of research.* Chicago: Rand McNally.

Kohn, J. B., & Kohn, W. K. (1978). *The widower.* Boston: Beacon Press.

Krantzler, M. (1975). *Creative divorce.* New York: New American Library.

Kraus, A. A., & Lilienfeld, A. M. (1959). Some epidemiological aspects of the high mortality rate in the young widowed group. *Journal of Chronic Disease, 10,* 207–217.

Kreis, B., & Pattie, A. (1969). *Win from grief.* New York: Seabury Press.

Krupp, G., Genovese, F., & Krupp, T. (1986). To have and have not: Multiple identifications in pathological bereavement. *Journal of the American Academy of Psychoanalysis, 14*(3), 337–348.

Kulka, R. A., & Weingarten, H. (1979). The long-term effects of parental divorce in childhood on adult adjustment. *Journal of Social Issues, 35*(4), 50–77.

Kurdek, L. A. (1981). An integrative perspective on children's divorce adjustment. *American Psychologist, 36*(8), 856–866.

Kurdek, L. A., & Siesky, A. E. (1980). Children's perceptions of their parents' divorce. *Journal of Divorce, 3,* 339–378.

Laws, J. L., & Schwartz, P. (1977). *Sexual scripts: The social construction of female sexuality.* Fort Worth, TX: Dryden Press.

Lentfoehr, T. (1979). *Words and silence: On the poetry of Thomas Merton.* New York: New Directions.

Leslie, G. R., & Leslie, G. M. (1977). *Marriage in a changing world.* New York: John Wiley and Sons.

Levine, S. (1987). *Healing into life and death.* New York: Doubleday.

Lipchick, E. (1988). Purposeful interviewing for beginning the solution-focused interview. In E. Lipchick (Ed.), *Interviewing.* Rockville, MD: Aspen.

Lopata, H. Z. (1972). Role changes in widowhood: A world perspective. In D. Cowgill & L. Holmes, (Eds.), *Aging and modernization* (pp. 275–303). New York: Appleton-Century-Crofts.

Lopata, H. Z. (1973). *Widowhood in an American city.* Cambridge, MA: Schenkman.

Lopata, H. Z. (1975). On widowhood: Grief work and identity reconstruction. *Journal of Geriatric Psychiatry, 8,* 41–55.

Lowenthal, M., & Robinson, B. (1976). Social networks and isolation. In R. Binstock & E. Shanas (Eds.), *Handbook of aging and the social sciences.* New York: Van Nostrand Reinhold.

MacKinnon, C. E., Stoneman, Z., & Brody, G. H. (1984). The impact of maternal employment and family form on children's sex-role sterotypes and mother's traditional attitude. *Journal of Divorce and Remarriage, 8*(1), 51–60.

MacNamee, S., & Gergen, K. (1993). *Therapy as social construction*. New York: Sage.

Madanes, C. (1981). *Strategic family therapy*. San Francisco: Jossey-Bass.

Maddison, D., & Raphael, B. (1975). Conjugal bereavement and the social network. In B. Schoenberg et al. (Eds.), *Bereavement: Its psychosocial aspects* (pp. 26–40). New York: Columbia University Press.

Magrab, P. R. (1978). For the sake of the children: A review of the psychological effects of divorce. *Journal of Divorce, 3*, 233–245.

Mahler, M., Pine, F., & Bergman, A. (1975). *The psychological birth of the human infant: Symbiosis and individuation*. New York: Basic Books.

Manning, D. T., Barenberg, N., Gallese, L., & Rice, J. C. (1989). College students' knowledge and health beliefs about AIDS: Implications for education and prevention. *Journal of American College Health, 37*(6), 254–259.

Marital status and living arrangements: March 1979. Current Population Reports (Series P-20, No. 349). Washington, DC: U.S. Government Printing Office, 1980.

Marsh, H. W. (1990a). Family configurations. *Journal of Educational Psychology, 82*, 327–340.

Marsh, H. W. (1990b). Two-parent, stepparent, and single-parent families: Changes in achievement attitudes during the last 2 years of high school. *Journal of Educational Psychology, 82*(2), 321–340.

May, R. (1969). *Love and will*. New York: W. W. Norton.

McCombs A., & Forehand, R. (1989). Adolescent school performance following parental divorce: Are there family factors that can enhance success? *Adolescence, 24*(96), 871–880.

McGoldrick, M. (1988). Women and the family life cycle. In B. Carter & M. McGoldrick (Eds.), *The changing family life cycle* (Vol. 2, pp. 35–49). New York: Gardner Press.

McGoldrick, M. (1989). Sisters. In C. M. Anderson & F. Walsh (Eds.), *Women in families: A framework for family therapy*. New York: W.W. Norton.

McLanahan, S. S., Garfinkel, I., & Ooms, T. (1987). Female-headed families and economic policy: Expanding the clinician's focus. In M. Lindblad-Goldberg (Ed.), *Clinical issues in single-parent households*. Rockville, MD: Aspen.

McLanahan, S. S., Wedemeyer, N. V., & Adelberg, T. (1981). Network structure, social support, and psychological well-being in the single-parent family. *Journal of Marriage and the Family, 43*, 601–611.

McPhee, J. (1984). Ambiguity and change in the postdivorce family. Towards a model of divorce adjustment. *Journal of Divorce, 8*(2), 1–15.

Meichenbaum, D. (1977). *Cognitive behavior modification: An integrative approach*. New York: Plenum Press.

Mendes, H. (1979). Single-parent families: A typology of life-styles. *Social Work, 24*,(3), 193–199.

Meyer, G. (1992). Family therapy with divorcing and remarried families. In J. Atwood (Ed.), *Family therapy: A systemic-behavioral approach*. Chicago: Nelson-Hall.

Mince, J. (1992). Discovering meaning with families. In J. Atwood (Ed.), *Family therapy: A systemic-behavioral approach*. (pp. 189–210). Chicago: Nelson-Hall.

Minuchin, S. (1974). *Families and family therapy*. Cambridge, MA: Harvard University Press.

Minuchin, S., & Fishman, H. C. (1981). *Family therapy techniques.* Cambridge, MA: Harvard University Press.

Molnar, A., & de Schazer, S. (1987). Solution-focused therapy: Toward the identification of therapeutic tasks. *Journal of Marital and Family Therapy, 13*(4), 349–358.

Morawetz, A., & Walker, G. (1984). *Brief therapy with single-parent families.* New York: Brunner and Mazel.

Morgan, (1976). A re-examination of widowhood and morale. *Journal of Gerontology, 31*(6), 687–695.

Newman, G., & Nichols, C. R. (1960). Sexual activities and attitudes in older persons. *Journal of the American Medical Association, 173,* 33–35.

Nichols, W. C. (1984). Therapeutic needs of children in family system reorganization. *Journal of Divorce, 7*(4), 23–44.

Norton, A., & Glick, P. (1986). One-parent families: A social and economic profile. *Family Relations, 35,* 9–17.

Okun, B. F. (1984). Family therapy and the schools. In B. F. Okun (Ed.), *Family therapy with school-related problems.* Rockville, MD: Aspen.

Ourth, J., & Zakariya, S. B. (1982). The school and the single parent student: What schools can do to help. *Principal, 62,* 24–38.

Papero, D. V. (1990). *Bowen family systems theory.* Boston: Allyn and Bacon.

Parkes, C. M. (1972). *Bereavement: Studies of grief in adult life.* New York: International Universities Press.

Parkes, C. M. (1975). Determinants of the outcome following bereavement. *Omega, 6,* 303–323.

Parkes, C. M., & Weiss, R. S. (1983). *Recovery from bereavement.* New York: Basic Books.

Parkes, M. C., Benjamin, B., & Fitzgerald, R. G. (1969). Broken heart: A statistical study of increased mortality among widowers. *British Medical Journal, 1,* 740–743.

Parsons, T., & Bales, R. (1955). *Family, socialization, and interaction process.* New York: The Free Press.

Peck, J. S., & Manocherian, M. S. (1988). Divorce in the changing life cycle. In B. Carter & M. McGoldrick (Eds.), *The changing family life cycle: A framework for family therapy* (2nd ed., pp. 137–162). New York: Gardner Press.

Penn, P. (1985). Feed forward: Future questions, future maps. *Family Process, 24,* 299–311.

Perls, F. (1969). *Gestalt therapy verbatim.* Lafayette, IN: Real People Press.

Persson, G. (1980). Sexuality in a 70-year-old urban population. *Journal of Psychosomatic Research, 24*(6), 335–342.

Petrowsky, M. (1976). Marital status, sex, and the social networks of the elderly. *Journal of Marriage and the Family, 38*(4), 749–756.

Pffeifer, E., & Davis, G. C. (1972). Determinants of sexual behavior in middle and old age. *Journal of the American Geriatric Society, 20,* 151–158.

Pfeiffer, E., Verwoerdt, A., & Davis, C. (1972). Sexual behavior in middle life. *American Journal of Psychiatry, 128*(10), 262–267.

Piaget, J. (1952). *The origins of intelligence in children.* New York: International University Press.

Pollock, G. H. (1975). *The mourning process and creative organizational change.* Plenary session postpresidential address, American Psychoanalytic Association.

Portes, P. R., Haas, R. C., & Brown, J. (1991). Identifying family factors that predict children's adjustment to divorce: An analytic synthesis. *Journal of Divorce and Remarriage, 15*(3/4), 87–103.

Preto, N. (1988). Transformation of the family system in adolescence. In B. Carter & M. McGoldrick (Eds.), *The changing family life cycle: A framework for family therapy* (2nd ed.). New York: Gardner Press.

Rainwater, L. (1965). *Family design.* Chicago: Aldine.

Rando, T. A. (1984). *Grief, dying, and death: Clinical interventions for caregivers.* Champaign, IL: Research Press.

Rathus, S. A., & Nevid, J. S. (1992). *Adjustment and growth: The challenges of life.* Fort Worth, TX: HBJ College Books.

Reissman, (1990). *Divorce talk.* New Brunswick, NJ: Rutgers University Press.

Rogers, C. R. (1951). *Client-centered therapy.* Boston: Houghton Mifflin.

Romanowski, B., & Brown, J. (1986). AIDS and changing sexual behavior. *Canadian Medical Association Journal, 134*(8), 872–879.

Roe, A. (1953). *The making of a scientist.* New York: Dodd, Mead.

Rosenthal, K., & Keshet, H. (1978). The impact of child care responsibilities on the part time or single father. *Alternative Lifestyles, 1*(4), 165–492.

Rosenthal, K., & Keshet, H. (1979, July). The not-quite stepmother. *Psychology Today,* pp. 82–88.

Rynearson, E. K. (1987). Psychotherapy of pathologic grief: Revisions and limitations. *Psychiatric Clinics of North America, 10*(3), 487–499.

Sanders. (1989). *Grief: The mourning after.* New York: John Wiley and Sons.

Santrock, J. W., & Warchak, R. A. (1979). Father custody and social development in boys and girls. *Journal of Social Issues, 35,* 112–125.

Santrock, J. W. (1972). Relation of type and onset of father absence to cognitive development. *Child Development, 43,* 455–469.

Santrock, J. W., & Tracy, R. L. (1978). Effects of children's family structure status on the development of stereotypes by teachers. *Journal of Educational Psychology, 70*(5), 754–757.

Schwebel, A. I., Barocas, H., Reichmann, W., & Schwebel, M. (1990). *Personal adjustment and growth.* Dubuque, IA: Brown.

Seligman, M. E. P. (1973). *Helplessness: On depression, development, and death.* San Francisco: Freeman.

Sherman, F., & Fredman, N. (1986). *Handbook of structured techniques in marriage and family therapy.* New York: Brunner and Mazel.

Sherman, R., Oresky, P., & Rountree, Y. (1992). *Solving problems in couples and family therapy: Techniques and tactics.* New York: Brunner and Mazel.

Silverman, P., & Cooperband, A. (1975). On widowhood: Mutual help and the elderly widow. *Journal of Geriatric Psychiatry, 8*(1), 9–27.

Siegel, B. (1986). *Love, medicine, and miracles.* New York: Harper & Row.

Silverman, P., & Englander, S. (1975). The widow's view of her dependent children. *Omega, 6,* 3–20.

Simon, W., & Gagnon, W. (1973). *Sexual conduct.* Chicago: Aldine.

Simpkins, L., & Eberhage, M. G. (1984). Attitudes toward AIDS, herpes II, and toxic shock syndrome. *Psychological Reports, 55*(3), 779–786.

Simpkins, L., & Kushner, A. (1986). Attitudes toward AIDS, herpes II, and toxic shock syndrome: Two years later. *Psychological Reports, 59*(2), 883–891.

Starr, B. D., & Weiner, M. B. (1981). *The Starr-Weiner report on sex and sexuality in the mature years*. New York: Stein & Day.

Stein, P. (1976). *Single*. Englewood Cliffs, NJ: Prentice-Hall.

Stolberg, A. L., & Garrison, K. M. (1985). Evaluating a primary prevention program for children of divorce. *American Journal of Community Psychology, 13*(2), 111–124.

Strong, B., & Reynolds, R. (1979). *The marriage and family experience*. St. Paul, MI: West.

Tannahill, R. (1982). *Sex in history*. Lanham, MD: Madison.

Thirot, T. L., & Buckner, E. T. (1991). Multiple predictors of satisfactory postdivorce adjustment of single custodial parents. *Journal of Divorce and Remarriage, 15*(1/2), 27–49.

Thorburg, H. (1979). Behavior and values: Consistency or inconsistency? *Adolescence, 8*, 513–520.

Tillmon, J. (1976). Welfare is a woman's issue. In R. Baxandall, L. Gordon, & S. Reverby (Eds.), *America's working woman: A documentary history—1600 to the present* (pp. 157–182). New York: Vintage Books.

Titler, B. I., & Cook, V. J. (1981). Relationships among family, school, and clinic: Towards a systems approach. *Journal of Clinical and Child Psychology, Fall*, 184–187.

Tombari, M., & Davis, R. A. (1979). Behavioral consultation. In G. O. Phye & D. J. Reschly (Eds.), *School psychology: Perspectives and issues*. New York: Academic Press.

Tschann, J. M. (1989). Family process and children's functioning during divorce. *Journal of Marriage and the Family, 51*(2), 431–444.

Van Coevering, V. (1974). *Exploring group counseling as a technique for ameliorating morbidity, mortality, and lowered life satisfaction of widowhood*. Paper presented at the Gerontological Society annual meeting, Portland, OR.

Veevers, J. E. (1990). Trauma versus strengths: A paradigm of positive versus negative divorce outcomes. *Journal of Divorce and Remarriage, 14*(1), 99–126.

Viney, L. L., Benjamin, Y. N., & Preston, C. (1988). Constructivist family therapy with the elderly. *Journal of Family Psychology, 2*(2), 241–258.

Vinick, B. H. (1978). Remarriage in old age. *The Family Coordinator, 27*, 359–363.

Visher, E. B., & Visher, J. S. (1990). Dynamics of successful stepfamilies. *Journal of Divorce and Remarriage, 14*(1), 3–12.

von Bertalanffy. (1968). *Geneeral systems theory: Foundations, developments, applications*. New York: George Braziller.

Waller, W. (1967). *The old love and the new: Divorce and readjustment*. Carbondale: Southern Illinois University Press.

Wallerstein, J. S. (1984). Children of divorce: Preliminary report of a 10-year follow-up of young children. *American Journal of Orthopsychiatry, 54*(3), 444–458.

Wallerstein, J. S., & Kelly, J. B. (1974). The effects of parental divorce: The adolescent experience. In G. J. Anthony & C. Koupernik (Eds.), *The child and his [or her] family—children at a psychiatric risk, III*. New York: John Wiley and Sons.

Wallerstein, J. S., & Kelly, J. B. (1980a). California's children of divorce. *Psychology Today, 13*(8), 67–76.

Wallerstein, J. S., & Kelly, J. B. (1980b). Children and divorce: A review. *Social Work, 24*, 468–475.

Walsh, F. (Ed.) (1982). *Normal family process.* New York: Guilford Press.

Walsh, F., & McGoldrick, M. (1991). Loss and the family: A systemic perspective. In F. Walsh & M. McGoldrick (Eds.), *Living beyond loss: Death in the family.* New York: W.W. Norton.

Warren, N., & Amara, I. (1985). Educational groups for single parents: The parenting after divorce programs. *Journal of Divorce, 8*(2), 79–96.

Warren, N., Illgen, E. R., Grew, R. S., Konac, J. I., & Amara, I. (1982, August). *Parenting after divorce: Evaluation of preventive programs for divorcing families.* Paper presented at the American Psychological Association meeting, Washington, DC.

Watts, D. S., & Watts, K. M. (1991). The impact of female-headed single-parent families on academic achievement. *Journal of Divorce and Remarriage, 15*(1/2), 97–114.

Watzlawick, P. (1978). *The language of change: Elements of therapeutic communication.* New York: Basic Books.

Watzlawick, P. (1984). *The invented reality.* New York: W.W. Norton.

Watzlawick, P., Weakland, J. H., & Fisch, R. (1974). *Change: Principles of problem formation and problem resolution.* New York: W.W. Norton.

Weinstein, E., Rosen, E., & Atwood, J. (1991). Adolescents' knowledge of AIDS and behavior change: Implications for education. *Journal of Health Education, 22*(5), 313–318.

Weiss, R. S. (1975). *Marital separation.* Basic Books.

Weiss, R. S. (1979). Growing up a little faster: The experience of growing up in a single-parent household. *Journal of Social Issues, 35*(4), 97–111.

Weiss, R. (1980). Strategic behavioral marital therapy: Toward a model of assessment and intervention. In J. Vincent (Ed.), *Advances in family intervention. Assessment and theory, 1* (pp. 210-243). Bristal, PA: Taylor & Francis.

Weitzman, L. J. (1985). *The divorce revolution: The unexpected social and economic consequences for women and children in America.* New York: The Free Press.

Weltner, J. S. (1982). A structural approach to the single-parent family. *Family Process, 21*: 203–210.

Whipple, B., & Scura, K. W. (1989). HIV and the older adult: Taking the necessary precautions. *Journal of Gerontological Nursing, 15*(9), 15–19.

White, M. (1985). Fear busting and monster taming: An approach to the fears of young children. *Dulwich Centre Review*, pp. 29–34.

White, M. (1986a). Family escape from trouble. *Family Therapy Case Studies, 1*(1), 29–33.

White, M. (1986b). Negative explanation, restraint and double description: A template for family therapy. *Family Process, 25*(2), 169–184.

White, M. (1989, Summer). The externalization of the problem. *Dulwich Centre Newsletter*, pp. 87–92.

White, M., & Epston, D. (1990). *Narrative means to therapeutic ends.* New York: W.W. Norton.

Wood, J. I., & Lewis, G. J. (1990). The coparental relationship of divorced spouses: Its effect on children's school adjustment. *Journal of Divorce and Remarriage, 14*(1), 81–95.

Wood, F., & Smith, C. (1985). Assessment of emotionally disturbed/behaviorally disordered students. *Diagnostique, 10*, 40–51.

Woody, J. D., Colley, D., Schlegelmilch, J., & Maginn, D. (1984). Parental stress and adjustment following divorce. *Crisis Intervention, 13*(4), 133–147.

Wyly, M. V., & Hulicka, I. M. (1975). *Problems and compensations of widowhood: A comparison of age groups.* Paper presented at annual meeting of the American Psychological Association, Buffalo, NY.

Yankelovich, D. (1981). *New rules.* New York: Random House.

Ysseldyke, J. E. (1979). Issues in psychoeducational assessment. In G. O. Phye & D. J. Reschly (Eds.), *School psychology: Perspectives and issues* (pp. 21–48). New York: Academic Press.

Zakariya, S. B. (1982). Another look at the children of divorce: Summary report of school needs of one-parent children. *Principal, 62,* 34–37.

Zeiss, R. A., & Zeiss, A. M. (1979). *The role of sexual behavior in the postdivorce adjustment process.* Paper presented at the annual meeting of the Western Psychological Association, San Diego.